LITTLE BOOK OF

LOUIS VUITTON

First published in 2021 by Welbeck
An imprint of Headline Publishing Group

Text © Karen Homer 2021
Design and layout © Carlton Books Limited 2021

A CIP catalogue record for this book is available from the British Library.

ISBN 978-1-78739-741-5

Printed in China

29

Headline's policy is to use papers that are natural, renewable and recyclable
products and made from wood grown in well-managed forests and other
controlled sources. The logging and manufacturing processes are expected
to conform to the environmental regulations of the country of origin.

HEADLINE PUBLISHING GROUP
An Hachette UK Company
Carmelite House
50 Victoria Embankment
London EC4Y 0DZ

www.headline.co.uk
www.hachette.co.uk

LITTLE BOOK OF

LOUIS VUITTON

The story of the iconic fashion house

KAREN HOMER

WELBECK

CONTENTS

INTRODUCTION..........................06

EARLY YEARS 10

FAMILY AFFAIR 22

THE SECOND WORLD WAR

   AND BEYOND 42

GLOBAL EXPANSION 52

MARC JACOBS 66

HERITAGE REBORN...................106

SIGNATURE PIECES 134

NOTES 156

INDEX 157

CREDITS 160

INTRODUCTION

"Louis Vuitton is the most visible, the most showy, in a way. Some people think it's terrible, some people love it, some people just have a fascination with it."

– Nicolas Ghesquière[1]

When Louis Vuitton, a poor country boy from Jura, France, opened his first workshop in 1854 – a bespoke packing and luggage-making service – he could not have dreamed that one day his family name would be associated with the pinnacle of luxury. Similarly, when his son Georges Vuitton, frustrated by competitors copying the company's trunks, designed a pattern he dubbed the "Monogram", little did Georges imagine it would one day be one of the most iconic prints in the world.

Since those early days, first as a family business and later as the jewel in the crown of luxury goods conglomerate LVMH, Louis Vuitton has catered to the highest echelons of society, from royalty to actresses and celebrities. Its luggage is not only the most recognizable, but often the most innovative. In its early days, the brand created trunks that revealed travelling wardrobes, sets carrying essential toiletries or drink-making equipment, and even a portable bed. And with the invention

OPPOSITE Jackie Onassis photographed at the airport in Washington in 1980, as always carrying her beloved, well-worn, Louis Vuitton Keepall bag.

in 1890 of their famous unpickable tumbler lock, which even Harry Houdini wouldn't challenge, Vuitton luggage became thief-proof too.

Louis Vuitton's strength has always lain in an ability to move with the times and capitalize on changing trends. In the 1920s and 1930s, as sedate train and ocean-liner travel gave way to a vogue for leaping into automobiles to weekend in the South of France, stacks of heavyweight trunks were replaced by a capacious soft-sided holdall, the aptly named "Keepall". And in the 1950s, a breakthrough in fabric design, which added PVC to their trademark canvas, meant Louis Vuitton bags were not just stylish but practical too. Toted by celebrities, including Brigitte Bardot and Audrey Hepburn, the bags became increasingly aspirational, setting a precedent for the status symbols they would later become.

In 1997, a new era began as Louis Vuitton entered the world of high fashion with the appointment of designer Marc Jacobs. The Monogram bag was no longer just a timeless classic, it was a fashion statement – and with it came a wardrobe of clothes that combined the elegance and heritage of Louis Vuitton with cutting-edge style. Throughout Marc Jacobs's 16-year tenure and into the reign of menswear designer Virgil Abloh and current artistic director Nicolas Ghesquière, Louis Vuitton continues to reinvent itself – most recently as a current, streetwise brand. It is as appealing to celebrities as to its loyal old guard of clients, and remains among the very top luxury brands in the world.

OPPOSITE A new generation of Louis Vuitton fans: Jaden Smith and Willow Smith in the front row at the Louis Vuitton Autumn/ Winter 2019/20 catwalk show.

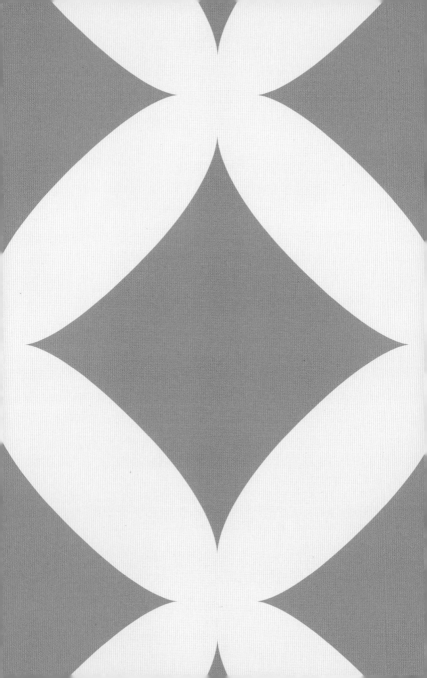

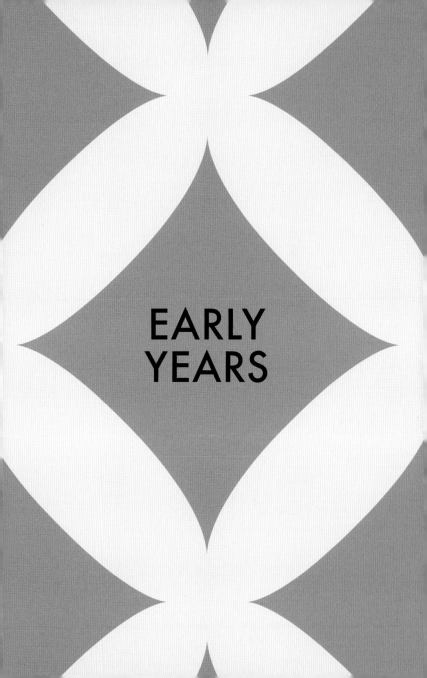

EARLY
YEARS

HUMBLE BEGINNINGS

Louis Vuitton was born on 4 August 1821 in Anchay,
a hamlet in the mountainous Jura region of France, into
a work-toughened family of five generations of joiners,
carpenters, millers and farmers. The life they led was hard,
and the family valued qualities like self-sufficiency and
perseverance, which would stand the young Louis in good
stead in later years.

I n 1835, at just 13 years old, he left to try his fortunes in Paris.
As was common in nineteenth-century France, his travels took
several years, as he embraced the tradition of the journeyman
worker. Apprenticing himself to various craftsmen along the way,
he finally arrived in Paris in 1837 and was taken under the wing
of box-maker and packer Monsieur Maréchal. Quickly proving
himself to his employer, he remained with Maréchal for the next
17 years, learning time-honoured skills that would be invaluable
in his later career as a trunk-maker. In Maréchal's workshop
on Rue Saint-Honoré, Louis was not far from the luxurious
shops and boulevards of Paris, which seduced him with their
fashionable displays and sophisticated clientele.

The role of the box-maker (*layetier*) and packer (*emballeur*) was
an important one – especially to the French court, which travelled

OPPOSITE A portrait of Louis Vuitton (1821–92) who founded the
company in 1854.

ABOVE A painting by Giuseppe Canella in 1832 of Île de la Cité and the Flower Market in Paris, just a few years before Louis Vuitton arrived to make his fortune.

regularly from Paris to Fontainebleau, as well as on extended tours of the country. In 1853, the young and glamorous Empress Eugénie, the Spanish wife of Napoleon III (the nephew of Napoleon Bonaparte), was impressed by the young Louis Vuitton. He became her personal packer, responsible for her elaborate gowns and crinolines. Her patronage sealed his destiny as a high-end craftsman and set a precedent for the aristocrats who came to admire Louis Vuitton luggage.

On 22 April 1854, Louis Vuitton married 17-year-old Clémence-Émilie Parriaux, the daughter of a mill owner. In the same year, he founded a workshop of his own, specializing in packing high-fashion and fragile items, at 4 Rue Neuve-des-Capucines, close to the Place Vendôme. With royal

ABOVE Empress Eugénie, shown here surrounded by her ladies-in-waiting in 1855, took a liking to Louis Vuitton and employed him as her personal *emballeur*, or packer. Her patronage sealed his future as trunk-maker to the highest members of society.

endorsement, his reputation quickly grew, and Vuitton's skill in creating lightweight poplar-wood trunks, which were far more stylish than traditional, heavy, pigskin-covered luggage, won him loyal customers.

Always searching for innovations that would create trunks that were both practical and aesthetically pleasing, he experimented with a treated canvas in a light grey that became known as the "Trianon". In 1858, he further developed this design, replacing the then-commonplace domed lid – designed to allow water to run off leather-coated trunks – with a flat lid. Thanks to the glue-based treatment used on the Trianon canvas, the trunk was entirely watertight and, combined with its lacquered iron trim, was both more stylish and better designed than its predecessors.

It was strong yet lightweight and the trunks stacked neatly atop each other for efficient travel.

The new flat-lid style of trunk was a huge success, so much so that competitors were quick to copy the design. In response, Vuitton added nailed beechwood slats for further reinforcement and in doing so, created an iconic look. Demand grew so fast that in 1859, Louis Vuitton moved his workshop and family home to Asnières, just outside Paris, continuing to supply his store in the city. He concentrated on creating trunks for every requirement, spurred on by the explosion in travel by rail and boat in the mid-nineteenth century, which heralded a new, modern era in travelling luggage. In 1867, Vuitton was honoured with a bronze medal for his designs at the Exposition Universelle in Paris. Legendary English designer Charles Worth had set up his haute couture atelier close to Vuitton's luggage store, and fashionable women bought custom-made trunks to carefully accommodate Worth's dresses crafted from reams of beautiful fabric.

LEFT The village of Asnières just outside Paris where Louis Vuitton moved his home and workshop in 1859.

OPPOSITE TOP Designed in the 1850s, this iconic trunk was reinforced with beechwood slats. The flat lid replaced the more commonplace domed style so that trunks could be efficiently stacked, and the box was covered in a glue-treated watertight canvas.

OPPOSITE BOTTOM A luggage label from the 1860s that advertised Louis Vuitton services as an *emballeur*, or packer.

OVERLEAF An image of the 1867 Exposition Universelle in Paris where Louis Vuitton was honoured with a bronze medal for his designs.

Fête De L'Espa[...]
De [...]

universelle

Imp. LEMERCIER et Cie. rue de Seine 57, Paris.

Louis Vuitton's success was in no small part thanks to his patronage by the aristocracy and the high society of Napoleon III's Second Empire. By 1869, Louis Vuitton was supplying trunks and other specially designed luggage to many heads of state, including Isma'il Pasha, Khedive of Egypt. Isma'il Pasha was instrumental in completing the Suez Canal, the transformative marine passage that allowed the wealthy and influential to travel easily between Europe and Asia, their belongings protected, more often than not, by Louis Vuitton.

The business thrived until July 1870, when the Franco-Prussian War, the fall of Napoleon III and the end of the Second Empire changed everything. A socialist government proclaimed the advent of the Third Republic, and Napoleon III was exiled to England. Prussian forces surrounded Paris, leading to a siege that lasted four months, throughout a brutal winter of food shortages and attack. Louis Vuitton's great-grandson Henry-Louis Vuitton described how his great-grandfather immediately organized

BELOW The opening of the Suez Canal in 1869 which allowed wealthy travellers easy maritime passage between Europe and Asia. Isma'il Pasha, Khedive of Egypt, who was instrumental in the completion of the canal, was a patron of Louis Vuitton.

ABOVE A picture from the late 1880s showing Louis Vuitton's employees in front of a delivery truck outside his Asnières factory. Louis's grandson Gaston-Louis, here shown as a child lying on a trunk-bed, would grow up to be a huge influence on the company.

supplies of rationed food in his district and offered his stock of canvas to make balloons, airborne messages being the only means by which the beleaguered capital could communicate to the rest of the country.

After the surrender of Paris in January 1871, Louis Vuitton returned to Asnières to find his workshop and home devastated. His stock of poplar wood for trunk-making had been burned for fuel by soldiers and his tools stolen. Determined not to be defeated, Vuitton rebuilt and expanded the workshops, finding new Parisian premises at 1 Rue Scribe, in the Opéra district. It was an inspired location: close to railway stations, the opera house and most importantly, the opulent Grand Hôtel. Completed in 1862 and the largest and most luxurious hotel in Europe, Le Grand Hôtel provided a ready new market in the shape of the elite travellers who stayed there. The Maison Louis Vuitton on Rue Scribe thrived, remaining the company's Paris address until 1914.

FAMILY
AFFAIR

A NEW GENERATION

Louis Vuitton passed his passion for crafting beautiful luggage onto his son Georges, and later his grandson Gaston-Louis took up the mantle of the family business. Both men were extremely talented artisans in their own right and helped shape the company into the luxury brand that it was to become.

GEORGES VUITTON: TRADEMARK PATTERNS FOR AN ERA OF MODERN TRAVEL

After fighting to rebuild his company after the Franco-Prussian War, Louis Vuitton was determined that his son, Georges, would carry on the family business. Born in 1857, Georges Vuitton was a natural craftsman, happily spending hours as a child in the workshops of Asnières. Even then, he was full of innovative ideas, and, after two years in a British boarding school studying and learning English, Georges was put in charge of the Rue Scribe store. His marriage to Joséphine Patrelle, the daughter of a wealthy businessman, allowed Georges to buy the flagship store from his father, who retreated to Asnières to concentrate on new designs, leaving the salesmanship up to his son.

OPPOSITE Louis Vuitton's son Georges with his wife Joséphine Patrelle, photographed circa 1900 with their children, Gaston-Louis and twins Pierre and Jean.

RIGHT London's Bond Street, where in 1900 Louis Vuitton moved its store finally finding a London location where the business thrived.

OPPOSITE An English catalogue cover from 1901 advertises Louis Vuitton and the new London store.

Georges set his sights on expansion, ready to convince the world that the French trunks designed by Maison Louis Vuitton should be as highly regarded as traditional English-made luggage. In 1885, he opened a store on London's Oxford Street, but it took five years for Georges to conquer the city. Initially, his exuberant pride in his French heritage – using the French *Tricolore* flag on his shop signs and dressing the window mannequins in French uniforms – went down badly. He also poorly judged the store locations, first on Oxford Street and then on the Strand, which was, ironically, a stone's throw from Nelson's column celebrating Britain's defeat of the French. However, in 1900, Louis Vuitton finally moved to more appropriate premises at 149 New Bond Street and the company began to thrive. The style of Louis Vuitton trunks, inevitably copied by other makers, even became colloquially known as "French trunks".

I, RUE SCRIBE.
PARIS.
Louis Vuitton
149. NEW BOND ST.
OPPOSITE CONDUIT ST
LONDON, W.
TELEGRAPHIC ADDRESS,
"VUITTON, LONDON."
TELEPHONE Nº 2587, GERARD.
L.V.
London
L. V.
London
Travelling Requisites

During the last decades of the nineteenth century, Georges Vuitton was also responsible for creating Louis Vuitton's most iconic designs. The ongoing problem of counterfeit copies of the trademark grey Trianon and the striped Rayée canvas needed to be solved, which Georges did by creating a chequerboard pattern of brown and beige squares with the Louis Vuitton registered trademark etched into the design. The resulting "Damier" canvas was presented at the Exposition Universelle in 1889 and is still one of Louis Vuitton's most recognizable patterns.

In 1896, four years after Louis Vuitton's death, still struggling with forgeries, Georges created the Monogram canvas. The design combines the LV of Louis Vuitton, a diamond with a four-petal flower in its centre, a block-colour flower and a circle containing a flower with four rounded petals. Georges drew on a wide range of historical aesthetic influences, from the Gothic to Japanese art, and the Monogram's graphic yet romantic tone still strikes a pleasing visual chord today. Despite early resistance from customers who preferred the original Damier chequerboard, it has become the most iconic of Louis Vuitton's signature prints.

BELOW In 1896, Georges Vuitton created a second iconic print: the Monogram canvas shown here on a 1911 Malle Idéale trunk.

OPPOSITE An early selection of Louis Vuitton trunks featuring the Damier check canvas from the 1890s. The London store advertised is 454 the Strand, which Vuitton later vacated in favour of Bond Street in 1900.

MALLES ET SACS DE LOUIS VUITTON

Fabrique à ASNIÈRES (Seine)

SAC DE CABINE

MALLE CUIR POUR HOMMES

PARIS

1, Rue Scribe

TÉLÉPHONE 239-48

SUCCURSALE :

57, AVENUE MARCEAU

Téléphone 518-67

LONDRES

454. Strand

En face la Gare

de

CHARING CROSS

MALLE POUR CHAPEAUX DE DAMES

CATALOGUE

franco

MALLE POUR HOMMES

BOITE POUR CHAPEAUX D'HOMMES

THE UNPICKABLE LOCK

Innovative design was always key to the success of Louis Vuitton luggage, but it was the addition of the virtually impenetrable tumbler lock that revolutionized the world of luggage. Always a skilled locksmith, Louis Vuitton had experimented with different locking mechanisms since beginning to make trunks, first using spring buckles and then replacing these with locks fitted with mobile disc tumblers, each registered with their own serial number. In 1890, Georges and Louis patented the tumbler lock and provided each lock with a unique, numbered key. In this way, an array of luggage belonging to one person could be opened only by the owner and new trunks could be commissioned that opened with the same key. Wealthy travellers who regularly moved around with important papers, cash and jewellery locked into their trunks flocked to buy the new, thief-proof trunks, and the essentials of the locking mechanism are still used today. The locks were

OPPOSITE An advertisement for Louis Vuitton luggage that appeared on the inside cover of Paul Derval's book on the Folies-Bergère published in 1955.

RIGHT In 1890, Louis and Georges Vuitton patented their own invention, the virtually impenetrable tumbler lock. Each lock and key carries a serial number unique to its owner. Even master escapologist Houdini could not crack it.

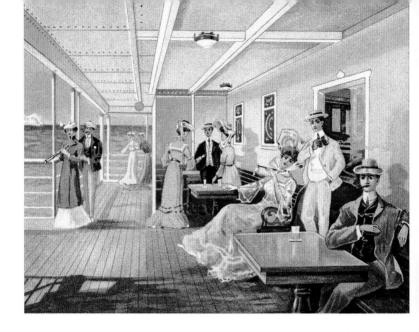

ABOVE The wealthy classes' passion for luxurious transatlantic travel, pictured here on deck in 1907, saw demand for Louis Vuitton luggage grow.

so well regarded that rumour has it that when the Vuittons challenged Harry Houdini to free himself from a trunk, the master escapologist declined the challenge.

The early part of the twentieth century saw a boom in transatlantic sea crossings on luxury liners, for which wealthy travellers required numerous pieces of luggage to safely transport their many possessions. The company found great success with designs including the "Idéale", a nested trunk that would hold a capsule collection of suits, shirts, shoes, hat and canes for the well-dressed man. And to counter the issue of onboard space, the large, unstructured "Steamer" bag – which could be emptied and folded neatly away in a wardrobe – was created in 1901. This is widely regarded as the forerunner of Louis Vuitton's soft-sided bags.

Sea crossings and steam train travel remained popular. However, new modes of transport were evolving that would

ABOVE In this 1909 image, passengers waiting to board an ocean liner in New York City have their Louis Vuitton trunks subjected to rigorous customs checks.

change the type of luggage people needed. First came the automobile, which Georges had predicted would become hugely popular before the turn of the twentieth century. The automobile trunk, released in 1897, was inspired by a zinc trunk Louis Vuitton had created for exotic travel. Hard-wearing and waterproof, it could be securely attached to the rear of the vehicle (before it became commonplace for a car to have an inbuilt "trunk"), ideal for bumpy, dusty roads in an automobile with little protection against the weather. Roof trunks were similarly designed to create more storage space in a semi-open vehicle. This luggage proved immensely popular, as the new fashion for holidaying in locales such as the Côte d'Azur meant automobiles needed to be packed to the rafters with glamorous clothes and accessories. In fact, Georges Vuitton decided to open his third store on the Côte d'Azur in 1908.

LEFT Automobile travel was a passion of Georges Vuitton, and he and his twin sons even ventured into the design of small vehicles. This image shows a collapsible Tilbury carriage by Louis Vuitton and Morel-Grummer, complete with Louis Vuitton trunks, which were commissioned by socialite Blanche de Clermont-Tonnerre in 1910.

OPPOSITE Aviation became hugely popular in the early twentieth century. Meetings, like the one in Monte Carlo advertised in this poster from 1910, featured competitions among the leading aviators and the latest aeronautical innovations. Very early on Georges Vuitton designed lightweight trunks to suit all kinds of aircraft.

Like many forward-thinking people of his generation, Georges was hugely keen on automobiles, so much so that he even ventured into designing them. With the help of his young twin sons, Jean and Pierre, the family designed a small, light vehicle known as a "*voiturette*". It was furnished with many of the items from the Louis Vuitton automobile range, including a spare-parts trunk, a mobile washbowl and lunch sets. But perhaps Georges's most ambitious mobile project was a type of early camper van he created in partnership with the Kellner coach-building company in 1908, which came complete with a washbasin, rooftop sleeping area, open-out bar and, of course, plenty of storage.

The other new mode of transport, and the one that inspired the most awe of all, was air travel, first by hot air balloon and finally by aeroplane. Exhilarated by this incredible feat

MONTE-CARLO
CONCOURS D'AVIATION
FEVRIER ET MARS
100.000 F DE PRIX
Grün
ATELIERS GRÜN-TEL-540.47
TOUT POSSESSEUR DE CETTE AFFICHE SERA POURSUIVI

ABOVE These two compact suitcases with their Louis Vuitton luggage labels were typical of the luggage Georges Vuitton designed for air travel.

– being able to fly like a bird – Georges started creating luggage designed for the skies even before air travel was commonplace. The featherlight "Aéro" trunk was designed in 1910 to be fixed to either side of a hot-air balloon's basket, and proved to be adaptable to all aircraft. Georges's twins, who were precocious children, graduated from designing automobiles to a promising early form of helicopter. However, their aeronautical careers were tragically cut short when Jean

BELOW Georges
Vuitton and his
son Gaston-Louis
were passionate
about aeronautical
adventures,
witnessing Charles
Lindbergh's landmark
transatlantic flight
in 1927.

Vuitton died after an illness in 1909, aged just 10 years old. His twin, Pierre, continued to experiment, but was sent to fight in the First World War in 1914 and died in September 1917. Despite these tragic losses, Georges's obsession with air travel, shared with his eldest son, Gaston-Louis, continued and culminated when the pair witnessed Charles Lindbergh land in Paris after his historical 3,600-mile flight from New York in May 1927. Lindbergh later visited the Louis Vuitton store to buy several trunks.

GASTON-LOUIS VUITTON: MODERN LUXURY DESIGN

Born in January 1883 at Asnières, Gaston-Louis Vuitton was the only surviving child of Georges Vuitton after the death of Gaston-Louis's twin brothers in 1909 and 1917. He suffered from childhood illnesses and as a result was a bookish child who enjoyed reading, writing and sketching. He grew into a cultured adult, an aesthete and collector of beautiful objects who was keenly interested in all aspects of design. Like his father before him, it was expected that he would inherit the family business. In 1897, he began an apprenticeship at the Asnières workshops before moving to the store on Rue Scribe two years later. He showed a flair for salesmanship and continued selling at the store for eight years. After marrying his childhood sweetheart, Renée Versillé, in 1906, Gaston-Louis was promoted by his father to the management of the company, creating a partnership with him that saw the company's trade name change to Vuitton et Fils.

In 1914, Georges moved the Paris flagship store to larger premises at 70 Avenue des Champs-Élysées, and Gaston-Louis took charge. The seven-storey building, designed by Ritz architects Bigaux and Koller in early Art Deco style, was the world's largest travel-goods store and its vast windows became the showcase for Gaston-Louis's inspired displays. Every week the window displays were changed, with Gaston-Louis drawing detailed sketches of exactly how they would appear. His passion for creating singular and compelling window art never dimmed, and in 1927, he described it as "an enjoyable preparation involving the arts of architecture and stage direction".[1] Never afraid to experiment and amuse, Gaston-Louis saw his windows become legendary – such as the early 1930s display in which two live giant tortoises appeared, much to the delight of passers-by.

During the First World War, like so many other luxury goods manufacturers, Maison Louis Vuitton found sourcing raw materials difficult. What remained at the factory at Asnières was used for making folded stretchers and sturdy military trunks rather than the usual luxury luggage. After the war ended, the factory gradually built up production again, and as America rose to become a global superpower, Georges and Gaston-Louis looked to the New World. It was the golden age of oceanic travel, with colossal liners offering those moving between the two continents ultimate comfort and luxury. Louis Vuitton had already opened two department-store outlets in the United States in 1905, in Chicago and San Francisco, followed by stores in Washington in 1907 and New York

BELOW The stunning seven-storey early Art Deco Louis Vuitton flagship store at 70 Champs-Élysées (pictured here in 2018) was designed by architects Bigaux and Koller and opened in 1914.

OPPOSITE TOP
Obsessed with the
Art Deco aesthetic,
Gaston Louis
collaborated with
other notable names
to create stunning
pieces such as this
ladies' travelling case
featuring delicate cut
glass bottles made
by René Lalique and
silverware by Jean
Puiforcat.

OPPOSITE BOTTOM
All eventualities were
catered for by Louis
Vuitton, including
this 1930s picnic set
housed in an elegant
case.

in 1912. Over the next two decades, with the rise of a new, wealthy, transatlantic jet set, the brand thrived, opening stores in several more US cities before the Great Wall Street Crash of 1929 and subsequent economic depression.

Gaston-Louis's passion for the arts and architecture greatly influenced the style of the Louis Vuitton brand. As a child, he had collected antique luggage, tools and shop signs as well as hotel luggage labels. In a lecture in 1920, he explained that these labels, which were routinely given by hoteliers to their guests to adorn their trunks, were in effect like mini advertisements to encourage travellers to return to a favourite destination or encourage others to visit for the first time. This innate understanding of how customers came to form an emotional attachment to their travels, and to the trunks that recorded them, allowed Gaston-Louis to successfully build the brand loyalty Louis Vuitton enjoyed throughout the following decades.

His infatuation with Art Deco also saw Gaston-Louis collaborate with many notable artistic names of the period. Ladies' travelling cases featured delicate cut-glass bottles made by René Lalique and silverware by Jean Puiforcat. His love of the design movement even led him to experiment away from travelling goods, designing everyday objects from furniture to a hugely successful range of dressing-table nécessaires, as the French dubbed them, including scent bottles, manicure sets and a selection of brushes which were included in Louis Vuitton travelling sets. Everything was beautifully designed, with even the ivory-backed brushes carved in a geometric Art Deco style. Inevitably, he saw an opportunity to fill his beautifully designed crystal bottles and in 1927, he launched Maison Louis Vuitton's first perfume: Heures d'Absence, created to invoke the magic of travel and adventure.

THE SECOND
WORLD WAR
AND BEYOND

OCCUPATION, LIBERATION AND A NEW FREEDOM

The Second World War was a challenging time for both
the Louis Vuitton company and the family themselves. The
invasion of France and the subsequent occupation of Paris in
June of 1940 threatened many businesses, and how to survive
became a very personal decision. Much has been made of the
divide within the Vuitton family during the war years.

According to author Stéphanie Bonvicini, Gaston-Louis
and his son Henry-Louis were seduced by Philippe
Pétain, the Nazi puppet French premier who promised
that collaborating with the Germans was the only way to save
France. Gaston-Louis's other two sons, twins Claude-Louis and
Jacques-Louis, saw through the charade and opposed the Vichy
regime, instead joining the resistance and fighting for the exiled
Charles de Gaulle. Although the company was allowed to trade
during the war years, the Asnières workshop could no longer
easily supply Paris, and foreign business was impossible.

After the liberation of Paris on 25 August 1944, it was a
time to rebuild both family relationships and the business itself.
Gaston-Louis gave each of his sons a role, putting Henry-Louis

OPPOSITE Pictured in *Vogue* in 1954, socialite Mrs Amory Carhart Jr
poses in front of the New York skyline as a man loads her Louis Vuitton
luggage onto a seaplane.

OPPOSITE AND ABOVE Style icon Audrey Hepburn was a longtime client of Louis Vuitton who helped boost the popularity of the brand, always travelling with her trusty Speedy bag. The luggage appeared on-screen too. This shot from her 1957 film *Love in the Afternoon* shows a large Louis Vuitton Monogram trunk.

in charge of sales in Paris, placing Claude-Louis at Asnières to oversee the workshop and making Jacques-Louis administrative and finance director. Within a couple of years, with supplies of raw materials flowing freely again, the business picked up, in part thanks to Gaston-Louis's work in supporting and promoting the manufacture and reputation of French luxury goods after the war. In 1954, on its 100th anniversary, the company moved from the Champs-Élysées, which had become overrun by brasseries and entertainment venues, to an elegant private mansion more befitting their clientele, at 78 Avenue Marceau.

Towards the end of the 1950s and into the 1960s, society was changing fast, influenced greatly by French cinema's New Wave – in which dynamic young directors embraced a spontaneous new way of filming, using handheld cameras to shoot

BELOW New Wave
cinema had a huge
influence on the
1960s aesthetic and
stars such as Brigitte
Bardot, shown
here in Jean-Luc
Godard's 1963 drama
Contempt, or *Le
Mépris*, were studied
and emulated both
on- and off-screen.

OPPOSITE Brigitte
Bardot, shown here
newly married to
Gunter Sachs in 1966.

contemporary subjects in real-life locations. The new face of this modern lifestyle was Brigitte Bardot, who was studied both on- and off-screen by the young women who rushed to emulate her. Saint-Tropez became the new "It" destination for celebrities and the wealthy, their glamorous lifestyles captured by the paparazzi, and it became commonplace to travel down for a weekend or even just for a one-night party. This new way of travelling needed a similarly flexible style of luggage, and so the soft-sided style of Louis Vuitton bags exploded in popularity, in particular the Keepall, a much-photographed favourite of Bardot's.

Another influencing factor on the reputation and success of Louis Vuitton during the 1950s and 1960s was fashion editorial. Photographers including David Bailey and Richard Avedon created stunning imagery featuring elegant models in the latest

RIGHT Catherine Deneuve and husband, fashion photographer David Bailey, arriving in London in 1966 with a complete set of Louis Vuitton Monogram luggage.

OPPOSITE Fashion editorial also played a big part in establishing the desirability of Louis Vuitton bags, as shown here in this shot of model Twiggy from *Vogue* in 1967.

haute couture for magazines such as *Vogue* and *Harper's Bazaar*. In many of these spreads, a Louis Vuitton travelling case or bag is the perfect foil to the exquisitely tailored suits of the 1950s – or complements the free, sassy mood of liberated young women of the 1960s, epitomized by the model Twiggy. Such pictures heightened the aspirational quality and social cachet of Louis Vuitton bags that continues to this day.

Gaston-Louis Vuitton, who was so influential in the design ethos and success of the family company, died in 1970. He remained devoted to the business, and from 1954 until his death, he divided his time between Asnières, where he spent his mornings, and the Paris store, to which he was driven by chauffeur at exactly 1.30 p.m. each day.

GLOBAL EXPANSION

CONQUERING THE WORLD OF LUXURY

In the years immediately following Gaston-Louis Vuitton's death in 1970, the company did little more than tread water. The Paris store and its sister store in Nice were still popular, but sales were stagnating rather than growing. By 1977, Gaston-Louis's three sons, along with his daughters' husbands, realized the company had enormous potential, but they needed to take action to exploit it.

The role of president was, after some heated family debate, given to Henry Racamier, Odile Vuitton's husband. Despite initial misgivings among some of the Vuittons, he proved to be an inspired choice. Hard-working and astute, Racamier was, like Louis Vuitton before him, a son of Jura, where tenacity and resilience were instilled from birth. After the Second World War, he had founded a massively successful steel manufacturing business, which he sold for a large profit before taking the helm at Louis Vuitton at the age of 65. His experience, particularly that of international trade, proved invaluable in increasing the global reach of the company.

At the time, the company's model of international selling was based on franchises, where local businessmen bought the

OPPOSITE Louis Vuitton's first soft-sided bag, designed in 1901 to be packed for ocean liner travel, was named The Steamer. Here Catherine Deneuve rests her feet on a classic Monogram version in 1970.

right to use the Louis Vuitton name and the licence to sell their products, but otherwise were essentially left to their own devices as to how they promoted the goods. When Racamier took over, this system was replaced with one focused on local subsidiaries, which allowed Louis Vuitton far more control over stores in other countries. Working closely with the heads of the subsidiaries, the family had input into store architecture, interior design and choice of product lines. Tapping into associates' knowledge of local markets and customer preference allowed the stores to thrive, and partnerships were forged which proved vital to the company's growth.

BELOW Since Gaston-Louis Vuitton's time, architecture, interior design and window displays have been hugely important to the success of the brand, exemplified by this display at the New York Fifth Avenue store.

Japan was an early success, with stores opening in Tokyo and Osaka in 1978. The rest of Asia soon followed, with stores opening in locations such as Singapore in 1979. Counterfeiting in Asia had been a particular problem, something Gaston-Louis had tried to address shortly before his death. Offering legitimate Louis Vuitton merchandise resolved the problem to a certain extent, and stores situated within large hotels were perfectly placed to attract international travellers. In 1981, a prestigious New York store opened, raising the company's profile stateside, and Europe followed, the highlight being a successful reopening of the London store on Bond Street that had first welcomed Louis Vuitton in 1900.

BELOW The opulent Louis Vuitton store on London's Bond Street, established 1900, and reopened in 1981.

LEFT In 1986, a new flagship Paris store was opened on Avenue Montaigne, which has since become renowned for its interior design and dramatic window displays.

OPPOSITE Asia has become a thriving market for Louis Vuitton with stores including this architecturally striking building in Hong Kong.

The 1980s was a successful decade for the brand, which grew from a handful of stores generating 11 million euros in sales in 1977 to 125 stores and 600 million euros in sales in 1989.[1] In 1986, a flagship Paris store on the elite Avenue Montaigne was unveiled with modern interior design and dynamic product placement. To further promote the brand's international profile, the company started looking for sponsorship opportunities, and in 1983, the Louis Vuitton Cup, a sailing race that was a required preliminary to the renowned America's Cup, was established. Three years later, the brand created the Louis Vuitton Foundation for Opera, which funded the training of new and talented young musicians and raised the profile of opera worldwide. These cultural partnerships with other brands and institutions that shared the core values of tradition and high quality helped seal the reputation of Louis Vuitton as one of the world's most prestigious luxury goods brands.

ABOVE To promote Louis Vuitton as a prestigious international brand, Henry Racamier sought sponsorship opportunities such as the Louis Vuitton sailing cup, a preliminary to the illustrious America's Cup.

ADVERTISING AND PHOTOGRAPHY: JEAN LARIVIÈRE

BELOW In 1978, Louis Vuitton commissioned photographer Jean Larivière, shown here at a retrospective of his work with the brand in 2007, to create advertising images. The collaboration would last over three decades, producing stunning photography under the banner "The Spirit of Travel".

Since the days when Gaston-Louis sketched out window displays that were almost works of art in themselves, the value of creating strong brand imagery was paramount at Louis Vuitton. With this in mind, in 1978, the company commissioned photographer Jean Larivière to shoot an advertising campaign. So began a collaboration that lasted more than three decades. His first series, titled "The Spirit of Travel", took Larivière to some of the most spectacular places in the world, including Thailand, China, Greenland, Myanmar and Nepal. The thrust of the campaign was to celebrate timeless luxury, and the locations sought out by Larivière placed Louis Vuitton products among some of the most mesmerizing landscapes on Earth.

A purist, Larivière obsessively planned the composition of his photographs before taking numerous versions to find the perfect shot. Sometimes he waited hours for the right light and thought nothing of trekking miles to get it. He recalled:

"It took five hours in an off-road vehicle to reach the location which is the largest impact crater in Chile. When I got there the sun was going down and I didn't have time to put a camera stand, I threw a sandbag on the ground, balanced my camera on it, I took two photos with two different rockets."[2]

Influenced by legendary photographers including Richard Avedon, Robert Mapplethorpe and Irving Penn, the stripped back, black-

and-white style of Larivière's early photographs for Louis Vuitton made an immediate impact on the public. He continued travelling over the years, creating meticulously composed photographs that cemented the association between Louis Vuitton and the most luxurious and exotic destinations. In addition to his advertising work, Larivière was commissioned to photograph a series commemorating the heritage of the brand, including shots of the workshops at Asnières. Despite Larivière being less well known than many of his contemporaries, retrospectives of his work, encompassing portraits, fashion editorial and reportage as well as advertising campaigns, show him to be a true artist.

LVMH: THE BIRTH OF A MEGA-BRAND

By the late 1980s, Henry Racamier had already started to expand Louis Vuitton by discreetly buying controlling interests in other high-end brands, including the fashion houses Givenchy and Loewe and champagne producer Veuve Clicquot. However, his ambitions were for greater penetration into the luxury goods market, so in 1987, Louis Vuitton merged with Moët Hennessy to create the mega-brand LVMH (Moët Hennessy Louis Vuitton).

Moët Hennessy had spent several decades investing heavily in businesses worldwide, including other champagne producers (their main competitor, Ruinart Père et Fils, was bought out in 1962), wine and spirit producers, and prestigious brands such as Christian Dior Parfums. Although successful, the company had overstretched itself financially; in June 1987, the legendary $4 billion merger took place. The impetus behind the merger was to allow Louis Vuitton to expand globally and save Moët Hennessy from takeover bids. Each party was to retain control of its own subsidiaries. Alain Chevalier, president of Moët Hennessy, which was the larger company, was named chairman and Henry Racamier was named executive vice president.

Unfortunately, disagreements soon arose as Racamier and the rest of the Louis Vuitton board accused Alain Chevalier and Moët Hennessy of trying to absorb the company into its own operations. The 60 per cent ownership the Vuitton family had held in Louis Vuitton as minority shareholder became worth just 17 per cent of LVMH[3]. To level the playing field, Racamier sought back-up from Bernard Arnault, a young property developer and financial engineer who invested in LVMH. Unfortunately for Racamier, the tactic backfired as Arnault himself had designs on the leadership of the conglomerate. Arnault, with the support of British firm Guinness plc (which had been persuaded to buy shares in LVMH by Chevalier to stand with him against Racamier), secured a controlling interest in Arnault's name. Chevalier left LVMH and Arnault and Racamier were left to battle control of the company out in the courts. Despite the fact that Louis Vuitton accounted for 32 per

ABOVE In 1987, after a turbulent decade for the brand, Louis Vuitton merged with Moët Hennessy in a ground-breaking $4 billion deal. Bernard Arnault, pictured here in the 1980s, invested in the company on the invitation of Henry Racamier but soon sought leadership himself, which resulted in Racamier and other Louis Vuitton family members being forced out.

cent of all LVMH sales, Arnault was supported by the Moët and Hennessy families. Along with other top executives, Racamier was forced out, and Arnault took control of Louis Vuitton.

While LVMH was still easily the world's most valuable luxury goods group, by the early 1990s the Louis Vuitton label began to struggle. Throughout the 1980s, the Monogram print had been used on a large number of new products to generate increased sales, but had become somewhat ubiquitous as a result. This overselling of the design devalued its worth as a status symbol, a problem compounded by counterfeiting. In 1989, LVMH brought French textile executive Yves Carcelle on board as CEO of Louis Vuitton, with a view to expanding product lines and boosting sales. However, during the first half of the 1990s, Louis Vuitton continued to struggle. It would take until 1996 for things to start to change, first with the redesign of the iconic Damier canvas on a new line of luggage and second, a celebration of the Monogram motif's centenary.

Reinventing the overused Monogram print was a priority. Louis Vuitton needed a high-profile campaign to show the brand was modern and dynamic rather than traditional and staid. The company invited seven contemporary fashion designers to create their perfect piece of luggage. It could be anything so long as it featured the Monogram canvas. The designs of the seven – Azzedine Alaïa, Vivienne Westwood, Manolo Blahnik, Helmut Lang, Romeo Gigli, Sybilla, and Isaac Mizrahi – were exhibited across the world and gained much press attention. The items themselves became sought after by collectors and Louis Vuitton found itself presenting a new, fashionable face to the world of luxury luggage. The obvious next step was to move into the world of fashion design. With this aim, in 1997 Arnault appointed a visionary designer, Marc Jacobs, to revitalize the brand.

MARC
JACOBS

LAUNCHING A FASHION LINE

Born in New York in 1963, Marc Jacobs was determined to be a fashion designer from a young age. His father died when he was seven and his mother subsequently remarried several times, uprooting Jacobs and his siblings so much that when he was in his teens he chose to live with his grandmother.

The move provided much-needed stability for the passionate and creative teenager, and his grandmother, a seasoned traveller who surrounded herself with beautiful objects, not only accepted but actively encouraged Jacobs's passions. She allowed him many freedoms and he was a regular at New York's fashionable nightclubs by the age of just 15. Despite his active social life, his dedication to fashion did not waver. A student at the High School of Art and Design, he also worked at an upmarket fashion boutique, Charivari, where he was allowed to design sweaters. This experience gained him a place at the prestigious Parsons School of Design. He excelled there, winning both the Perry Ellis Gold Thimble Award and Chester Weinberg Gold

OPPOSITE Model Naomi Campbell is a long-time muse of Marc Jacobs. As she walks the catwalk for one of his earliest Louis Vuitton shows, the bank of photographers behind reveals the huge media interest in the young designer's new venture.

Thimble Award as well as Design Student of the Year upon his graduation in 1984. Soon after, he created a collection for Sketchbook for Reuben Thomas, which won him the Council of Fashion Designers of America Perry Ellis Award for New Fashion Talent.

Marc Jacobs also met his long-time business partner Robert Duffy at this time and within a year had launched his eponymous fashion label. The next few years saw Jacobs face many challenges, as he sought backers for his company and encountered downright bad luck when one collection was stolen and a terrible fire destroyed his studio. His fortunes changed when, in November 1988, it was announced that the 25-year-old Jacobs was to be appointed head of womenswear for Perry Ellis. Ellis, who had died in 1986, was a renowned name in American fashion, comparable to Ralph Lauren or Calvin Klein. The company needed young, fresh talent and this was a huge opportunity for Jacobs, who was determined to put his own mark on the casual clothing and sportswear brand.

Over the eight collections he designed for Perry Ellis, what would become Jacobs's iconic grunge look began to emerge. Taking supermodel Linda Evangelista as his muse, he produced designs that left the fashion press divided and were also not commercially successful for Perry Ellis, who fired him in 1992. But by the time he left to focus on his own label once more, it was clear that he had started a monumental trend. Ironically, the collection that cost Jacobs his job – an array of printed granny dresses, heavy Doc Martens boots and flannel shirts – won him great critical acclaim and the 1992 CFDA Womenswear Designer of the Year. *Women's Wear Daily* (*WWD*) christened the designer "the guru of grunge", and the hottest style of the early 1990s was born.

In a 1992 interview with *WWD*, Jacobs described his deconstructed grunge style as "a hippie, romantic version of

OPPOSITE In 1997 Bernard Arnault appointed the young designer Marc Jacobs to launch Louis Vuitton into the world of fashion ready-to-wear.

punk". He went on to explain, "There is no wrong or right now. It's all about giving people choices."

Grunge captured the anti-capitalist mood of the early 1990s perfectly, offering an antidote to the greedy overconsumption and status symbols of the 1980s. But by 1995, the backlash against high fashion was waning, minimalism was growing in popularity and traditional French fashion houses were popular once again. There was a difference, however, in that many of these old-school labels were now employing young avant-garde designers to shake things up. British designers included Stella McCartney, who joined Chloé, and the two *enfants terribles,* John Galliano and Alexander McQueen, whom Bernard Arnault had enticed to head up Dior and Givenchy, respectively.

Perhaps to balance the theatrics Galliano and McQueen offered, or perhaps because American designer Tom Ford had made such a huge impact at Gucci in the years since he joined in 1990, Arnault looked to the United States for designers who might take over at other LVMH labels. In 1997, he chose Michael Kors to design for Céline, and Narciso Rodriguez to head up Loewe. But it was his appointment of Marc Jacobs to launch ready-to-wear collections at Louis Vuitton that generated the biggest headlines.

Marc Jacobs's first collection for Louis Vuitton appeared in March 1998, and in a somewhat perverse decision, the collection featured just one handbag, with a discreet LV logo. In fact, the whole show confirmed the move towards a more stripped-back look that the designer had been experimenting with under his own label for the previous few seasons. Minimalism during the 1990s was the antithesis of mix-and-match grunge, with designers such as Jil Sander, Helmut Lang and Calvin Klein creating clothes for women who wanted a beautiful yet functional wardrobe. Jacobs fully embraced this aesthetic in his debut show, offering plain, well-cut dresses and coats and elegant separates in subtle shades of blue and grey, with little ostentation. It fitted perfectly with how Louis Vuitton wanted the brand to appear, a homage to understated luxury that above all was eminently wearable. As Marc Jacobs told fashion writer Sarah Mower:

"We couldn't make it look like old Vuitton, because there was no tradition … So I started from zero, without putting an insignia on the outside of things – just in the linings, pieces in pale grey like the original Vuitton trunks and in fabric like bonded cotton that had both luxury and practicality."[1]

Jacobs also showed an aptitude for self-promotion when he pulled a brilliant publicity stunt a few days before the show. Naomi Campbell recalled how she and many other top models booked to walk the Louis Vuitton show were stuck in Milan, unable to find transport to Paris. Jacobs, a close friend of the supermodel, promptly sent a private jet complete with gift trunks for each model, and Campbell called the paparazzi. A subsequent shot of the line-up of the world's top models, all holding Louis Vuitton luggage, with Campbell in the foreground with a baby-blue Keepall hot off the production line, became iconic.

Marc Jacobs's second show confirmed his minimalist aesthetic, with plenty of all white or grey outfits – although, perhaps foreshadowing his successor Nicolas Ghesquière's obsession with sci-fi, the designer did send some of the models down the runway in jumpsuits accessorized with space helmets. The neutral palette of his clothes lent itself to the bolder accessories that Louis Vuitton produced that season. He opted for an embossed logo on Monogram bags, which appeared in a range of lollipop colours in patent leather, both in traditional and newer styles, like the backpack, cross-body and bum-bag versions.

OPPOSITE The high-society elegance that epitomizes Louis Vuitton has always infused Jacobs's collections. This shot of Claudia Schiffer for Spring/Summer 2000 wearing a yellow belted raincoat with contrasting pastel patent bag is fresh yet still classic.

RIGHT For Autumn/ Winter 2000, Marc Jacobs presented minimalist Parisian chic with a hint of his beloved 1980s. Black crocodile suits, broken up by splashes of colour such as this oversized green fur jacket, were teamed with angled berets. Luxurious textures and fabrics quickly became a mainstay of the Louis Vuitton fashion collections.

For his Spring/Summer 2000 show, Marc Jacobs took inspiration from the travel ideology of the Louis Vuitton brand with a collection that would suit international jet-setters as at home on an African safari as they were strutting the sidewalks of Manhattan. Alongside the khaki and pale yellows, printed fabrics started to appear, both in the form of a mini-Monogram on coats and jackets and more graphic designs on silk jersey dresses.

By the Autumn/Winter 2000 collection, Jacobs was showing a keen awareness of how trends were moving among younger style-setters. He introduced just enough homage to the 1980s, albeit the uber-chic Paris of that decade, to ensure Louis Vuitton had its finger on fashion's pulse. The palette was mostly sophisticated tones of coffee and black, jazzed up in glossy satin or adorned with sequins. Oversized shoulders and asymmetrical tops slipping off on one side, teamed with angled berets, thoroughly summed up the retro mood. The showstopper was a blue crocodile-skin suit – just in case anyone had forgotten Louis Vuitton was the world's top luxury brand.

COLLABORATIONS: FASHION MEETS ART
STEPHEN SPROUSE

One of the ways in which Marc Jacobs brought the traditional Louis Vuitton to the attention of a new, younger, and cooler audience was through collaborations. Stephen Sprouse was a designer and artist popular in the early 1980s for his graffiti-printed fashion. He dubbed his clothes "cyber punk" and also gained permission to use iconic prints, Andy Warhol's *Camouflage* being the most high profile. Sprouse collaborated with artist Keith Haring and also worked as a graphic artist himself. Though critically acclaimed, Sprouse was not very well known outside the fashion and art worlds until his work for Louis Vuitton in 2001.

OPPOSITE AND LEFT Jacobs's collaborations with artists made a huge splash. His first, featuring graffiti-scrawled bags by Stephen Sprouse, debuted on the Spring/Summer 2001 catwalk and the design quickly became iconic.

The result was a series of graffitied bags that became a huge hit for the label. It was a daring move, as Marc Jacobs explained in an interview for the 2012 exhibition of the designer's work with Louis Vuitton at the Musée des Arts Décoratifs:

"I'm not really rebellious, but it was kind of a clever solution to doing what we were told by a certain old guard at Louis Vuitton we couldn't do: 'You don't deface the Monogram; you don't change the Monogram.' There was a certain respect and a disrespect (in scribbling on the Monogram). Again if anything we only amplified the attention to the Monogram by writing on top of it."[2]

Initially, the reception the bags had among the "suits" at Louis Vuitton was lukewarm. But the press response was hugely enthusiastic and sparked a mania for graffiti-painted bags that spilt over into fashion everywhere. Jacobs recalls: "It was everywhere. And even now to this day some of those bag souvenir places right by our office in Paris have the little nylon bags that are so clearly taken from that Sprouse graffiti."[3]

LEFT AND OPPOSITE
For Spring/Summer
2002 Jacobs revisited
his grunge years with
long paisley print
dresses. Accessories
were a toned-down
version of the
graffiti bag, which
was suffering from
over-exposure, with
cute woodland animal
themes that suited the
collection's whimsical
mood.

It was at Jacobs's Spring/Summer 2001 show that the graffiti bags were first revealed, finding a place among the contrasting trends of the season, which ranged from a military vibe, complete with an "SS Vuitton" naval cap, to soft florals and a smattering of Day-Glo bright fluorescents with a 1980s-punk feel.

Marc Jacobs continued to be fêted by the press for his work at Louis Vuitton. For Autumn/Winter 2001, he presented an almost entirely monochrome palette, breaking up the severe black and white with playful details, including mini polka dots masquerading as oversized buttons, and fur collar trims. The overall impression was of a classic, timeless collection and yet it managed to be modern and sophisticated too. Jacobs was certainly fulfilling his brief to bring a fresh, new eye and younger customers to Louis Vuitton without betraying the heritage of the brand or its old guard of clientele.

By Spring/Summer 2002, the clean lines and discreet tailoring had been replaced by a more bohemian look. Long, paisley-printed peasant dresses might have been taken from Jacobs's grunge years, but the grown-up elegance of his designs was pervasive. This season showed a new spin on accessories, too. With the street-style graffiti bag having suffered from overexposure, Jacobs instead offered cutesy, animal-themed bags in the shape of a butterfly, or with oversized owl eyes peering from above the flowers of the Monogram print.

Autumn/Winter collections lend themselves to sophisticated clothes, perfectly in line with Louis Vuitton's brand values, and 2002 did not disappoint. The 1950s feel that had lurked in the background of some of Jacobs's more recent shows came to the fore with elegant pencil skirts teamed with silk camisoles, tailored two-piece suits and three-quarter-length, fur-trimmed coats. A familiar nod to the 1980s, in the form of silk bomber jackets and corset-style tops, as well as a few oversized blazers, capitalized on Vuitton's love of luxurious fabrics. Mink, cashmere, washed silk and traditional herringbone tweed all felt perfectly on message, the statement underlined by a metallic mesh Monogram evening bag.

TAKASHI MURAKAMI

The collaboration between Takashi Murakami and Louis Vuitton that began in 2002 and lasted for 13 years was a groundbreaking initiative that saw the traditional French luggage company meet the world of Japanese pop culture.

Murakami is a Japanese contemporary artist who, since the early 1990s, has created work inspired by a wide range of influences, including traditional Japanese art, anime and manga, sci-fi and pop culture. He works in a variety of media, spanning painting, sculpture and film. His invented cartoon characters –

RIGHT The collaboration between Japanese pop culture artist Takashi Murakami and Louis Vuitton began in 2002 and lasted for 13 years.

ABOVE Murakami
superimposed cute
kawaii emblems onto
the Monogram canvas
such as this tote from
the Cherry Blossom
collection.

some anime, others smiling flowers, bears and lions – are often interpreted as symbols of contemporary themes like technology, fantasy or violence. Kawaii, the Japanese culture of cuteness and childlike vulnerability, has a big influence on his work.

In 2002, Marc Jacobs approached Murakami with the idea of transforming the Monogram emblems into cartoon characters. The designer envisioned the collaboration as a kind of Warholian pop art and gave Murakami complete freedom in how to interpret the commission. The resulting designs have become iconic. In the "Multicolore" range, a vibrant version of the Monogram is reimagined in 33 colours on a white background, and in some versions the circular flowers of the traditional Monogram are replaced by cutesy kawaii characters. The "Cherry Blossom" collection featured Murakami's version of the traditional Japanese

flower emblem repeatedly interwoven onto a background of the traditional Monogram brown and beige, which in other limited pieces hosted Murakami's trademark comic characters. The designs were wide-ranging, with successes including the "Monogramouflage", which was a camouflage version of the iconic Monogram print and was launched in 2008.

In a further intermingling of art and business, Murakami took the Monogram designs and reincorporated them into his own paintings and sculptures. In 2009, a retrospective of the Japanese artist's work, which showcased many of his designs for Louis Vuitton, was held at the Museum of Contemporary Art in Los Angeles. The exhibition also featured a boutique that sold the collaborative pieces.

In keeping with the kawaii nature of Murakami's bags, Spring/Summer 2003 was similarly upbeat and optimistic. Slightly dimmed versions of the bright colours on the new bags were echoed in charming satin dresses with neat Peter Pan collars and tied belts with a large bow. Again, the vibe was retro, this time 1950s going on 1960s, but the collision with pop culture brought the collection right up to date, especially with the inventive use of neoprene and rubber in several of the outfits.

This experimentation with new and exciting textiles, pairing them with the most traditional of luxury fabrics, has been a trademark of Marc Jacobs at Louis Vuitton. For Autumn/Winter 2003, the Monogram appeared printed on futuristic vinyl – only to be teamed with ladylike tweed. By his following collection, the emphasis was still on texture, this time channelling silver-screen glamour in the form of crushed velvet, crêpe de Chine, peacock-blue silk and gold lamé. The collection conjured up evenings in cocktail bars or perhaps dinner in grand country houses, but as always, with Jacobs it didn't feel dated and had plenty of appeal for Louis Vuitton's younger customers as well. This season, the perfectly matched

OPPOSITE The Multicolore range of bags saw the traditional Monogram print reimagined in 33 colours on a white background and was presented on the Spring/Summer 2003 catwalk.

RIGHT Always
experimenting and
casting a wide net for
inspiration, Jacobs
gave a nod to designer
Vivienne Westwood in
Autumn/Winter 2004
with a collection that
visited the Scottish
Highlands.

accessories came as a series of neat Monogram bags: some rich with gold, others in coordinating patent leather.

As Jacobs's tenure at Louis Vuitton progressed, collections with mixed reviews were interspersed with runaway hits. For example, Autumn/Winter 2004, for which the mood was based in the Scottish Highlands, saw a deluge of tartan – trimmed with fur for a belted coat, or as a suit complete with swinging skirt and net petticoat. There was even a bustier in case it became too fusty. The homage to Vivienne Westwood was clear, but there was also a nod towards the East, as Jacobs acknowledged the inspiration of Tsuguharu Foujita, a Japanese traditionalist painter who worked in Paris in the 1920s. The legions of Japanese Louis Vuitton customers must have been pleased – as were the accountants at LVMH, as Japan was a significant market for the company.

It is important to remember that alongside his work for Louis Vuitton, Marc Jacobs was also designing seasonal

BELOW Accessories are the mainstay of the Louis Vuitton brand, and Marc Jacobs designed new bags each season, here echoing the luxury of his clothes with an embellished velvet Monogram evening bag.

LEFT Elegance and sumptuous fabrics presented in his unique style became a trademark of Marc Jacobs at Louis Vuitton. This knitted suit patched with leather and crocodile for Autumn/Winter 2005 is a perfect example.

collections for his eponymous label, meaning he quite often opened the show circuit in New York and closed it in Paris. Inevitably, the mood of one would influence the other, albeit unintentionally. In general, Jacobs's own line revealed the designer's penchant for whimsical, fairy-tale clothes, his grunge background never completely forgotten. But for Autumn/Winter 2005, a more sombre mood prevailed at Marc Jacobs, which was echoed on the Louis Vuitton catwalk.

The abundance of all-black outfits raised a few eyebrows, but Jacobs's ability to tailor his designs for Louis Vuitton into beautifully structured outfits ultimately transformed what could have been a depressing spectacle. The essence of Parisian chic, pared down into elegant suits; cocoon coats with three-quarter-length sleeves, revealing delicate gloves; pencil skirts; and belted dresses with boat necks and capped sleeves was pure 1950s, and subtle decorative details transformed the evening wear. The bags from this collection were some of Jacobs's most spectacular yet, including a velvet bag with bejewelled handles and a quilted, embossed leather evening bag.

In 2006, the 1980s reared its head again, this time in several collections channelling Versace-style bling, but there was some old-school Italian glamour there, too, with a Pucci feel to some of the prints. The referencing of other legendary French designers is a continuing theme at Louis Vuitton, where it is quite possible to see

BELOW For Autumn/Winter 2006 pure old-school elegance echoed classic French designers including Balenciaga and Yves Saint Laurent.

a single show nodding to the legacies of Balenciaga, Dior and
Yves Saint Laurent. This makes sense given that, until Jacobs
came on board, Louis Vuitton was purely a luggage designer;
this referencing cleverly places the bags within the history of
French haute couture.

The bags are where the profit lies, the catwalk cementing
their covetable status and each season making a new statement.
In 2006 it was the turn of embossed vinyl and fur, more
Murakami Monogram prints, and striking, patent handheld
totes with a pair of golden headphones for a handle. Louis
Vuitton's continued popularity in Japan that began with the
Murakami collaboration was not lost on Jacobs and his design
team. The Spring/Summer 2007 show, for all its elements of
flouncy Victoriana, had a definite kawaii feel, as models with
cute floral hairpieces strutted down the catwalk in doll-like,
frilly dresses.

RICHARD PRINCE

The next headline-grabbing collaboration masterminded by Marc Jacobs for Louis Vuitton was with the artist Richard Prince. The controversial American painter and photographer has been working since the late 1970s creating art by rephotographing the work of other photographers. His work questions and redefines ownership of art and, at the same time, acts as a commentary on some of the most important themes in American culture, including racism, sexism, celebrity culture, pornography and pulp fiction. Prince has become increasingly well known as one of America's most prominent contemporary artists and his work has become highly sought after, especially pieces such as his *Nurse* paintings, which can fetch up to $10 million at auction.

Asked by Bernard Arnault to continue the successful series of artist collaborations, Marc Jacobs, who owns several of

OPPOSITE The launch of the Richard Prince collaboration complemented a collection rich in vibrant colour and texture during the Spring/Summer 2008 show.

LEFT This bag, where the words are superimposed over the Monogram canvas, was from the "Jokes" collection by Richard Prince.

Prince's pieces, approached the artist in early 2007. Jacobs and Prince worked closely together to brainstorm ideas, the artist experimenting with silk-screen paintings until an idea was born. The result was named the "After Dark" collection, and it debuted on the Spring/Summer 2008 catwalk.

The bags were carried by top models, including Naomi Campbell and Eva Herzigova, dressed as sexy nurses wearing semi-transparent, belted, plastic coats in reference to Prince's famous *Nurse* series of paintings. Richard Prince had created four patterns that were superimposed onto the Monogram canvas: the "Jokes" Monogram canvas; the "Pulp" screen-printed Monogram canvas in yellow or red on blue denim with large Louis Vuitton lettering; the "Watercolor" Monogram canvas, which used 17 superimposed colours; and the leather "Bonbon" canvas in pink and green.

The collection into which these bags fitted was similarly colourful and inventive, offering a kaleidoscope of yellow, lilac,

OPPOSITE AND ABOVE Marc Jacobs's third major collaboration was with Richard Prince and debuted on the Spring/Summer 2008 catwalk. The bags were carried by models including Naomi Campbell and Eva Herzigova dressed as sexy nurses in reference to Prince's famous "Nurse" series.

pink and purple in a mix of fabrics that included sparkling Lurex® knits, glossy silk organza and voluminous chiffon. The reception was part shock, part amusement, but the accessories – not only the bags, but also pointed flats and costume jewellery – saved the show and confirmed the designer's continued commercial awareness.

Over the next five years, until Marc Jacobs left Louis Vuitton to concentrate on his own label, the similarities between his own line and that of Louis Vuitton grew more noticeable, perhaps revealing the reason he was ready to concentrate on the former. Typically, though, the Louis Vuitton show was a more refined, tailored affair. Autumn/ Winter 2008 was no different; it was 1980s-inspired with a demure palette of browns, beige and mint green, about which Jacobs commented: "We just worked with shapes. Darts, folds, and pleats. I don't like to use these words because they sound

pretentious, but if you like, last season was painterly, and this season's sculptural."

At the end of 2008, showing his Spring/Summer 2009 collection against the shadow of a world facing economic depression, Jacobs reacted by offering a glitzy, cabaret-style collection that referenced the last-chance gaiety of Paris during the Second World War. The bags this season were similarly seductive, in a glorious array of multicoloured metallic tones, tactile suede and leopard and python prints. And for his Autumn/Winter collection, the 1980s were back, Christian Lacroix style – full of bubble skirts, puffed-sleeved peplum jackets and oversized bows. The accessories again stole the show, with a 1980s feel not only with bags, but also with thigh-high boots and leather chokers.

Marc Jacobs's final years at Louis Vuitton zig-zagged through time and influences. Spring/Summer 2010 offered models sporting huge Afro wigs and a collection that didn't quite know what it was. John Galliano seemed to be a reference, with fitted, bustier-accented minidresses teamed with brocade cycling shorts. The sportswear theme lived on, though rather messily, with mesh, fringing and raw edges. There was even a bit of military. Luckily, by his next collection, Jacobs had rediscovered his direction, taking us back to a Bardot-esque 1950s and 1960s. The models hired, including Elle Macpherson, were not the usual androgynous, blank-faced catwalk creatures, but womanly and voluptuous in cinch-waisted suits and low-cut dresses. Fittingly, the Louis Vuitton "Speedy" bag, an icon of the brand since 1930, was the star of the show, carried by almost every model – in classic, luxe leather and also reinvented, adorned with lace and sequins or covered in fur.

OVERLEAF The 1980s was a recurrent theme for Jacobs popping up again in Autumn/ Winter 2009 with bubble skirts and puff-shoulders.

RIGHT Asia is a huge market for Louis Vuitton and the cheongsam-inspired outfits of his Spring/Summer 2011 collection gave a nod to the East.

For Spring/Summer 2011, the designer started out in the East, with cheongsams, Nehru-collared silk evening pyjamas and heavily fringed cocktail dresses. By his Autumn/Winter show, things had hotted up, with a provocative series of hyper-sexualized outfits that bordered on kink, especially factoring in the thigh-high dominatrix boots, oversized, shiny, patent-leather belts and authoritarian military jackets and caps teamed with black stockings and spike heels. It sold, though. The rubber dominatrix boots sold 2,000 pairs in the first week, according to the designer.

In 2012, the Spring/Summer collection was delicate and ethereal, set against a backdrop of a carousel full of white horses. The broderie anglaise dresses and laser-cut florals in candy-pastel colours were demure, with a sense of 1950s about them, especially the two-piece suits, which had a Dior's New Look feel. Long-time friend and model/muse Kate Moss closed the show, leading to speculation as to how long the designer would remain at the brand. But back Jacobs came, and to coincide with the opening of the exhibition *Louis Vuitton / Marc Jacobs* at Musée des Arts Décoratifs, presented a homage to the house's travel heritage, with hatted and gloved models stepping off a steam train dressed in camel and tan double-breasted jackets with oversized crystal-flower buttons. The skill of both Jacobs and the workshops at Louis Vuitton was underlined by exquisite dresses and trouser suits offering a swirl of colour and pattern – and some truly extraordinary embroidery.

Jacobs's final full year at Louis Vuitton fell in 2013. For his Spring/Summer collection, the designer paid tribute to the original canvas, the chequerboard Damier print. The feel was very 1960s, with plenty of Mary Quant-style graphic minidresses in black and white – but also in lime green and acid yellow. Autumn/Winter offered more muted tones and the elegance and luxury that sit so well with the Louis Vuitton name. Silk, velvet and fur, over delicately floral-printed negligées and pyjamas and robes, against a backdrop of an Art Deco hotel, suggested 1930s society types lounging about during the day until changing into luxe evening wear, which came with Louis Vuitton's typical attention to detail.

Marc Jacobs's nostalgic final show for Louis Vuitton was Spring/Summer 2014, and he recreated many of the themes and sets from his 16 years at the brand. The outfits were almost all black, but it didn't feel like a funeral for the designer – rather, a celebration of all that he had achieved. The outfits – adorned with black jet and beads, with every model wearing Stephen Jones ostrich-feather headpieces – were suitably glamorous, but with enough street style to remind the audience that despite his imminent departure, this was a designer with his finger still on the pulse of fashion. He signed off his show notes with the words: "To the showgirl in all of us."

BELOW Marc Jacobs signed the show notes for his final flamboyant show for Louis Vuitton off with the words: "To the showgirl in all of us".

OPPOSITE As Jacobs neared the end of his tenure at Louis Vuitton, he presented a Spring/Summer collection for 2013 that paid tribute to the Damier check, with outfits that channelled a 1960s Mary Quant vibe.

HERITAGE
REBORN

NICOLAS GHESQUIÈRE AND VIRGIL ABLOH

After the departure of Marc Jacobs, the pressure was on Louis Vuitton to find a designer who could both match Jacobs's success and bring a fresh perspective to the brand. The appointments of Nicolas Ghesquière, and later Virgil Abloh for menswear, proved to be inspired choices.

NICOLAS GHESQUIÈRE

Nicolas Ghesquière was revealed as the new artistic director of Louis Vuitton at the beginning of November 2013, just a few weeks after Marc Jacobs announced his departure. Jacobs immediately praised the appointment, commenting during a talk at the Tate Modern shortly afterwards:

"He is a brilliant designer and he'll do something completely different ... I've always admired Nicolas. I'm curious to see what he'll do ... I'm really glad someone I respect and admire, and think is a really great talent, is there."

Ghesquière was similarly complimentary about Jacobs, "whose legacy I wholeheartedly hope to honour."[1]

OPPOSITE Nicolas Ghesquière has continued to explore the heritage of Louis Vuitton but give it a modern twist. This exquisitely tailored coat from Spring/Summer 2016 is made from butter-soft leather in contrasting red and black with one sleeve in Monogram print, the other in the red stripe that traditionally lined Louis Vuitton trunks.

Born in 1971, Ghesquière was brought up in Loudun, a small town in western France. Like his predecessor, he started in the fashion business at a young age, when he interned with French fashion designer agnès b., a job for which he was paid in clothes. In 1990, instead of attending fashion college, he moved to Paris to work as an assistant to Jean-Paul Gaultier. Two years later, he took a job at Pôles, designing their knitwear line. Despite relatively inauspicious roles in the interim, in 1997, Ghesquière was the surprise appointment as creative director of struggling French fashion house Balenciaga, after Dutch designer Josephus Thimister was fired. At Balenciaga,

Ghesquière was responsible for designing clothes and accessories as well as overseeing advertising and store design. He rose to the challenge admirably, and over the next 15 years, transformed Balenciaga into a critically acclaimed fashion house, injecting it with his thoroughly modern aesthetic.

When considering a replacement for Marc Jacobs, Ghesquière was attractive to Bernard Arnault for a number of reasons. Not only had he massively increased both the status and profit of Balenciaga (owned by LVMH's main competitor, the luxury goods brand Kering), he had created one of the most iconic "It" bags of the 2000s: the luxe-vintage "Lariat" bag, or the "Motorcycle" bag, as it became known. Handbags and luggage remained the main profit driver at Louis Vuitton. A designer who had the vision to create a product that was fresh and new, but felt like you could own and use it forever, was exactly what Arnault wanted.

BELOW Before his official appointment, Ghesquière impressed Bernard Arnault with a mock-up of a miniature Louis Vuitton trunk to be worn as a handbag. The result was the now-iconic Petite Malle, shown here in the Damier check.

Ghesquière has summed up his skill in creating modern designs with a traditional feel in a 2019 interview with the *New York Times*, explaining that his "favorite way to start a collection is with an anachronism", and reminding us that "what you think of as normal and classic was once new".

After his first meeting with Arnault, Ghesquière created a mock-up of a miniature Louis Vuitton trunk to be worn as a handbag. When the designer presented the idea, Arnault immediately saw the merchandising opportunities, imagining the bag displayed in large quantities in stores. This ability to take a creative idea and show how it could be made into a profitable product was something that Ghesquière had not considered before. He realized that Arnault was "someone who could consider what I was doing and imagine the steps after I designed. It's clearly what I was missing in my previous career … I wanted that kind of vision. I wanted someone that I would work with on a story like that."[2]

The design that so impressed Arnault, eventually dubbed the "Petite Malle", is now a mainstay of the Louis Vuitton collection, retailing at $5,500.

His talent at designing accessories notwithstanding, Ghesquière is first and foremost a clothes designer and although Louis Vuitton ready-to-wear accounts for just 5 per cent of the company's sales – 90 per cent of which come from leather goods[3] – the catwalk collections mould the image of the brand. For this, Ghesquière was an inspired choice. When he joined Louis Vuitton, he was already at the top of his game, one of a handful of "genius" fashion designers who had influenced trends worldwide for over a decade. His aesthetic at Balenciaga, which continued to influence his designs when he moved to Louis Vuitton, drew on historical silhouettes from periods as wide-ranging as the eighteenth century to the 1940s and 1980s. His brilliance at melding traditional garments with futuristic

OPPOSITE This rock-androgynous multi-coloured biker jacket and printed trouser combination for Spring/Summer 2016 shows Ghesquière has a talent for mixing patterns that few designers could pull off.

elements, along with his talent for structure and tailoring, have seen him author some of fashion's most striking looks. Despite his wide-ranging themes and challenging sartorial combinations, Ghesquière has managed to create a remarkable number of wearable and sought-after pieces, from shearling aviator jackets to floral prints and biker boots, all of which heavily influenced the high-street fashion scene.

The new partnership suited both sides. The ability to create popular trends appealed to Arnault, and Louis Vuitton's position as the world's top luxury brand (and the resources it offered) seduced Ghesquière. The expectation was that the designer's clothes would offer the ultimate in luxury; he was encouraged to experiment with indulgent fabrics, including cashmere and the highest-quality silks and plush velvets, detailed with the most expensive silver- and gold-embroidered brocade and handmade lace.

Ghesquière's debut show for Louis Vuitton was for Autumn/Winter 2014, and was given the coveted spot of closing Paris Fashion Week. As he was following in the footsteps of the talented and theatrical Marc Jacobs, expectations were high. On each seat, Ghesquière had left a typewritten note reading: "Today is a new day. A big day. Words cannot express exactly how I am feeling at this moment … Above all, immense joy."

Joy was in abundance in the internal courtyard of the Louvre where, instead of his predecessor's moody and dramatic backdrops, Ghesquière chose to bathe the catwalk in glorious sunlight. The silhouette was predominantly 1960s, in some looks verging on 1970s, with thigh-skimming, A-line coats and skirts but, as always with Ghesquière, fabrics were thoroughly modern. Leather and suede, mainstays of the brand, were not the butter-soft luxury versions you might expect but patent or cracked, and included a coat of black

OPPOSITE Futuristic fabrics in heritage styles are a mainstay of Ghesquière's collections, as shown here in this luxe gold cavalry-style jacket from Spring/Summer 2017.

RIGHT Brocade frock coats teamed with satin running shorts and LV trainers sum up Ghesquière's unique mix of contrasting influences.

crocodile, one of the world's most expensive skins. Texture and colour was rife with accents of orange and red, but Ghesquière included some of his trademark florals, as well as patterned knits. Belts in red, black and tan leather were knotted to pull in the flared silhouette. Coats associated with a more traditional Parisian style, including trench and luxe fur coats, nodded to the heritage of the brand, reminding the audience that for once in the global world of fashion, Louis Vuitton's new designer

was a native of the city.

The emphasis on bags was noticeable, with almost every model carrying one (unsurprisingly, given that these bags would soon be flying off the shelves as predicted). The Petite Malle mini-trunk bag was joined by several others featuring the Monogram print – some very traditional, others offering a modern twist, with a stripe of print alternating with vibrant colours. The Speedy, Louis Vuitton's mainstay, appeared in several guises, and there were also offerings for those who preferred something less structured.

All in all, Ghesquière's debut was relatively understated for a designer famous for his love of experimentation, but it was also perfectly pitched at those who were nervous about him meeting expectations. However, there was no reason to fear. By Spring/Summer 2015, Ghesquière had settled into his role with a second show that continued the theme of wearability, but heightened in a way that only he could pull off. Classic tailoring, including a peacoat and several blazers, was paired with simple white tops made from what appeared to be lace. Dresses and more tops in white, black and blue were made from the same fabric, which on closer inspection revealed itself to be an intricate meshwork of thin leather strips woven together with metal rings. The creativity was remarkable, and yet the end result incredibly wearable. Leather featured again in minidresses in stripes of red or orange and black, and a skirt featuring a humorous print of hairdryers, cars and vacuum cleaners added a little frivolity. As Ghesquière himself put it: "No rupture with last season … It's still a wardrobe, it's about an instinctive mix."[4]

By Autumn/Winter 2015, the retro vibe of Ghesquière's two previous collections had vanished to be replaced by a futuristic bent, the Louis Vuitton traveller racing lightyears ahead. Metallic fabrics reigned, including figure-hugging ribbed knitwear and a tweed-like gold skirt and blouse combination that still had an air of traditional Parisian lady about it. Similarly wearable, if a little extravagant, were the enormous white sheepskin coats that opened the show, the models carrying metal handbag-sized trunks. The ultra-modern accessories included a transparent-glass vanity trunk and the metallic trunk-handbags. The latter became instant bestsellers, cleverly designed to offer style but also practicality with inbuilt

OPPOSITE
Ghesquière, like Jacobs before him, frequently harks back to the 1980s but often with a futuristic bent. For Autumn/Winter 2020, metallic gold fabric trims the puffball skirt of a sleeveless dress, its bodice carrying a space-age geometric print.

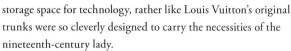

storage space for technology, rather like Louis Vuitton's original trunks were so cleverly designed to carry the necessities of the nineteenth-century lady.

By 2016, Ghesquière's Balenciaga boldness was re-emerging. Sci-fi and futuristic sartorial imaginings had always inspired the designer, and fans were delighted to see this influence emerging on the Louis Vuitton catwalk. But again, the aggressive edge of biker jackets and leather gilets was tempered by peasant-style dresses. Fabrics looked synthetic but in fact, in keeping with Louis Vuitton's purist aesthetic, were cleverly constructed leathers and layers of pinhead-sized metallic studs. The Autumn/Winter collection offered something new again, still a sci-fi feel for a digital age, but with heritage prints appearing reimagined as slinky dresses. An

edge of streetwear emerged too, with fluid athleisure pieces and aggressive lace-front combat boots.

As his time at Louis Vuitton continues, Ghesquière is exploring more and more of Louis Vuitton's heritage, but always giving it a modern twist. For his Spring/Summer 2017 show, he commented: "I didn't explore that much yet the sophistication and the more dressed-up part of Louis Vuitton." In answer, he offered his trademark exquisite tailoring, albeit with quirks like cut-out panels as well as elegant block-colour and geometric-print draped jersey dresses. The accessory of the moment was a "Petite Malle" phone case, which rendered the carrying of a status-symbol handbag almost obsolete.

Ghesquière's experimentation with fabrics reached new heights in his Autumn/Winter 2017 ready-to-wear show. It had the usual abundance of leather, but in contrast to previous shows, this was

highly polished – or broken-down and cracked. That staple of the luxury fashion house, fur, was used more than on previous occasions, including in a striking patchwork coat. But perhaps the most impressive piece of craftsmanship was the creation of a denim that was actually wool, treated to create the effect of faded blue jeans.

The brief for Ghesquière when he joined Louis Vuitton was to take the brand's heritage but propel it firmly into the present and future, something that he performs admirably to this day. His Spring/Summer 2018 collection took elements of pre-revolutionary French courtiers, with brocaded frock coats and Marie Antoinette-style gowns, but teamed them with

BELOW AND
OPPOSITE
Ghesquière is
particularly talented
at accessory design,
reflected in the
wide variety of
covetable bags,
often referencing the
heritage Monogram
and Damier prints,
that Louis Vuitton
has produced since
he joined.

satin running shorts or LV trainers. By Autumn/Winter 2018, Ghesquière was looking up into space again, but with one foot still securely on the ground among the Paris bourgeoisie. Neat-fitting short jackets and skirts appliquéd with gold metallic brocade accessorized with envelope-style clutch bags had a very real appeal to the social elite, including then President Emmanuel Macron's wife, Brigitte, who was reputedly a fan of the fashion house.

Over the last three years, Ghesquière, who renewed his contract with Louis Vuitton in 2018, has continued to play with a combination of heritage, retro influences and thoroughly futuristic visions. The 1980s have been a recurring theme, with

wide-shouldered, sharply tailored jackets blended with space-man references. Darting further back in time also continues to inspire the designer, as he visits both the 1800s and Paris of the belle époque, with flared peplum-style jackets nipped at the waist and puffed shoulders and sleeves. And as always, there is a modern accent, often in the form of logo trainers or parachute-style trousers to offset the sculptural elements. Most recently, streetwear in the form of oversize parkas has been added to the mix. Loyal to his employers, Ghesquière makes sure to include the history of Louis Vuitton, often in the most ingenious ways. For his Spring/Summer 2020 collection, he included a Monogram tote bag with 1980s VHS video-cassette tapes,

OPPOSITE
Ghesquière's Spring/
Summer 2021 show
included a jab at
politics with a T-shirt
inscribed with the
word "Vote", aimed
at his US fans.

the names of the films altered so that instead of *Thelma and Louise* he had *Gaston and Louis*, referencing Gaston-Louis, the legendary head of the company.

He continues to experiment with different fabrics, such as moulded rubber and sequin-embroidered mesh. The shows also reference past and current cultural touchstones like the TV show *Stranger Things*, and imagine what we might wear in a virtual reality life. His Spring/Summer 2021 show, transmitted virtually as the world grappled with a viral pandemic, even included a jibe at politics with a T-shirt bearing the word "Vote", aimed at his US fans. Like other high-profile contemporary designers, most notably Gucci's Alessandro Michele, Ghesquière has also begun to play with gender-neutral clothes, explaining:

"My question this season was less about one theme; it was about this zone between femininity and masculinity. This zone is highlighted by non-binary people, people that are taking a lot of freedom dressing themselves as they want, and, in turn, giving a lot of freedom to all of us."

Ironically, despite being so fixated on space and the future, Ghesquière says that his philosophy is to recreate a sartorial world before social media dictated our dress choices, the argument being that Instagram has effectively homogenized style. There is certainly no homogeneity in Ghesquière's world; his designs for Louis Vuitton continue to be truly original, just like the man himself.

VIRGIL ABLOH

In March 2018, Louis Vuitton appointed fashion designer and DJ Virgil Abloh as artistic director of menswear. The American, who was born in 1980 to Ghanaian parents and grew up on the outskirts of Chicago, studied both civil engineering and architecture before focusing on a career in fashion. In 2009, he became creative director for Kanye West (with whom he had interned at the fashion label Fendi), overseeing the rapper's shows and merchandising. In 2012, Abloh created his first fashion label, Pyrex Vision, but it was the launch of luxury streetwear label Off-White a year later that brought him to the attention of the fashion world. Off-White became a sought-after brand worn by celebrities like Jay-Z, Rihanna and Beyoncé. In 2015, the brand was an LVMH Prize finalist. Abloh's designs for the label included collaborations with Nike, Levi's and Warby Parker, offering a buzz of street cool that instantly upped the desirability of those brands.

It was inevitable that a major fashion house would snap up the designer, and the fit with Louis Vuitton seemed particularly neat. As Louis Vuitton's chairman, Michael Burke, acknowledged in an interview with *The Times*, Abloh had a unique talent for "creating bridges between the classic and the zeitgeist of the moment".

Interviewed by the *New York Times* after the news of his appointment was released, Abloh admitted to being "elated". He went on to say:

"This opportunity to think through what the next chapter of design and luxury will mean at a brand that represents the pinnacle of luxury was always a goal in my wildest dreams. And to show a younger generation that there is no one way anyone in this kind of position has to look is a fantastically modern spirit in which to start."

OPPOSITE
Designer and DJ Virgil Abloh, shown here attending the 2019 CFDA Fashion Awards, was appointed in March 2018 as Louis Vuitton's artistic director of menswear.

BELOW AND
OPPOSITE Abloh's
catwalk debut for
Spring/Summer
2019 started with
all-white outfits that
referenced his own
brand Off-White
but soon morphed
into fluorescent
colour with plenty of
accessories inspired
by current culture.

Abloh was among the relatively few Black designers in leading creative roles within the fashion industry and the first African American artistic director at Louis Vuitton. His mission was not just to make high fashion wearable but, in his own words, to "define new codes".

Abloh explained, "My muse has always been what people actually wear, and I am really excited to make a luxury version of that."

His predecessor Kim Jones, who had headed up menswear since 2011, had already begun to blend Louis Vuitton with street style. Jones had collaborated with brands to inject a new buzz into the luxury label, most noticeably

with skate brand Supreme in 2017. And by the time of his departure – a mutual and amicable decision with Louis Vuitton – Jones had managed to make the prohibitively expensive clothes and accessories not just aspirational but also appealing to a young, Instagram-savvy audience.

Abloh's debut for Louis Vuitton, the Spring/Summer 2019 menswear show, was titled "We Are The World", a brilliantly inclusive sentiment, bringing to mind not only Louis Vuitton's travel heritage but also Michael Jackson and Lionel Richie's 1985 charity single in support of Ethiopian famine relief. The designer's opening outfits, a range of all-white tailored jackets, pleated trousers and LV logo semi-transparent tops, subtly reminded us of the success of his own brand, Off-White. The accessories, a white crocodile-skin tote and trainers, completed the monochrome theme. But soon, the

RIGHT For Autumn/
Winter 2020
Abloh explained he
wanted to look at
male dress codes,
deconstructing
and rebuilding
the business suit,
offering both
traditional looks
and bold colours.

catwalk thrummed with colour: plenty of fluorescents and an unmistakable casual feel.

Abloh continued to change things up at Louis Vuitton right up until his death from cancer in November 2021, at the age of only 41. Just bringing a streetwear vibe to the collections was not inventive enough for the designer who, for his Autumn/Winter 2019 show, changed the focus to choice of fabrics, tailoring and embellishments. The hybrid of pop culture and sophisticated luxury – Michael Jackson was cited as inspiration – saw a collection of deeply covetable clothes, full of seductive texture and accents of colour. His Spring/Summer 2020 show, while completely different in tone – full of light pastels and floral motifs – continued to bring all sorts of fashion together into a universal whole. As journalist Sarah Mower put it in the *Vogue* show notes:

"Abloh is the fulcrum point of these changing times in fashion, creating common ground between the aesthetics of the cultures of streetwear and the exclusive domain of luxury."

BELOW For Autumn/Winter 2019 Abloh paid tribute not only to Louis Vuitton's travel heritage but also his own, with outfits including African flags and the American stars and stripes.

For Autumn/Winter 2020, Abloh questioned male dress codes, citing observation of commuters and how he could deconstruct and rebuild the typical business suit. Who could have predicted that Spring/Summer 2021 would be live-streamed from China in the midst of worldwide pandemic lockdowns and social unrest, including the murder of George Floyd? In response to these events, Abloh presented a deeply personal collection, part playful and childlike as he examined his role as a Black father, and part eco-warrior, questioning fashion's carbon footprint by producing some of his pieces from leftover fabric. The Damier print made a reappearance, as Abloh drew his audience's focus on looking forward but with an eye to the past.

In an essay to accompany the show, Abloh explained that quarantine had given him "time to question the status quo of fashion. I got to be a lot more thoughtful about man's relationship to Earth. I decided there's so much placed on 'the new' in fashion. I'm saying to my consumer that value doesn't deteriorate over time." A worthy sentiment, and one that Louis Vuitton himself might have expressed.

OPPOSITE
Remodelling the classic Monogram print to produce small accessories to be worn casually has been hugely profitable for Louis Vuitton.

BELOW Like Ghesquière, Abloh experimented with fabrics, this time luxury high tech rather than traditional leathers and fur.

SIGNATURE PIECES

THE WORLD'S MOST ICONIC BAGS

Louis Vuitton bags are some of the most recognizable in the world. To this day, the company uses its original designs: the 1889 chequerboard Damier canvas, and the Monogram canvas, a pattern created by Georges Vuitton in 1896 that combines the LV of Louis Vuitton, a diamond with a four-petal flower in its centre, a block-colour flower and a circle containing a flower with four rounded petals.

L ouis Vuitton bags are some of the most recognizable in the world. To this day, the company uses its original designs: the 1889 chequerboard Damier canvas, and the Monogram canvas, a pattern created by Georges Vuitton in 1896 that combines the LV of Louis Vuitton, a diamond with a four-petal flower in its centre, a block-colour flower and a circle containing a flower with four rounded petals.

Originally, these canvases covered rigid trunks in varying sizes, designed to pack everything from travelling wardrobes to toiletry sets and picnics – and, in one case, a portable bed concealed in a large trunk. The only soft-sided option was the 1901 "Steamer" bag, a foldable holdall designed to fit in a wardrobe compartment. By 1930, however, customer demands were changing and the first of Louis Vuitton's signature

OPPOSITE The structured "Alma" bag, named after Paris's Alma Bridge, was designed in 1934.

RIGHT An early example of a Louis Vuitton trunk in the iconic Damier canvas created in 1889.

BELOW This 1969 Monogram Louis Vuitton vanity case belonged to the American socialite Wallis Simpson, later the Duchess of Windsor, when she became wife to the former King Edward VIII.

lightweight soft bags, the Keepall, was created. Initially made from monogrammed cotton with leather trimmings, it was an instant hit with the fashionable Côte d'Azur crowd.

In 1932, Louis Vuitton released the Speedy, a smaller, more compact version of the Keepall for everyday use, and in the 1950s, the company began using PVC to strengthen the monogrammed cotton and coated linen. The new bags were supple and hard-wearing, didn't crease or crack and were far more durable. The celebrity crowd embraced the stylish and practical handbags and a paparazzi shot of Audrey Hepburn carrying a Speedy in the 1960s sparked a surge in sales. To this day, the Speedy reappears each season in many different guises. In 2011, it was relaunched with a shoulder strap as part of the "Speedy Bandoulière" collection.

In 1932, just after the Speedy was released, Gaston-Louis Vuitton was asked by a champagne producer to create a bag that would carry five bottles, and the result was the "Noé" bag, the world's first bucket bag. The drawstring bag is today more likely to be used for carrying mobile phones and eco-friendly water bottles than champagne, yet it remains a Louis Vuitton classic.

BELOW The Noé bucket bag was originally designed in 1932 to carry champagne bottles and has become another classic Louis Vuitton style.

The year 1934 saw the appearance of another icon that has been reinvented countless times, the structured "Alma" bag (although it was not called this until 1955; its original name was the Louis Vuitton "Squire" bag). Named after the Alma Bridge, which connects two Paris neighbourhoods, it has a reinforced leather base with protective studs and rolled-leather handles, as well as a shoulder strap for versatility.

During the 1950s, Louis Vuitton bags became a staple of wealthy celebrities and the social elite. In 1958, the company released the "Lockit", named for the leather patch with a padlock on the side of the bag. Already famous for the unpickable locks on its trunks, the company found that the addition of this security to a handbag proved immensely popular.

In 1985 Louis Vuitton introduced the brand's characteristic textured Epi leather, its first plain design appearing in many styles and colourways and quickly becoming a house icon. One of the enduring designs of the 1980s was 1988's "Pochette Trapèze", an Epi-leather clutch bag shaped like an upside-down trapezoid, which the current artistic director Nicolas Ghesquière reinvented for his Spring/Summer 2019 collection. The Trapèze clutch also inspired Ghesquière's 2015 "Twist Lock" bag.

With the appointment of Marc Jacobs in 1997 to launch a ready-to-wear collection, the brand's bags became correspondingly high fashion, with some of the most striking items coming from collaborations with contemporary artists.

BELOW The Lockit bag, released in 1958, was named for the leather patch with a padlock on the side of the bag. Originally appearing in Monogram and Damier checks it, has become an elegant classic in a range of leathers and colours.

Takashi Murakami's kawaii-inspired take on the Monogram, Stephen Sprouse's graffiti-covered designs and Richard Prince's screen-printed "Jokes" collection flew off the shelves and brought Louis Vuitton bags to a new generation.

Jacobs also launched a few daring bags of his own invention, including a leather version of the ubiquitous chequered laundry bag, complete with LV logo, that graced the catwalks for Spring/Summer 2007. The same year, Louis Vuitton launched its most popular bag of the twenty-first century, the "Neverfull". The capacious tote bag, with leather trim and attached wallet, comes in three sizes and with the choice of the Damier, Monogram or textured Epi leather, as well as various limited-edition styles.

Despite its eye-catching limited-edition bags, Louis Vuitton's mainstay is the classic Monogram bag, which the house regularly releases in new and traditional styles. The now-discontinued "Looping", a Monogram shoulder bag

RIGHT The Neverfull tote, shown here in a pale Damier check, was designed by Marc Jacobs in 2007 and is the newest in a line of stylish but practical Louis Vuitton bags.

with a looped single handle, arrived in 2002. So did the revived Pochette series, which ranges from a small leather or chain-link-handled bag to the 2012 structured satchel, the Pochette "Metis".

One of Louis Vuitton's most popular contemporary classics is the 2013 "Capucines" bag, named after the first store Louis Vuitton opened on Rue Capucines in 1854. The elegant, structured handbag, available in a wide range of finishes, has both a neat handle and cross-body strap and bears the LV logo. Carrying on the tradition of collaboration with artists, in 2019 Louis Vuitton launched the "Artycapucines" collection, in which the bag was reinterpreted by six contemporary artists: Beatriz Milhazes, Liu Wei, Henry Taylor, Jean-Michel Othoniel, Josh Smith and Zhao Zhao.

When Nicolas Ghesquière was being considered for creative director, he created a miniature handbag version of the iconic Louis Vuitton trunk which soon found its way into

BELOW Miniature bags designed by Nicolas Ghesquière include the Petite Malle trunk bag from 2013 and Petite Boîte Chapeau, based on a Louis Vuitton hatbox, in 2018.

the new season's collection as the Petite Malle, now a staple of the brand. The "Petite Boite Chapeau", released in 2018, is a similarly clever take on the heritage of Louis Vuitton, this time recreating a miniature hat box as a circular shoulder bag. Originally very rigid, like a real hatbox, the bag was updated as the "Boite Chapeau Souple", in a more flexible canvas offering both style and functionality.

Ghesquière has worked hard to honour Louis Vuitton's heritage by creating a strong collection of bags. One of his first designs was the neat "Dora" tote, launched on his Autumn/Winter 2014 catwalk in classic Monogram and leather calfskin. Following the theme of elegant, wearable bags, in 2015, Ghesquière introduced the "City Steamer" bag, which has the feel of a classic Hermès Birkin bag, and the discreet "Cluny" bag in iconic Epi leather with an embossed LV logo.

BELOW The Twist Lock, as its name implies, features a metallic LV clasp.

OPPOSITE The Keepall has been reinvented many times since its debut, most recently as a street menswear bag the "Keepall Prism" worn here by influencer André Borchers in 2020.

CELEBRITY CLIENTELE

BELOVED BY THE RICH AND FAMOUS

From its inception, Louis Vuitton was a luggage maker that appealed to the cream of society who were happy to pay for the company's exquisite workmanship and design. The Second Empire of Napoleon III and Empress Eugénie saw both French and British socialites flock to the newly established sea and spa resorts on the French coast, their extensive wardrobes packed into Louis Vuitton travelling cases until the 1870 Franco-Prussian War forced Napoleon III into exile.

By the turn of the century, the Côte D'Azur had become an essential destination for an artistic and bohemian crowd. Extravagant villas were built by those who wanted to spend the cold winter months somewhere more clement. Boating regattas, horse racing and taking the sea air by day turned into parties and gambling at night. Grand receptions, where invitees included Winston Churchill, Pierre-Auguste Renoir and Claude Debussy, lent a gravitas to an otherwise frivolous social scene. In 1908, Louis Vuitton opened its third store on the Côte D'Azur, catering to English, American and Russian aristocracy, including the Russian Imperial family, who were loyal customers until

OPPOSITE French singer and actress Juliette Gréco with her Louis Vuitton bag in 1970.

the tragedy of their mass slaughter in the 1917 Russian Revolution. Dynastic American families such as the Rockefellers, Vanderbilts and Fords used Louis Vuitton luggage for their frequent travels on glamorous ocean liners.

During the 1920s, the Art Deco travel cases designed by Gaston-Louis Vuitton were favoured by the fashionable artistic crowd, including *The Great Gatsby* author F. Scott Fitzgerald and his glamorous wife Zelda, Ernest Hemingway and Pablo Picasso. American novelist Edith Wharton was particularly proud of her set of Louis Vuitton trunks.

The 1950s saw a second surge in celebrity patronage at Louis Vuitton, this time thanks to cinema's New Wave. Again, the South of France and Saint-Tropez were at the epicentre, with Brigitte Bardot becoming the iconic face of freedom and hedonism. The paparazzi flocked to photograph the actress, often carrying her Louis Vuitton Keepall, along with the other stars of the day. During the 1960s, Louis Vuitton bags were beloved of style ambassadors like Audrey Hepburn and Jackie Kennedy. The accessories regularly graced the editorial pages of fashion magazines such as *Vogue*, displayed on the arms of the world's first supermodels, including Twiggy.

Since the 1997 launch of the Louis Vuitton fashion ready-to-wear and accessories labels, initially under the creative direction of Marc Jacobs, there has hardly been an influential celebrity who has not owned a Louis Vuitton. As the company's vision evolved, so did the women who came to embody the Louis Vuitton ideal, summed up by Paul-Gérard Pasols, author of *Louis Vuitton: The Birth of Modern Luxury*, as "eternally feminine … with high heels and a handbag".

OPPOSITE American heiress and socialite Gloria Vanderbilt and her aunt Gertrude Vanderbilt Whitney sit on top of their Louis Vuitton trunk after returning from a cruise in the early 1940s.

RIGHT Kate Moss is a long-time friend and muse of Marc Jacobs. She is pictured here leaving Louis Vuitton head office in 2011.

OPPOSITE Supermodel Naomi Campbell, pictured here carrying a specially designed Alma handbag by Azzedine Alaïa to celebrate the centenary of the Louis Vuitton Monogram fabric.

Marc Jacobs had a series of muses whom he dressed in Louis Vuitton, including Kate Moss, Sofia Coppola and Winona Ryder. Other actresses and models, including Naomi Campbell, Madonna, Jennifer Lopez and Scarlett Johansson, have represented the brand both in advertising and editorial shoots, as well as being photographed wearing the brand while off-duty by paparazzi.

A cutting-edge photographic campaign for Louis Vuitton, shot in 2007 by Annie Leibovitz, featured less obvious figures like Mikhail Gorbachev, Andre Agassi and Steffi Graf, and Catherine Deneuve. Antoine Arnault, the company's director of communications at the time, described the choice of celebrities for the campaign, which went on to feature the likes of Angelina Jolie, Sean Connery and Keith Richards, as "timeless models that are Louis Vuitton's strength and history".

A MODERN ICON

Over the last few years, Louis Vuitton has reached a younger, hipper audience. Actresses and celebrities who are regularly spotted carrying the bags include Hailey Bieber, Miley Cyrus, Taylor Swift and the entire Kardashian-Jenner family.

High-profile American DJ, record producer and media personality DJ Khaled is also a fan of the label, especially the collaboration with Supreme that was engineered for Autumn/Winter 2017 by then menswear designer Kim Jones. Kanye West has long been a patron, even more so now that his good friend Virgil Abloh is menswear designer, adding even more street cred to the label.

Rappers have long name-dropped luxury labels. Louis Vuitton is no exception, for example, Nicki Minaj name-checked the brand in her track "Whip It". Other rappers who have referenced the label include Kanye West, 2 Chainz, Jay-Z and Big Sean.

As Nicolas Ghesquière and Virgil Abloh blur the boundaries between luxury and street style, tradition and modern style, Louis Vuitton looks set to remain relevant for generations to come.

OPPOSITE Billy Eilish is often seen wearing Louis Vuitton. Shown here at The Billie Eilish Experience in Los Angeles in 2019.

RIGHT Over recent years Louis Vuitton has continued to appeal to a younger audience, helped by the endorsement of celebrities including Kim and Kourtney Kardashian.

NOTES

FAMILY AFFAIR
1.   Pasols, Paul-Gérard (2012). *Louis Vuitton: The Birth of Modern Luxury*, London: Abrams.

GLOBAL EXPANSION
1.   Pasols, Paul Gérard (2012). "Relaunch and international growth" in *Louis Vuitton: The Birth of Modern Luxury*, London: Abrams.
2.   Larivière, Jean (n.d.). The Spirit of Travel. Available at: louisvuitton.com
3.   Funding Universe.

MARC JACOBS
1.   Mower, Sarah (2001). "Interview with Marc Jacobs", *Arena Homme +*.
2.   Golbin, Pamela (ed.) (2012). "Interview with Marc Jacobs" in *Louis Vuitton / Marc Jacobs*, Italy: Rizzoli, p.153.
3.   Golbin, Pamela (ed.) (2012). "Interview with Marc Jacobs" in *Louis Vuitton / Marc Jacobs*, Italy: Rizzoli, p.153.

HERITAGE REBORN
1.   Cartner-Morley, Jess (2014). "Nicolas Ghesquière Brings joy to Louis Vuitton at Paris fashion week", *Guardian*, March 5, 2014.
2.   Gregory, Alice (2019). "The Greats, Nicolas Ghesquière", *New York Times*, October 18, 2019.
3.   Cartner-Morley, Jess (2014). "Nicolas Ghesquière Brings joy to Louis Vuitton at Paris fashion week", *Guardian*, March 5, 2014.
4.   Phelps, Nicole (2014). "Louis Vuitton Spring Summer 2015 Ready-to-Wear", *Vogue*, October 1, 2014.

INDEX

(Page numbers in **bold** refer to main subjects, including photographs; *italic* refer to all other photographs/captions)

Abloh, Virgil 8, 109, **126–33**, 154
advertising *16*, *17*, **26–9**, *34*, **61–5**, 111, 153
Aéro 36
After Dark collection 94
Agassi, Andre 153
air travel **34–7**, 41, *44*, *45*
aircraft trunks 34–6, *34*, *36*
Alaïa, Azzedine 65, *153*
Alma bag *136*, *137*, 140, *152*, *153*
architecture **38–9**, 41, **56–9**, 127
Arnault, Antoine 153
Arnault, Bernard **64–5**, *70*, 73, 93, *110*, 111–15, *111*
Art Deco 38, *39*, 40, 41, *41*, 104, 150
Asnières 16, *16*, 21, *21*, 25, 38–9, 45–7, 50, 63
automobile travel 33, *34*
Avedon, Richard 48, 61
Avenue des Champs-Élysées *39*, 40, 47
Avenue Marceau 47
Avenue Montaigne *58*, 60

Bailey, David 48, *50*
Balenciaga *89*, 110–11, 120
Bardot, Brigitte 8, 48, *48*, *49*, 99, 150
Beyoncé 127
Bieber, Hailey 154
Big Sean 154
Bigaux and Koller *39*, 40
Billie Eilish Experience *155*
Blahnik, Manolo 65
Boite Chapeau Souple bag 144
Bonaparte, Napoleon 14
Bond Street 26, *26*, 28, 57, *57*
Borchers, André *145*

branding 7, 8, 25, 41, *47*, *56*, **60–5**, **70–7**, 81, *87*, **99–104**, **109–22**, **127–31**, 141, 144, 153
Burke, Michael 127

Calvin Klein 70, 73
Campbell, Naomi *68*, *69*, 74, 94, *94*, *95*, *152*, 153, *153*
Canella, Giuseppe *14*
Capucines bag 143
Carcelle, Yves 65
Carhart Jr, Mrs Amory *44*, *45*
catalogues *26*, *27*, *29*
celebrity **7–9**, **48–9**, 93, 127, 139, 140, **146–55**
Céline 73
CFDA 70, *127*
Chainz 154
Cherry Blossom collection 83
Chevalier, Alain 63–4
China Girl feel *102*, 103
Chloé 73
Christian Dior 63
Churchill, Sir Winston 149
City Steamer bag 144
Clermont-Tonnerre, Blanche de *34*
Cluny bag 144
Coachella *155*
collections:
    Autumn/Winter 2000 *8*, *9*, *76*, 77
    Autumn/Winter 2001 **80–1**
    Autumn/Winter 2003 84
    Autumn/Winter 2004 *86*, 87
    Autumn/Winter 2005 *88*, 89
    Autumn/Winter 2006 *89*
    Autumn/Winter 2009 **99–101**
    Autumn/Winter 2011 103
    Autumn/Winter 2013 103–4
    Autumn/Winter 2014 104, *104*, 115, 144
    Autumn/Winter 2015 118
    Autumn/Winter 2016 120

    Autumn/Winter 2017 120–2, 154
    Autumn/Winter 2018 123
    Autumn/Winter 2019 *8*, *9*, *118*, *119*, *131*, *140*
    Autumn/Winter 2019/20 131
    Autumn/Winter 2020 *130*, 133
    Spring/Summer 2000 *75*
    Spring/Summer 2001 *79*, 80
    Spring/Summer 2002 *80*, 81
    Spring/Summer 2003 84, *84*, *85*
    Spring/Summer 2007 90, *90*, 142
    Spring/Summer 2008 **92–6**
    Spring/Summer 2009 96, *98*
    Spring/Summer 2010 99
    Spring/Summer 2011 *102*, 103
    Spring/Summer 2012 103
    Spring/Summer 2013 103, *104*, *105*
    Spring/Summer 2015 118
    Spring/Summer 2016 *108*, *109*, *112*, *113*
    Spring/Summer 2017 *114*, *115*, 120
    Spring/Summer 2018 122–3
    Spring/Summer 2019 128, *128*, *129*, 141
    Spring/Summer 2020 *120*, *121*, 124, 131
    Spring/Summer 2021 124, *124*, *125*, 133
Connery, Sean 153
Coppola, Sofia 153
Côte d'Azur 33, 139, 149
Council of Fashion Designers of America (CFDA) 70
counterfeiting 28, 57, 65
Covid-19 133
Cyrus, Miley 154

Damier print:
    first designed **28–9**, 137, *138*

reimagined 65, 103, *104*, *105*, *118*, *119*, *123*, *124*, *133*
de Gaulle, Charles 45
Debussy, Claude 149
Deneuve, Catherine 50, *54*, *55*, 153
Dior 73, 90, 103
DJ Khaled 154
Doc Martens 70
Dora tote bag 144
dressing-table nécessaires 41
Duffy, Robert 70
dynastic families *138*, 150

Edward VII *138*
Eilish, Billy *154*, *155*
Ellis, Perry 69–70
Epi leather 141, 142, 144
Eugénie, Empress 14, *15*, 149
Evangelista, Linda 70
Exposition Universelle 16, *16*, *18–19*, 28, *28*

fashion awards 69–70, 127
fashion editorial 48, *50*, 63, *63*
Fendi 127
Fifth Avenue *56*, 57
Fitzgerald, F. Scott 150
Fitzgerald, Zelda 150
Floyd, George *133*
Forde, Tom 73
forgery 28, 57, 65
Foujita, Tsuguharu 87
franchising 55–6
frock coats *116–17*, 123

Galliano, John 73, 99
Gaultier, Jean-Paul 110
Ghesquière, Nicolas 7, 8, 74, **109–25**, *133*, 141, 143–4, *143*, 154
Gigli, Romeo 65
Givenchy 63, 73
Godard, Jean-Luc *48*
Gorbachev, Mikhail 153
Graf, Steffi 153
graffitied bags *78*, 79, *79*
Greco, Juliette *148*, 149
grunge **70–4**, *80*, 81, 89
Gucci 73, 124
Guinness plc 64

Hepburn, Audrey 8, *46*, *47*, 139, 150
Hermès Birkin bag 144
Herzigova, Eva 94, *94*, *95*
Heures d'absence 41
High School of Art and Design 69
hot-air balloons 36
Houdini, Harry 32

Idéale 32
Île de la Cité and the Flower Market in Paris 14
Instagram 124, 128
interior design **56–60**
Isma'il Pasha, Khedive of Egypt 20, *20*
"It" bags 111

Jackson, Michael 128, 131
Jacobs, Marc 8, **67–105**, 109, *110*, 111, *118*, 141–2, 150, *153*
Jay-Z 127, 154
Johansson, Scarlett 153
Jokes collection *93*, 94, 142
Jolie, Angelina 153
Jones, Kim 128, 154

Kardashian-Jenner family 154, *154*
kawaii **83–4**, 90, *90*
Keepall bag *6*, 7, 8, 48, 74, 139, *144*, *145*, 150
Kemper, Nan *62*, *63*
Kennedy, Jackie *6*, 7, 150
Klein, Calvin 70, 73
Kors, Michael 73

Lacroix, Christian 96
ladies' travelling cases *40*, 41, *41*
Lalique, René 41, *41*
Lang, Helmut 65, 73
Lariat bag 111
Larivière, Jean **61–3**
Lauren, Ralph 70
Leibovitz, Annie 153
Les Arts Décoratifs 103
Levi's 127
Lindbergh, Charles 37, *37*
Liu Wei 143
locking mechanisms *7*, 8, 31–2, *31*, 141
Lockit bag 141, *141*

Loewe 63
Looping bag 142–3
Lopez, Jennifer 153
Louis Vuitton:
 founding of 7, *13*, 14
 global expansion **52–65**
 as LVMH 7, **63–5**, 73, 87, 111
 100th anniversary 47
Louis Vuitton Cup 60, *60*
Louis Vuitton Foundation for Opera 60
Louis Vuitton—Marc Jacobs 103
Louis Vuitton (Pasols) 150
LOVE bag 90
luggage 7–8, *14–20*, 26
LV hatbox *143*, 144
LVMH Prize 127

McCartney, Stella 73
Macpherson, Elle 99
McQueen, Alexander 73
Macron, Brigitte 123
Macron, Emmanuel 123
Madonna 153
Maison Louis Vuitton 21, 26, 39, 41
Malle Idéale *28*
Mapplethorpe, Robert 61
Maréchal, M. 13
Marie Antoinette 123
Mary Quant 103, *105*
Metis bag 143
Michele, Alessandro 124
Milhazes, Beatriz 143
Minaj, Nicki 154
miniature bags **111–12**, 117, 120, **143–4**
Mizrahi, Isaac 65
Moët Hennessy 63–4, *64*
Monogram print:
 becomes fashion statement 8
 first designed 7, 137
 reimagining 83–4, *96*, *97*, *123*, *124*
 superimposed *93*, 94
Monogramouflage 84
Morel-Grummer *34*
Moss, Kate 103, 153, *153*
Motorcycle bag 111
Mower, Sarah 74, 131
Multicolore range 83, *84*, *85*
Murakami, Takashi **82–7**, 90, 142

Murphy, Carolyn *72*, *73*
Musée des Arts Décoratifs 79

Napoleon III 14, 20, 149
Neverfull bag 142
New Look 103
New Wave cinema 47–8, *47*, 150
New World 39–41
Nike 127
Noé bucket bag 139, *139*
Nurse paintings **93–5**, 94

ocean travel *30*, *31*, 32, *32*, *33*,
    41, *55*, *140*, 150
Off-White 127, 128, *128*
Onassis, Jackie *6*, *7*, 150
Othoniel, Jean-Michel 143
Oxford Street 26

paparazzi 48, 74, 139, 150,
    150–3, 153
Paris Fashion Week 115
Parriaux, Clémence-Émilie
    (wife) 14
Parsons School of Design 69
Pasols, Paul-Gérard 150
Patrelle, Joséphine (daughter-in-
    law) *24*, *25*
Penn, Irving 61
perfumes 41, 63
Perry Ellis 69–70
Pétain, Philippe 45
Petite bags **111–12**, 117, 120,
    143–4
photography **61–3**, **93–6**, 153
Picasso, Pablo 150
picnic sets *40*, *41*
Pochette series 141, 143
pop culture 77, **82–5**, 93–4, 124
Prince, Richard **93–6**, 142
Pucci 89
Puiforcat, Jean 41, *41*
Pyrex Vision 127

Racamier, Henry 55–6, *60*,
    63–5, *64*
Ralph Lauren 70
Rayée 28
Renoir, Auguste 149
Richards, Keith 153
Richie, Lionel 128
Rihanna 127

Rodriguez, Narciso 73
roof trunks 33
Rue Capucines 14, 143
Rue Scribe 21, 25, 38
Ruinart Père et Fils 63
Ryder, Winona 153

Sachs, Gunther *48*, *49*
Saint-Tropez 48, 150
Sander, Jil 73
Schiffer, Claudia *74*, *75*
sci-fi imaginings 74, 82, 85, 115,
    115, 118, 120, 123–4
silverware *40*, 41, *41*
Simpson, Wallis 138
Sketchbook for Reuben Thomas 70
Smith, Jaden *8*, *9*
Smith, Josh 143
Smith, Willow *8*, *9*
Speedy bag *47*, 99, 118, 139
Speedy Bandoulière collection 139
Spirit of St. Louis 37
"The Spirit of Travel" 61, *61*
Sprouse, Stephen **77–9**, 142
Squire bag 140
SS Vuitton cap 80
The Steamer bag 32, *54*, *55*
Steamer bag 137, *140*
Strand 26, *28*
Supreme 128
Swift, Taylor 154
Sybilla 65

Tate Modern 109
Taylor, Henry 143
Thimble Awards 69–70
Thimister, Josephus 110
Thomas, Reuben 70
Tilbury carriage *34*
transatlantic travel, *see* air travel;
    ocean travel
Trapèze clutch bag 141
travelling sets *40*, 41, *41*
Trianon 15, 28
Tumbler lock *7*, 8, 31–2, *31*
Twiggy *50*, *51*, 150
Twist Lock bag 141, *144*

Versace 89
Versillé, Renée (granddaughter-
    in-law) 38
Veuve Clicquot 63

Vogue 7, *44*, *45*, *50*, *63*, 131
"Vote" T-shirt 124, *124*, *125*
Vuitton, Claude-Louis (great-
    grandson) 45, 47, 55
Vuitton, Clémence-Émilie
    (wife) 14
Vuitton et Fils 40
Vuitton, Gaston-Louis (grandson)
    24, 25, *25*, 37, *37*, **38–41**,
    45–7, 55, *56*, 57, 61, 124,
    139, 150
Vuitton, Georges (son) 7, *24*,
    25–37, *25*, 38, 39, 137
    1920 lecture 41
Vuitton, Henry-Louis (great-
    grandson) 20, *21*, 45–7, 55
Vuitton, Jacques-Louis (great-
    grandson) 45, 47, 55
Vuitton, Jean (grandson) *24*,
    25, *34*
    death of 36–7, 38
Vuitton, Joséphine (daughter-in-
    law) *24*, *25*
Vuitton, Louis *12*, 55
    birth of 13
    death of 28
    first workshop 7, *13*, 14
Vuitton, Odile (great-
    granddaughter) 55
Vuitton, Pierre (grandson) *24*,
    25, *34*, 36
    death of 36, 38
Vuitton, Renée (granddaughter-
    in-law) 38

Wallis, Duchess of Windsor *138*
Warby Parker 127
Warhol, Andy 77
"We Are The World" 128
Weinberg, Chester 69
West, Kanye 127, 154
Westwood, Vivienne 65, *86*, 87
Wharton, Edith 150
window display 38, **56–60**, 61
Women's Wear Daily (*WWD*) 70
Worl 45
Worth, Charles 16

Yves Saint Laurent *89*, 90

Zhao Zhao 143
zinc trunk 33

CREDITS

The publishers would like to thank the following sources for their kind permission to reproduce the pictures in this book.

Akg-images: 14; © Les Arts Décoratifs, Paris/Jean Tholance 17 (top and bottom), 28, 40 (top); Olivier Martel 64; Mondadori Portfolio/Angelo Deligio 148

Alamy: dpa picture alliance archive 60, 111; Delphotos 56; Directphoto Collection 58; Everett Collection 33, 47, 49, 79; Peter Horree 93; Ovidiu Hrubaru 126; The Print Collector 20; Prisma by Dukas Presseagentur GmbH 59; Reuters 89; Reuters/Benoit Tessier 102, 105; United Archives GmbH 48; World History Archive 18-19

Bridgeman Images: Christie's Images 31, 34, 36, 40b; PVDE 21, 29

Getty Images: 44, 62; David M.Benett 152; Bettmann 26; Giancarlo Botti 54; Victor Boyko 128, 131, 133; Gustavo Caballero 154; Stephane Cardinale-Corbis 68, 91, 97, 100, 120; Dominique Charriau 125; Victor Chavez 61; Thomas Coex 75; Corbis Historical 37; Michel Dufour 87; Estrop 119; Ron Galella 6; Francois Guillot 90; Julien M.Hekimian 82; Heritage Images 12, 15; Hulton Archive 24, 27; Michelle Leung 96; Mirrorpix 46, 50; Jean-Francois Monier 139; Antonio de Moraes Barros Filho 113; Jean-Pierre Muller 80, 86; Thierry Orban 81; Marc Piasecki 153; Pool Bassignac/Benainous 84; Karl Prouse/Catwalking 101; /Rindoff/Dufour 104; Bertrand Rindoff Petroff 110; Eric Robert 71; Lorenzo Santini 95 (left); Joe Scarnici 155; Science and Society Picture Library 35; Pascal Le Segretain 9, 108, 123; Streetstyleshooters 145; Bob Thomas/Popperfoto 32; Pierre Vauthey 72; Pierre Verdy 76, 78, 88, 92, 94, 95 (right), 98, 99; Victor Virgile 122, 129; Peter White 114, 116-117, 121, 130, 132, 140

Kerry Taylor Auctions: 83, 136, 138 (top), 138 (bottom)

Shutterstock: Willy Barton 57; DKSStyle 142; Papin Lab 141, 143, 144; Kiev.Victor 39

Topfoto: 30; Roger-Viollet 16

Every effort has been made to acknowledge correctly and contact the source and/or copyright holder of each picture and Welbeck Publishing apologises for any unintentional errors or omissions, which will be corrected in future editions of this book.

LITTLE BOOK OF

YVES SAINT LAURENT

For Dusty Rose who really doesn't like knees.

I am indebted to my brilliant editor Issy Wilkinson for her wise observations, and many thanks to the excellent team at Welbeck.

Published in 2021 by Welbeck
An Imprint of HEADLINE PUBLISHING GROUP

18

Design and layout © 2021 Carlton Books Limited
Text © 2021 Emma Baxter-Wright

Cataloguing in Publication Data is available from the British Library
ISBN – 978-1-78739-554-1
Printed in China

HEADLINE PUBLISHING GROUP
An Hachette UK Company, Carmelite House
50 Victoria Embankment, London EC4Y 0DZ

www.headline.co.uk
www.hachette.co.uk

LITTLE BOOK OF

YVES SAINT LAURENT

The story of the iconic fashion designer

EMMA BAXTER-WRIGHT

WELBECK

CONTENTS

INTRODUCTION 06
EARLY LIFE 10
SUCCESSOR TO CHRISTIAN DIOR.....20
ARTISTIC EXPLOSION OF COLOUR 34
A DECADE OF STYLE INNOVATION ...46
THE SCANDALOUS 70S 68
THEATRE, BALLET AND CINEMA 90
THE ICONIC PERFUMES................100
ACCESSORIES AND JEWELLERY 112
GLOBAL INSPIRATION..................128
THE LEGACY OF YVES 140
INDEX 156
RESOURCES 159

INTRODUCTION

"I felt myself drawn to the past, whilst the future
drove me ahead."

YVES SAINT LAURENT

*I*f the act of artistic genius requires equal amounts of talent
and suffering, then Yves Saint Laurent, with an abundance
of both firmly embedded in his DNA, successfully utilized
these traits to propel his career from prodigious boy wonder to
that of arguably the most influential designer of the twentieth
century. With a career initially shaped by the traditions of haute
couture, the designer had no hesitation in shaking off the shadow
of his former employer Christian Dior and striking out in new
directions to accommodate an era of change.

Recognized throughout his lifetime for a fragile disposition
shielded behind trademark glasses, in truth his reclusive
personality masked a steely determination to conquer the
competition and secure iconic status as the author of modern
womenswear. Saint Laurent made headlines in a life that was to
become as mythologized as his dazzling designs: he scandalized

OPPOSITE The legendary couturier, known always as a great
trailblazer, at the height of his success in 1976.

the world by posing naked to promote his own merchandise, shocked the fashion elite with trouser suits for women and transparent fabrics and solidified his international appeal by launching a range of ready-to-wear collections that democratized fashion for an audience of younger women. Innovation came from exploring new horizons in art and culture, from the perfect geometry of the Mondrian dress to the extravagant fantasy of the Opéras-Ballets Russes collection. Revered as a "legend", "God" and "idol" by every successful designer that trailed in his footsteps, and named by Coco Chanel as the rightful successor to her indisputable crown, Saint Laurent famously declared that his only regret in a visionary career was not to have invented blue jeans.

ABOVE: As a young designer, scrutinizing the shape and silhouette of a toile in search of perfection.

OPPOSITE: An early example of a trouser suit designed for women, 1967.

More than any other designer, Saint Laurent transcended the mere aesthetics of fashion and caused a revolution, trusting his instincts to empower women from the salon to the street through a seductive style that shaped the attitudes of the times.

EARLY LIFE

BUDDING TALENT

Surrounded by love, laughter and the shimmering heat of the
North African sun, Yves Henri Donat Mathieu-Saint-Laurent
was born into wealth and privilege in the melting-pot
cosmopolitan port of Oran, Algeria, on 1 August 1936.

*A*s the eldest of three children, with two younger
sisters, Michèle and Brigitte, the slight, shy boy with
a flashing smile was raised as a pampered prince of
the family, by Lucienne, his glamorous party-loving mother,
in an extended female household which included his maternal
grandmother, Madame Marianne Wilbaux, and Great-Aunt Renée.

His handsome, athletic father, Charles Mathieu-Saint-Laurent,
cut a distinguished figure in the town, overseeing an insurance
company and managing a string of cinemas in Algeria, Morocco
and Tunisia. Business often took him away from home, but
the relationship between father and son in a loving family
atmosphere was always strong, with the designer later recalling
him as "an exceptional human being". In summer, the family
decamped from their large three-storey house in Oran to their
villa in Trouville, one of the most prestigious coastal resorts in

OPPOSITE: Yves Saint Laurent at the age of 21, buttoned
up in a suit and tie, sporting the trademark glasses he
was rarely seen without.

the region, where for several months they swam in the ocean, picnicked on the beach and entertained friends for the season.

It was Lucienne, Yves' stylish mother, who encouraged her son's early artistic efforts and captivated the fertile imagination of the budding designer. He watched her dress up to dazzle café society, with her infectious laughter and innate good taste, and by the age of 13 he would accompany her each week to purchase the latest fashion magazines like *Vogue* and *Le Jardin des Modes* at the Manes bookstore. As he recounted when interviewed in the *Globe* in 1986, "When you live in the provinces, magazines from the capital are hugely important. At the time there were fantastic magazines about the theatre, and also fashion magazines with designs by people like Bérard, Dalí, Cocteau. Those magazines had an enormous influence on me."

This visually tantalizing peek into the possibilities of an

RIGHT: With his glamorous mother Lucienne Mathieu-Saint-Laurent, the first woman Yves designed dresses for.

altogether different type of existence was reinforced in May 1950 when the teenager was taken to the municipal opera house in Oran to see a performance of Molière's *L'École des femmes* (School for Wives) with sets and costumes designed by Christian Bérard. Enthralled by the spectacle of this early theatrical exposure, Saint Laurent later claimed: "It was an extraordinarily emotional experience, the most extraordinary I have ever had." The magical illusion of the theatre consumed an impressionable young Yves and thinking this could be where his professional future lay, he invented a fantasy world in which he immersed himself. His parents provided a room for him, where, as self-appointed director, set designer and couturier, he staged secret performances by invitation only for his sisters. As creative mastermind for his productions, Yves painted scenic backdrops and invented cut-out cardboard characters dressed in fabric costumes made with scraps cut from his mother's gowns.

In sharp contrast to this idyllic home life where he was cherished as the blue-eyed boy, the Jesuit-Catholic boarding school he attended from the age of 12 provided him with nothing but ongoing misery. As a pale and timid outsider, who spent his free time alone without friends, Yves' teenage years were marked with trauma and unhappiness as he juggled a dual existence: " On the one hand there was the cheerful life with my family, the world I created with my drawings, costumes and plays. On the other, the ordeal of Catholic school, where I was an outcast." Years later, he told *Le Figaro* that he suffered the horrific beating and bullying at school knowing he was different to the other boys and that one day he would be famous. A passion for reading Marcel Proust, and a developing interest in the seasonal collections of the Parisian designers Hubert de Givenchy, Christian Dior and Cristóbal Balenciaga, all served as

At home in Oran,
an adolescent Yves
spent hours immersed
in a fantasy world
of fashion, creating
hundreds of outfits for
his paper dolls based
on models of the
1950s.

ABOVE: Saint Laurent
in Paris, with his
winning design for
the International
Wool Secretariat
competition in 1954.
Karl Lagerfeld, who was
awarded second prize,
is on the left.

welcome distractions from the terror of the playground.

From 1951 onward, Yves spent hours filling sketchbooks with
sets and costumes for the ballet and theatre, transcribing books,
illustrating text and providing detailed drawings for the ensembles
worn by fictional characters such as Madame Bovary and Scarlett
O'Hara. As well as designing outfits for his mother, which were
given to her seamstress to make up, Yves created his own fashion
collections using paper dolls he had made in the guise of Suzy
Parker and Bettina Graziani, the most famous mannequins of
the day. The imaginative wardrobes he invented for 11 paper
dolls were extensive, producing over 500 different garments and
accessories, and writing detailed programme notes to accompany
each collection. The young artist always signed and dated his work
"YMSL" or "Yves Mathieu-Saint Laurent" and only later, around
1957, dropped the Mathieu and settled on the signature "YSL".

Encouraged by his family, Yves submitted work into the
International Wool Secretariat fashion competition, and in autumn
1953 set off for Paris with his mother, Lucienne, to collect third

prize. Through his father's contacts he was introduced to the influential magazine editor Michel de Brunhoff during his short stay in the capital. De Brunhoff, who had founded *Gazette du bon ton*, and now edited *Vogue (Paris)*, was very impressed with what he saw. Recognizing Yves' flair for fashion, he encouraged him to keep drawing but also to finish his baccalaureate exams. When college was over, de Brunhoff suggested Yves enrol at the Ecole de la Chambre Syndicale de la Couture Parisienne, the best fashion school in Paris, to improve his couture technique. His parents agreed and at 18, he began a new life in the capital, renting a furnished room at 209 Boulevard Pereire in the 17th arrondissement. Later that year, competing with 6,000 other entrants, Yves won first prize for his elegant designs in the dress category of the 1954 International Wool Secretariat competition, where his winning design – a black wool cocktail dress which provided an early example of his instinctive eye for wearable style – was made up in the atelier of Hubert de Givenchy.

His victory was reported in the local paper, *L'Echo d'Oran*, but despite this early validation of success, Yves was suffering from what would be the first of many bouts of depression. Recognizing the unhappiness in his son, Charles Mathieu-Saint-Laurent wrote in confidence to Michel de Brunhoff to ask again for his help. After a productive holiday in Oran, Yves returned to the offices of *Vogue* in Paris armed with 50 original sketches to show de Brunhoff his latest work. Stunned by the similarity of his drawings to those of Christian Dior's new A-line collection he had seen the previous day, the journalist telephoned his great friend and arranged a time to introduce his talented protégé to the feted designer. The meeting was a great success and on 20 June 1955, the boy from Oran who fantasized about working for Christian Dior, the greatest couturier in Paris, realized his dream.

Successor to Christian Dior

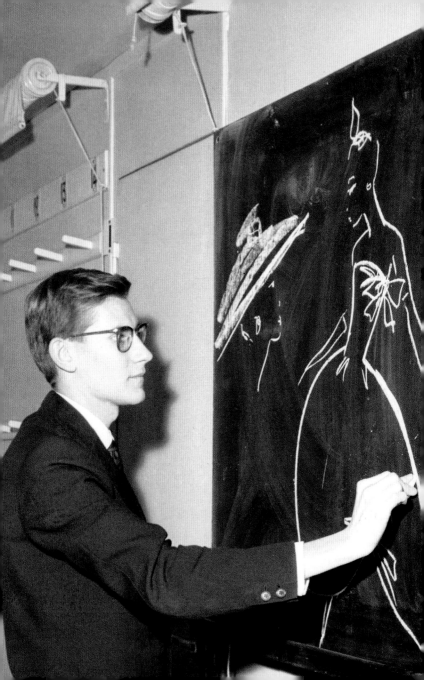

Heir to The Throne

Stepping through the hallowed doors of 30 Avenue Montaigne for his first day at work as an apprentice, Saint Laurent began the important process of learning how to run a successful couture house from the bottom up.

T he Parisian fashion house had a global reputation, thanks to the unrivalled success of Christian Dior's post-war silhouette of glamorous femininity, which he called *La Ligne Corolle* and which Carmel Snow, editor of American *Harper's Bazaar*, dubbed the "New Look". In a single collection Dior's international fame had been assured and when a painfully shy Saint Laurent arrived at the Maison eight years later, Dior was widely acknowledged as the most celebrated and financially successful couturier in the world.

Owned by Marcel Boussac, then the wealthiest man in France, the company employed around 1,000 people, owned 27 ateliers and was responsible for nearly half of all haute couture exports to America. Royalty, Hollywood's A-List and the best-dressed

OPPOSITE: An extraordinarily gifted illustrator, seen here sketching early designs on a chalkboard at the House of Dior in the early 60s.

ABOVE: One of the last
photos taken of Yves
Saint Laurent with his
mentor Christian Dior,
backstage at a fashion
show in 1957.

women in the world all clamoured to be adorned by Monsieur
Dior. His enviable client list included Elizabeth Taylor, Margot
Fonteyn, Marlene Dietrich and Wallis, Duchess of Windsor, as well
as the aristocratic beauties Gloria Guinness and Daisy Fellowes.

Dressed in a white lab coat and working each day from a
wooden desk in the studio, Yves was soon promoted to the role
of assistant with Marc Bohan and Guy Douvier, then elevated to
principal associate, working directly alongside Christian Dior. The
Maison operated under a strict hierarchy, with a rigorous structure
that ensured everyone knew their place and what was expected of
them within the townhouse premises. To rise up through the ranks
to reach the level of premiére was a great honour and demanded
the dedication of around 20 years of work that was continually
examined and graded for elegance, finishing and execution. As
head of a successful couture house, Dior was under pressure.
Although celebrated as the most famous couturier in the world,
the ongoing expectations to excite an international audience

of clients and press at every new show had become a relentless treadmill and the designer was quick to recognize and value the assured competence of his youthful employee. Yves' first sketches dated from July 1955 remain in the Dior archives and his mentor began to include his designs in the bi-annual shows from as early as autumn of that year. For his part, Yves admired his new boss immensely, was thrilled to learn his professional craft within the confines of such a prestigious environment and felt the individual creativity of both men benefited from working closely with one another.

"I arrived in the morning and spent the day alongside Christian Dior without talking very much. I have to say that I learned a great deal. Christian Dior overstimulated the imagination, and he trusted me totally with his work. One of his ideas would give me ideas, and one of my ideas might give him ideas. There was no discussion between us. I had an idea. I drew it. I showed him the sketch. The big demonstration between us was the proof. Since I am not talkative, I prefer that, it's a *tour de force*."

Influential tastemaker Carmel Snow picked up on one of Yves' early designs for Dior and included it in her 1955 "Paris Report" for the September issue of American *Harper's Bazaar. Soirée de Paris*, an elegant black sheath dress with contrast satin bow, was modelled by the aristocratic beauty Dovima and captured on film by the genius young photographer Richard Avedon in a sensational photographic setting at the Cirque d'Hiver in Paris. The classic fashion photograph that went on to become an iconic image of understated 1950s style set a record price for an Avedon photo when it sold at Christie's Auction House for $1.2 million in November 2010.

Yves was happy in his new role in an atmosphere that was reassuringly familiar to him, surrounded by a predominantly female workforce, the majority of whom were much older than him. Neatly buttoned up in a uniform of charcoal grey suits, sporting cropped school-boy hair and wire framed specs, the conservative youth had found a few allies of his own age and started to socialize with them after work. Anne-Marie Muñoz, a family friend of Dior's who had started off as a messenger in the workrooms and worked her way up, and the unconventional model Victoire Doutreleau, whose Saint Germain looks made her Dior's favourite muse, were both strong women who would remain friends and later participate in the opening of Saint Laurent's own haute couture house.

Having gained Dior's trust, Yves found an increasing number of his original designs included in every collection, with the grand couturier openly praising the skills of his young associate. In July 1957, the designer celebrated 10 years of success for the fashion house that bore his name. He made the cover of *Time* magazine brandishing a giant pair of cutting shears and told his business partner, Jacques Rouet, "Yves Saint Laurent is young, but he is an immense talent. In my last collection, I consider him to be the father of 34 out of the 180 designs. I think the time has come to reveal it to the press. My prestige won't suffer from it."

When Lucienne came to visit her son in Paris that year she was summoned by Monsieur Dior, who had asked to meet her. She spoke later of the encounter: "He made some complimentary remarks and then said, 'Yves is the one who'll succeed me.' At the time I didn't really understand. Dior was still young, 60 at most."

If the great Dior had vocalized his desire that Yves had been chosen to eventually succeed him, it was understood as something to be considered in the future when his protégé had matured into the role, not as a premonition forecasting his imminent demise. The wider world, however, was unaware that despite outward appearances of a calm demeanour, the couturier was riddled with

OPPOSITE: A triumphant debut collection for Christian Dior in 1957, featuring a new, less structured silhouette called the "trapeze" line.

RIGHT: With his team at Christian Dior, Madame Raymonde Zehnmacker (left) who ran the studio, and Madame Marguerite Carré, who oversaw the couture workshops.

anxiety and consumed by health worries about his weight. While taking an autumn trip to his spa clinic in Montecatini Terme, Italy, Dior collapsed suddenly and died of a heart attack, aged 52. The fashion world mourned the death of a man seen as the heroic saviour of Parisian couture and his funeral was attended by vast crowds and famous couturiers Pierre Balmain, Cristóbal Balenciaga and Hubert de Givenchy.

The unexpected death of Dior catapulted the frail-looking 21-year-old Yves centre stage into the reluctant role of successor. There was much deliberation as to whether the young pretender was mature enough to withstand the pressures demanded by the House of Dior, but Marcel Boussac, the industrialist billionaire who financed the company, was hesitant to close the door on a business that turned over two billion francs. On 15 November, 1957, a press conference was called at Avenue Montaigne, where business partner Jacques Rouet made the announcement to the assembled audience that the couture house would be run by a creative team consisting of four individuals, all of whom had been hired personally by Monsieur Dior: Madame Zehnacker, Marguerite Carré, Mitzah Bricard and Yves Saint Laurent. The news was well received by the French press, with the evening paper *Paris-Presse-L'intransigeant* printing congratulatory headlines: "The Invisible Yves Saint Laurent Was Tonight Crowned Christian Dior's Successor".

As was his usual custom, after the announcement Yves rushed back home to his family in Oran, where he locked himself away in his room and completed over 600 original sketches in 15 days for the upcoming collection. When he returned to Paris, the longstanding team of Zehnacker, Carré and Bricard edited a legion of fresh ideas into a streamlined collection of 178 looks dominated by a fluid silhouette that swung jauntily from shoulder to knee.

On the day of the show, 30 January 1958, Yves waited nervously backstage with a sprig of lily of the valley (Christian Dior's favourite good luck charm) in his buttonhole. His debut collection – called the "Trapeze" – relied on none of Dior's signature stiffening and padding. Instead, Yves' youthful line liberated female curves from the tyranny of a nipped-in waistline and skimmed the body in a similar style to that of Balenciaga's iconic "baby doll" dress. The applause was immediate, the collection hailed a triumph and Yves woke to find glowing headlines around the world, claiming Saint Laurent "has saved France".

Within weeks of his successful debut, Yves met the man who was to become a lifelong soulmate, partner, protector and tireless promoter in the years that lay ahead. At 27, Pierre Bergé was the opposite of Saint Laurent in almost every respect – short, ebullient, energetic and ruthlessly controlling, a man determined

to succeed in life whatever the costs. The couple were introduced
at a dinner party given by the influential fashion editor and
high society hostess Marie-Louise Bousquet. At the time Bergé
was the lover and enthusiastic business supporter of the artist
Bernard Buffet, but as his star faded and an acrimonious break up
followed, Bergé had already discovered a new artist to champion.
The pair made an unlikely double act and yet the combination
of their respective talents created a dynamic and enduring
partnership that went on to conquer the world of fashion for the
next five decades.

Yves trusted his instincts for the next few collections he
produced for Dior, with designs that reflected a more youthful
spirit than that of his predecessor. Influenced enormously by Coco
Chanel, who believed women wanted freedom of movement
without constraints, he declared in the press release for his spring/
summer 1959 Longue collection, "Line has been sacrificed to
the benefit of style." For his Beat collection of 1960, he took
inspiration from the French actress and cabaret singer Juliette
Gréco and the beatniks who hung around the jazz clubs of Saint-
Germain-des-Prés, producing an entirely black collection of ultra-
modern clothes that included motorcycle jackets in alligator, mink

coats with knitted sleeves, turtleneck cashmere sweaters and tight knit caps. This bold style statement was greeted with astonishment from a slightly bewildered Dior clientele and did little to impress Marcel Boussac, who was so alarmed at the customers' reaction that when Saint Laurent was conscripted into the army later that year, the House of Dior did not contest it.

The timid 24-year-old was drafted to fight in the Algerian colonial war but collapsed during the induction process and was sent briefly to a military hospital before being transferred for further treatment to Val-de-Grâce, a mental hospital in southern Paris. After a relentless campaign by Pierre Bergé to get him out, he was finally released from hospital in November 1960 and discharged from the army due to ill health. The impact of this terrifying ordeal, where he was given electric shock treatment and heavily sedated with a cocktail of psychoactive drugs, would scar for life a fragile man already prone to episodes of neuroses.

During this time Yves discovered he no longer had a job waiting for him at the House of Dior, who did not renew his contract and had instead appointed Marc Bohan to take over. Physically and mentally diminished by his recent hospital experiences but determined to start a new venture, Yves relied increasingly on the support of his partner to deal with the court case against Dior for breach of contract and to raise funds to finance his own couture house. Pierre Bergé took control of everything. He helped Yves settle back into his apartment on rue Vauban, successfully sued Dior for damages and raised additional finance from J. Mack Robinson, an entrepreneur from Atlanta, Georgia.

With just enough funding to make a start, the House of Yves Saint Laurent was officially launched on 4 December 1961, with the first couture show presented in January the following year from their newly acquired premises at 30 bis rue Spontini.

OPPOSITE: The Beat collection included a significant amount of soft leather, patent crocodile skin and dark colours. This was the final collection Yves Saint Laurent produced for the House, as it was considered too edgy for the sedate clientele of Dior.

Artistic Explosion of Colour

WEARABLE
WORKS OF ART

"Contrary to what people might think, the severe lines of
Mondrian's pictures worked well on the female form. The
results provoked a sensation."

YVES SAINT LAURENT, PARIS MATCH, *1981*

T he eminent graphic designer Cassandre created a logo
for the new company, a stylish monogram that consisted
of the initials of Yves Saint Laurent's name sensuously
intertwined in a style that reflected the modernist approach of
his haute couture house. Many Dior employees switched their
allegiance and started working for Saint Laurent, including the
very capable Anne-Marie Muñoz, who became a key figure and
went on to manage the studio for the next 40 years.

The public immediately saw a change of mood from the young
man who, working under his own name, had no obligations
to adhere to the traditional demands of the past. New shapes
and silhouettes tumbled out of him and onto his catwalk. The
double-breasted pea coat (*le caban*), wide-legged "sailor" trousers,

OPPOSITE: Saint Laurent's homage to the Dutch painter
Piet Mondrian provided huge international success for the designer
in his 1965 Autumn/Winter collection.

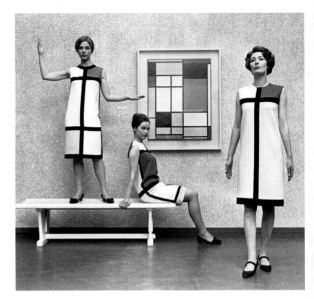

RIGHT: Superb cutting techniques were utilized to keep the geometry of the grid lines intact, with a variety of Mondrian-themed dresses produced, using different blocks of colour, and design.

simple tunic shifts, short evening dresses and a stylish trench coat all made their debut within a couple of seasons.

The company was a success as a youthful Saint Laurent could be relied upon to deliver a stylish injection of "street" in terms of practical modernism, while still maintaining the established principles of superb execution and finishing learnt through his training in Dior's couture salon. Saint Laurent (like some of his contemporaries) was quick to recognize the cultural shifts in society and women's changing role within it. He picked up on the phenomenal success of Mary Quant in London, acknowledged the futuristic space age outfits presented by Courrèges in 1964 and consequently understood the importance of creating something that would appeal to a younger generation who were rebelling against the long-established conventions of formal fashion. Several weeks before finalizing the line-up for his 1965 Autumn/

Winter show, Saint Laurent surveyed his work, decided it lacked modernism and set about re-designing brand new outfits: "I was getting bogged down in traditional elegance and Courrèges yanked me out of it. His collection stimulated me. I said to myself, I can come up with something better."

The catalyst that sparked the process of producing "something better" came from a book his mother, Lucienne, had recently given him. While leafing through Michel Seuphor's 1957 book, *Piet Mondrian: Life and Work*, a definitive biography about the abstract art and neoplastic style of the Dutch artist Piet Mondrian (1872–1944), Saint Laurent was struck by the idea that fashion needed to provide women with a new type of functional elegance more suited to contemporary life.

"I suddenly realized that dresses should no longer be composed of lines, but colours. I realized that we had to stop conceiving of a garment as sculpture and that, on the contrary, we had to view it as a mobile. I realized that fashion had been rigid up till then, and that we now have to make it move."

Taking inspiration from the geometric lines and asymmetric use of block colour exemplified by Mondrian and from the jigsaw paintings of the Russian-born French modernist Serge Poliakoff (1900–69), Saint Laurent produced 26 new designs which clearly paid homage to both men's artistic work and seamlessly transposed the visual dynamic of a two-dimensional painting into modern fashion. Constructed in fluid wool jersey from the House of Racine, the Mondrian-inspired collection consisted of perfectly proportioned straight shift dresses which incorporated primary colours, separated by black grid lines on a predominantly white background. Saint Laurent's genius lay in his skill in keeping the lines and colour blocks of Mondrian's paintings apparently geometrically aligned on the moveable shape of a woman's body, which he achieved by imperceptibly incorporating darts and seams

LEFT: Trompe-l'oeil pop art dresses inspired directly from Tom Wesselmann's Great American Nude series were interpreted into swinging sixties fashion for the Autumn/Winter collection in 1966.

into the graphic grid shapes. The fact that the ideal model figure in the 1960s was stick-thin without the obstacle of either rounded hips or a curvaceous bosom to distort the bold geometry of his designs certainly worked in his favour in the flawless execution of pared-down elegance.

The outfits were an immediate success story with both press and clientele, and marked a significant moment in the history of fashion. The "Ligne Mondrian" was hailed as groundbreaking and the global applause that followed did much to boost the reputation of both designer and artist, with copies of the dress produced all over the world. As a direct result of the publicity, a retrospective of Mondrian's work was held at the Musée de l'Orangerie in Paris a few years later. Sales to buyers took off and revenue for the house increased from 790,000 to 1.4 million francs in one season. Interviewed by a Sunday newspaper on the decision to take such a radical change of direction, Saint Laurent explained he was simply "fed up with making dresses for blasé billionaires."

The Mondrian dress kick-started an artistic theme that Saint Laurent would go on to explore in many inventive forms over the coming years. As a designer who was passionate about culture, who loved opera, ballet and the theatre, his antennae were finely tuned to the changing moods of abstraction and the American Op Art and Pop Art movements of the mid-sixties provided him with expressive new ways to translate a canvas to the catwalk. His collections for 1966 drew heavily on new pieces by Andy Warhol, Roy Lichtenstein, Tom Wesselmann and Bridget Riley. Working with an exceptionally vibrant colour palette and the visual witticisms of cut-out trompe-l'oeil profiles, as well as monochrome Op Art techniques, Saint Laurent produced Pop Art cocktail dresses with bubble-gum pink hearts, sun and moon motifs and graphic black and white chevrons styled into short,

OPPOSITE: Birds in flight were a favourite motif of the artist Georges Braque, re-interpreted into haute couture fashion by Yves Saint Laurent for his Spring/Summer 1988 collection.

RIGHT: Contemporary art remained an enduring influence throughout Saint Laurent's life, with the couturier adopting the symbolism of cubism from Georges Braque's guitar along with doves into a spectacular evening dress.

ABOVE: Detail of the exquisite embroidery and bead detailing produced by the House of Lesage for Yves Saint Laurent, to recreate the vibrance of Van Gogh's irises and sunflowers.

OPPOSITE PAGE: Naomi Campbell and Bess Stonehouse walk the runway in lavish Vincent van Gogh-inspired evening jackets, embellished with thousands of sequins and tiny seed pearls, for Spring/ Summer 1988.

sharp daywear. Most memorable were two outfits inspired by Wesselmann's *Great American Nude series*, which perfectly transposed the language of the Pop Art movement into sublime fashion. The visually fluid evening gown with its pink trompe-l'oeil profile of a woman's body that falls asymmetrically from shoulder to floor inlaid seamlessly in purple wool jersey is a masterclass in understated style.

Over the course of a 40-year career, Saint Laurent consistently revisited the idea that fashion and art were irrevocably linked, taking inspiration from the glittering colours of the Opéras-Ballets Russes collection in 1976, Picasso's cubism interpreted into flamboyant multicoloured satin appliqué dresses in 1979 and paid tribute to Louis Aragon and Jean Cocteau by embroidering lines of their poetry onto sumptuous bejewelled satin evening jackets in 1980. The Spring/Summer collection of 1988 was highly praised for its extraordinary beaded appliqué motifs produced in collaboration with the House of Lesage, headed up by François Lesage. The Van Gogh "Iris" cardigan made using 250,000 sequins and 200,000 individually threaded pearls in 22 different colours was just one example of Yves' masterful homage to the great twentieth-century artists.

A DECADE
OF STYLE
INNOVATION

THE STYLISH 1960s

"Fashions fade, style is eternal. My dream is to provide women
with the foundations of a classic wardrobe that escapes
the fashion of the moment, giving them greater confidence
in themselves."

YVES SAINT LAURENT

S aint Laurent had initiated a soaring trajectory that saw
his status rocket from ambitious young pretender to the
most influential designer in the world. He revolutionized
the way women thought about clothes, producing a series of
sensational innovations, many of which took inspiration from
classic menswear items and went on to become modern fashion
staples, such as the double-breasted reefer jacket or the trouser
suit. Like Coco Chanel, who had enhanced the reputation of her
own label by embracing her role as a celebrity figurehead, the
success of Saint Laurent's brand was magnified by a fascination
about the mythical stature of the man himself. Although buoyed
by his success and embracing a 1960s vibe of longer hair and
casual clothes, he continued to smoke incessantly and regularly
found himself derailed by debilitating dark depressions and
mental fragility.

OPPOSITE: With longer hair, and a bohemian style of dress, Yves Saint Laurent poses
for a CBS fashion special in June 1968, wearing sunglasses and a leather trench coat,
from his new collection of menswear.

Throughout his career, rumours of sickness and addiction propelled the public appetite for designer as introverted artist tortured by his own talent, a troubling image of genius which has never been so commercially utilized before or since.

Shielded by his partner Pierre Bergé from the day-to-day financial complexities of running the business, Saint Laurent was part of a fashionable set who regularly dined at Maxim's and later danced till the early hours at Régine's night club in the Latin Quarter. But his existence was not just one of gilded ivory tower entitlement, he was astute to the social changes in society and as *Vogue* journalist Hamish Bowles later observed, "Saint Laurent captured the zeitgeist with uncanny acuity".

Saint Laurent understood women. He hung out with his female friends, Betty Catroux (a tall, androgynous blonde who many claimed was the female double of the designer himself and was also his muse), Clara Saint, a Chilean heiress who went on to run the Rive Gauche press office, and Anne-Marie Muñoz. Through them he understood the need for clothing that empowered women in a society increasingly dominated by a female voice that demanded equality.

Though fully committed to the exacting processes involved in haute couture, Saint Laurent also recognized the limitations of a collection that was labour-intensive and prohibitively expensive to all but a few. The audience of women worldwide who could afford to spend thousands of pounds on a bespoke evening gown or hand-stitched, jewel-encrusted cocktail dress was dwindling before his eyes, while he felt himself part of a younger generation who took their cues from the spirit of the street. Inspired by the fast-moving world he could sense unfolding around him, Saint Laurent was on a mission to provide a viable and stylish alternative for those who could not afford his extremely expensive haute couture clothes. He was not the first couturier

OPPOSITE: Embracing his constant companions Betty Catroux and Loulou de la Falaise, in matching safari tunics, at the opening of the Rive Gauche boutique on Bond Street, London.

RIGHT: This understated cotton shirt dress with hooped chain belt typified the new younger style, worn with pilgrim buckle low-heeled pumps designed by Roger Vivier for Yves Saint Laurent.

OPPOSITE: French actress Catherine Deneuve modelling a double-breasted plaid wool trouser suit, from Yves Saint Laurent's prêt-à-porter collection on sale in the new Rive Gauche boutique in Paris. Her endorsement ensured it became an instant bestseller.

to offer ready-to-wear fashion – Madeleine Vionnet (1876–1975) and Lucien Lelong (1889–1958) both toyed with the idea of selling less expensive, off-the-peg ranges – but Saint Laurent was the first to develop the concept fully, defining the unique characteristics of each line with the explanation, "Rive Gauche is for the necessities, for the needs of daily life. In haute couture you can allow yourself to dream." His ambition to provide a collection of seasonal prêt-à-porter clothes in his signature designs made from quality fabrics with excellent production values was brought to life with the first Saint Laurent Rive Gauche boutique, which opened its doors at 21 rue de Tournon, on the Left Bank of Paris, on 26 September, 1966.

Situated in the narrow streets around Église Saint-Sulpice, off Boulevard Saint-Germain, the new boutique designed by Isabelle Heybey was painted with red and black lacquered ceilings and featured tubular Mies van der Rohe chairs to create a modernist but functional aesthetic. The "Rive Gauche" clothes, which were manufactured by sewing machine rather than handstitched, referenced similar themes to those shown in his couture collections but were not simply a cheaper, watered-down version. The ready-to-wear range allowed the couture rebel to express a more carefree attitude, targeted specifically to a generation who could not afford to indulge in the elitism of bespoke fashion, while his creative process remained intact: "The big difference between couture and ready-to-wear is not design. It is the fabrics, the handwork and the fittings. The act of creation is the same," the designer explained to *Women's Wear Daily* in 1968.

The new boutique featured a life-size portrait of Saint Laurent surveying his new venture in trademark suit and statement glasses, painted by the artist Eduardo Arroyo (1937–2018). Striped jersey dresses hung from the shop walls, while dazzling jewellery trinkets and accessories were presented in gleaming metal-and-glass display cabinets. Guest of honour at the grand opening was 23-year-old blonde beauty Catherine Deneuve, a young French actress whom Saint Laurent first encountered a year earlier when she approached him to design a dress for her to wear at a reception hosted by the Queen of England. In movie-star style, she arrived wearing oversized sunglasses, her glossy hair drawn back with a velvet hairband, dressed in a military-style pea coat with statement buttons. Saint Laurent helped her pick out some suede miniskirts and a new trouser suit, which quickly became a bestseller.

The "Rive Gauche" line was an immediate hit as young women seized the chance to own a little piece of Parisian style

created by the genius of Yves Saint Laurent with a price tag
they could afford. The shop became a go-to location for a
complete look of designer separates, accessories, jewellery and
shoes that could all be tried on in situ and bought on the spot.
The concept to roll out a chain of Rive Gauche boutiques to
the fashion capitals around the world began in 1968 with a
ready-to-wear boutique that opened on Madison Avenue, New
York, followed in 1969 by one in Bond Street, London. That
year, the designer also turned his attention to creating a similar
vein of contemporary modern menswear with the launch of his
first Saint Laurent Rive Gauche collection for men. The Parisian
boutique situated alongside his womenswear shop in rue de

Tournon provided a relaxed style of clothing that broke away from the traditional conformity of tailored suits.

Rejecting stereotypical menswear in favour of a newfound freedom of expression, the shop stocked patterned silk shirts, knitted twinsets, velvet jackets and easy trench coats, all of which reflected Saint Laurent's own wardrobe choices. The new venture proved as successful as the womenswear line, snapped up by an army of uninhibited young men ready to explore their own identity through a more flamboyant style of dress appropriate for the era. Less than 20 years later, there were nearly 200 Saint Laurent Rive Gauche boutiques worldwide.

From the inception of his own House, Saint Laurent experienced a whirlwind burst of creativity, exploring a wide range of influences that helped consolidate his personal fame and professional reputation. Decades earlier, Chanel – whom he admired greatly – had successfully re-appropriated menswear for women and now Saint Laurent also looked outside traditional female tropes to create new genres of clothing appropriate for the era's burgeoning sexual revolution. He dressed women in an elegant trench coat, designed trousers for day- and evening wear, feminized a gentleman's traditional after-dinner jacket for an androgynous female figure and borrowed military-style uniforms to create his iconic "Saharienne" safari jacket.

Each collection presented a fresh challenge to the established norms of good taste and all of his innovations consistently reinforced the ethos that women should be allowed the same freedom of movement as men. These visionary pieces celebrated at the time and ultimately recognized as Saint Laurent "classics" were referenced and reinterpreted many times over throughout his long career with the designer acknowledging "good things never go out of fashion".

RIGHT: Yves Saint Laurent produced endless variations of his trouser suit, taking a classic male uniform and re-appropriating for women, tweaking proportions, fabrics and details to revolutionize the way women wanted to be seen in an era of sexual ambiguity.

LEFT: A 1967 example of Le Smoking, the black tuxedo jacket that went on to become a recognized House of Yves Saint Laurent staple for the next four decades.

OPPOSITE: Known as a rebel couturier who loved to surprise and shock his audience, here the classic Le Smoking is re-invented with wool Bermuda shorts, mixing masculine and feminine tropes with the addition of a totally transparent, pussy bow blouse.

LEFT: Diana Ross, lead singer of the Motown girl group The Supremes, radiates glamour in fluid velvet pants and a belted tunic top to celebrate the arrival of the Rive Gauche boutique in New York, 1968.

Designed to make women feel powerful, Saint Laurent provided a modern alternative to a traditional evening gown when he first presented his black tuxedo jacket known as "Le Smoking" in 1966. Superb cutting of a masculine trouser suit juxtaposed with overtly feminine pussy bow silk shirts played with topical ideas of sexual ambiguity and, initially, the elegant tuxedo caused outrage, with women who wore his trouser suits refused service in hotels and restaurants. Nobody looked better in Le Smoking than his best friend Betty Catroux, whose slim, androgynous frame and angular features exemplified the trend for unisex style, and the success of his tuxedo would transcend all other designs to become the most recognized signature of his whole career.

Le Smoking went through many evolutions, initially worn with a white blouse and black wool trousers stitched with a wide satin side stripe along the outside leg. Two years later, it appeared with tailored Bermuda shorts and a totally transparent black blouse, creating another round of shockwaves and publicity. A range of sheer organza shift dresses exquisitely decorated with sequinned ribbons embellishing strategic points at the breast and lower torso also caused controversy.

In 1968, when Paris was rocked by student protests, Saint Laurent escaped to Marrakesh for several months, returning to present a collection full of audacity that paid homage to the riots by featuring a series of duffel coats and fringed leather jackets, as well as his daring black chiffon "see-through dress" that bared everything but revealed very little by virtue of an extravagant band of ostrich feathers positioned strategically around the hips.

Born in North Africa, the designer found an ongoing source of inspiration in the art and culture of the continent. His Bambara collection consisted of beaded and bejewelled

RIGHT: Sales of the trouser suit were boosted by the endorsement of celebrity fans like French actress Brigitte Bardot, seen here in a classic double-breasted suit.

LEFT: The 1967 Spring/ Summer collection drew inspiration from the art of Africa, with a series of intricately beaded mini dresses and elaborate headdresses.

OPPOSITE: In 1968, Yves Saint Laurent shocked audiences with the near total nudity of this transparent evening dress, trimmed only with a band of ostrich feathers around the hips and a Claude Lalanne gold serpent belt.

mini shifts, intricately appliquéd with jet and bronze coloured wooden beads, sequins and decorated with raffia. While a problematic style looked at through the lens of the present day, imbued as it is with its history of colonialism, Saint Laurent's "safari" or utility jacket – inspired by the gaberdine uniforms worn by military troops in Africa – was first debuted in the 1967 runway show to much acclaim. It was however a bespoke gaberdine utility tunic with metal ring belt made specifically for *Vogue Paris* the following year that caused an editorial sensation, shown on the statuesque six-foot German model Veruschka in a scrubland location shot by photographer Franco Rubartelli. The sexually powerful image captured the female liberation zeitgeist and ensured an avalanche of customers when the mass-produced version arrived on the Rive Gauche rails.

Trouser suits were a Saint Laurent staple in all forms, but as the decade progressed, the designer introduced an elegant jumpsuit into his repertoire, the basis of which came from the functionality of an all-in-one aviator suit. Embracing the practicality of the utilitarian workwear, he redesigned the concept as womenswear, replacing the original baggy silhouette with a refined cut that emphasized the shape of the female body. Immediately successful with the cigarette-slim models of the day, his new jumpsuit was produced in many versions, in fabrics ranging from sparkling sequins to demure wool jersey, and with a multitude of different design details. The new Saint Laurent creation was a particular hit with the American customers, who appreciated both the practicality and comfort of the jumpsuit. Within weeks, the New York boutique was out of stock.

From stylized versions of the practical pea coat to breaking the taboo of nudity, the design innovations debuted in this period anticipated the evolving roles of women within the context of a tumultuous period of change.

RIGHT: The first jumpsuits appeared on the runway in 1968, originally inspired by the functional all-in-one aviator suits worn by pilots. This version made in crepe de chine with flared pants and a revealing zip fastener could be worn for day or evening.

THE SCANDALOUS 70s

THE ERA OF LIBERATION

Internationally famous and seen as an integral part of the elite jet set crowd, Saint Laurent in his early thirties appeared to be more at ease with himself and his newfound image as celebrity couturier.

*P*aparazzi snaps capture him partying in New York with Andy Warhol, hanging out with Rudolf Nureyev at the hedonistic Club Sept in Paris and spending time with a revolving group of wealthy bohemians centred around John Paul Getty Jr. and his beautiful wife Talitha, in the laid-back atmosphere of Marrakesh.

Although Saint Laurent disliked international travel, he had long harboured a desire to return to the sunny climes and exotic colours of his North African childhood, which held vivid memories of happy times with his family. A holiday with Pierre Bergé, staying at La Mamounia in the hippy enclave of Marrakesh in 1967, had resulted in them purchasing a modest house located within the walls of the medina in a spot known as the Lemon Garden. The house was called Dar el-Hanch, which translated as "House of the Serpent", and was built around a stone courtyard several minutes away from the central square of Djemaa el-Fna.

OPPOSITE: Classic pin-stripe trouser suit, worn with an extravagant fox fur collar, photographed for a *Vogue* editorial in 1971.

Marrakesh provided an opportunity for escapism, away from
Saint Laurent's demanding role as creative figurehead of his own
couture house, and the couple retreated there for several weeks at
a time as often as they could.

Under dazzling skies in the permissive culture of North Africa,
Saint Laurent could wander freely through the bustling souk,
dressed casually in sandals and a cotton kaftan, without being
recognized – in stark contrast to the daily duties required of him
in Paris. A heady cocktail of narcotics was readily available to
enhance the chilled-out holiday vibe. Kif – the local marijuana
of Morocco – was smoked openly, but opiates like heroin and
a new wave of hallucinogens were also popular among the chic
bohemian visitors. As documented in Alice Rawsthorn's 1996
biography *Yves Saint Laurent*, within the close confines of his
intimate group of loyal friends who often stayed with the couple,
Fernando Sánchez (a classmate years earlier at the Chambre
Syndicale), Clara Saint and her boyfriend, Thadée Klossowski
(son of the painter Balthus) and Betty and François Catroux,

RIGHT: The couturier benefitted from frequent holidays at his homes in Marrakesh, where he felt able to relax and escape from the pressures of his strict routine in Paris.

Saint Laurent started experimenting with everything this relaxed environment could offer. As he explained years later to Anthony Burgess, "Drugs are more than an escape. They can open new imaginative vistas for the artist".

There was a dramatic feeling of change in Paris at the start of a new decade. President Charles de Gaulle had resigned after 11 years in power, America was still embroiled in the Vietnam War and the heady optimism of the sixties had been replaced with a darker cynicism. When Andy Warhol and his entourage of Factory disciples arrived in the capital in 1970, Saint Laurent had already acknowledged the American artist's cultural influence by referencing his work in his Pop Art collection. Warhol's crew were in Paris to shoot a short movie called *L'Amour* (1972) in Karl Lagerfeld's Left Bank apartment, with the German designer playing a minor role, and Saint Laurent visiting the set as a voyeur to mingle with the bohemian crowd of beautiful misfits. Warhol's underground art films were generally perceived as conceptual vanities, having low production values, dubious camerawork and baffling storylines, but always featuring a fascinating gang of creative people.

Saint Laurent and Lagerfeld had been youthful acquaintances since 1954 when the German designer came second in the International Wool Secretariat competition that had helped catapult Yves into his position at Christian Dior. Fiercely competitive individuals, as the success of YSL escalated, their friendship had somewhat soured and the polar differences in their respective personality traits had magnified to a point that they now existed in very different fashion cliques, with few people allowed to flit between both factions. Warhol knew both men but was captivated by the glowing magnetism that surrounded Saint Laurent, and in 1972 suggested he sit for a series of multicoloured silk screen portraits that captured the designer in reflective mood.

Paloma Picasso, who was living in Paris with her mother, the artist Françoise Gilot, was one of very few people who was allowed to hang out with the distinctly separate Saint Laurent and Lagerfeld fashion cliques. As a 22-year-old beauty, she presented herself in a way that was strikingly unforgettable: raven-black hair, porcelain skin and vivid red lips, all dressed up in an eclectic way that stylishly combined flea market finds from Portobello Road with pieces raided from her mother's wardrobe. Paloma looked remarkable in vintage clothes from the 1940s and often turned up wearing crepe de Chine dresses and elegant turbans which evoked memories for Saint Laurent of Christian Bérard's illustrations he had admired as a child, and also of the way his adorable mother

OPPOSITE: Inspired to produce his "Liberation" collection by the eclectic style choices of Paloma Picasso, who referenced the seventies decade with her Carmen Miranda turbans and silk tea dresses. Close friends of the designer, Paloma Picasso, Marisa Berenson and Loulou de la Falaise were placed strategically in the audience at the show to encourage support.

ABOVE: Photographic images taken by Helmut Newton from the 1971 "Liberation" collection, as well as the original 80 items of clothing were displayed at the Fondation Pierre Bergé – Yves Saint Laurent in Paris, in 2015.

OPPOSITE: Naomi Campbell in the Spring/Summer 2002 haute couture show, wearing a reproduction of the acid green fox fur "chubby" first seen as part of the "Liberation" collection that caused uproar.

Lucienne had dressed, back in Oran. It was these references that the designer was thinking of when he presented what came to be known as his "Scandal Collection" at the rue Spontini in January 1971.

The bombshell "Liberation" show inspired by 1940s wartime fashion quickly became known as "Paris's ugliest collection". It caused an uproar of disapproval from his regular clientele and an unprecedented wave of vitriol from the fashion press, who were shocked at the audacity of the 80-piece couture collection. Heavily influenced by retro fashion, first exemplified by the square-cut shoulders and boxy silhouettes adopted during the Second World War, Saint Laurent presented his audience with short dresses, wedge-heeled shoes, wide pleated pants and suits with square shoulders.

Support from friends Loulou de la Falaise, Marisa Berenson and Paloma Picasso, strategically positioned among the audience and wearing their own interpretations of this updated retro look, did little to counter the explosive reaction the show provoked.

Eugenia Sheppard, writing for the *International Herald Tribune*, did not hold back, proclaiming the collection "completely hideous", and even the French press attacked Saint Laurent for what they perceived as an unmitigated disaster in a way he could not previously have imagined.

Having championed an aesthetic style of elegant androgyny so successfully over recent years, the overt femininity of this collection, which featured sexy chiffon dresses with plunging necklines, short fox fur chubbies in garish colours, a velvet coat embroidered with red lips and puff-sleeved crepe de Chine dresses printed with erotic scenes from classical Greek art, provided a shocking departure from the traditional expectations of a Saint Laurent haute couture show. The models themselves appeared sexually blatant, visibly bra-less, heavily made up with red lips and nails and wearing chunky platform wedges, visual references that clearly stirred memories of the "horizontal collaborators" who slept with the Nazis under the Occupation. An overriding swell of anger was directed at Saint Laurent for reminding the middle-aged audience of their years lived in fear and deprivation, and the controversial show was described as "kitsch", the first time this word had been used in relation to bad taste vulgarity in fashion. The designer was prepared for the criticism and said in an interview with French *Elle* at the time: "I don't care if my pleated or draped dresses evoke the 1940s for cultivated fashion people. What's important is that young girls who have never known this fashion want to wear them."

In fact, the backlash was short-lived. Saint Laurent had broken the rules, drawing on nostalgia for a past he did not experience and representing it in a way that was bold, sexy and perfect for an audience of youthful women who demanded the right to choose their own style. The collection anticipated a new way of dressing that embraced ideas from a younger generation who casually mixed styles and influences from different eras, cultures and continents.

OPPOSITE: The fashion critics who sat in silence at the show declared the 1940s-style, silk slip dresses and crepe de chine suits "hideous".

Drawing parallels with the negative response the artist Edouard Manet received for his painting *Olympia* when it was first exhibited in 1865, Saint Laurent understood that exploring new directions of creativity would inevitably attract criticism, as he explained to *Women's Wear Daily* after universal condemnation of his show: "I did not think that in a profession as free as fashion that one could meet so many people so narrow-minded and reactionary, petty people paralyzed by taboos. But I am also very stimulated by this scandal because I know that which shocks is new."

In the wake of the Scandal collection, Nicaraguan-born Bianca Pérez-Mora Macías went to meet the designer for the first time in his offices in rue Spontini to commission her wedding dress, with a very clear idea of what she wanted. Unerringly modern, effortlessly chic and confidently assured of her own style, Bianca married Rolling Stone Mick Jagger wearing what was to become the most iconic wedding outfit ever seen. Paparazzi images of her sharp-shouldered, white tuxedo suit, worn with nothing but a glimpse of bare breast and an oversized sun hat, ricocheted around the world after the couple's quick ceremony on 12 May 1971 in the Town Hall in St Tropez.

Recalling the event nearly 40 years later, Bianca Jagger said, "Contrary to popular wisdom, it wasn't a trouser suit: it was a long, narrow skirt and a jacket. He made the wide-brimmed hat with a veil and we decided that instead of carrying a bouquet I should wear a flower corsage on my wrist to go with the suit." The 27-year-old groom – not known for his sartorial choices – was also wearing YSL couture, appearing alongside his partner in a pale green three-piece suit, dressed down with coloured sneakers. While marriage to Mick was brief and unsuccessful, Bianca remained a consistently loyal supporter and friend of Saint Laurent.

RIGHT: Extreme tailoring exemplified by the cut of the exaggerated lapels in this double-breasted jacket worn with wide legged pants, and a decorative turban.

PREVIOUS PAGE:
Bianca Pérez-Mora
Macías marries Rolling
Stones frontman Mick
Jagger in St. Tropez
1971, in a white Yves
Saint Laurent tailored
two-piece suit and
broad-brimmed
white sun hat.

LEFT: Classic Yves Saint
Laurent blazer worn
over white 1940s-style
slacks, 1971.

RIGHT: Original Saint
Laurent sketches on
show at the Fondation
Pierre Berge – Yves
Saint Laurent, "Scandal
Collection" exhibition
in Paris, 2015.

Creating a scandal to generate publicity was a profitable idea. Later that year, the designer caused another storm by starring in his own advertising campaign for the launch of *Pour Homme*, the first YSL male fragrance. French fashion photographer Jeanloup Sieff, who was responsible for the monotone Christ-like image of an unashamedly naked Saint Laurent bathed in a halo of heavenly light, remembers the concept was fully formed when his friend arrived at the studio: "He told me to photograph him in the nude, he said he wanted to create a scandal. It was all Yves's idea."

Sitting cross-legged on a pile of black leather cushions and naked save for his trademark glasses, Sieff captured the serenity of a man confident of his own sexuality and produced an image that resonated with an audience of young gay men. First shown in the November 1971 issue of *Vogue Paris* and *Paris Match*, with other publications refusing to run the campaign, the resulting frenzy of press detailing the shockingly distasteful content helped fuel the flames of publicity, ensuring more sales and coverage than any amount of paid for advertising might have generated.

A new muse who clearly charmed Saint Laurent with her aristocratic heritage and wild bohemian style had recently been adopted into the inner sanctum, where she would remain as long-time confidante, creative "collaborateur" and partner in crime. Loulou de la Falaise was a part-English, part-French *enfant terrible*; a wafer-thin occasional model and fashion journalist who burst through the doors of Avenue Marceau dressed like an exotic nomad, laden with junk jewellery and trailing a multitude of scarves. She enchanted Paris and amused Saint Laurent with her madcap hippy deluxe London style and boundless energy, and as she worked alongside him for the next 30 years the designer relied on both her professional opinion and

OPPOSITE: Yves Saint Laurent with his long-time collaborator Loulou de la Falaise in a fashion shoot for *Vogue* shot by Deborah Turbeville.

personal friendship. The pair would often escape after long hours spent at the studio (along with the glamorous Betty Catroux) to let loose in a nightclub until the early hours of the morning.

Both women adored Saint Laurent and as Pierre Bergé confirms in the 2011 documentary *L'Amour Fou*, the feelings were mutual: "Yves was very fond of both of them, they played a very important part in his life." At work, Loulou would unfailingly bolster his spirits and spur him on by praising his latest ideas when black moods consumed him, while the relationship with Betty was darker, as she explained: "We had a very negative relationship. He'd call to say, 'Life is Hell' and I'd say, 'You're right!' I certainly didn't have a positive influence". The trio were often found dancing together till dawn at Le Sept, with the more sensible Bergé and François Catroux trying their best to act as strict parents to their younger partners, who behaved like uncontrollable teenagers. Their efforts invariably failed and as the decade continued, Saint Laurent's conduct became increasingly decadent and out of control, with the mental strain of having to produce four collections a year resulting in hysterical outbursts in the studio and progressively dangerous behaviour after dark.

As the physical dependency on drink and drugs became harder to disguise, the gossip columns regularly blasted out stories of breakdowns, incurable illness and even rumours of suicide and death. Everyone understood that Bergé would be around to pick up the pieces, handle the practical details of the business, shield his lover's lifestyle choices from public scrutiny, and present a public face of calm. But after one too many visits to the American Hospital to be treated for depression, drug and alcohol dependency, an obsessive affair with Lagerfeld's protégé Jacques de Bascher and a blazing row, where Saint Laurent

ABOVE: Female friends Betty Catroux and Loulou de la Falaise both provided emotional support to the designer throughout his life.

disappeared completely for 24 hours, Pierre called time on their relationship. Defeated by an 18-year professional and personal partnership that required constant management of Saint Laurent's fragility, he finally moved out of their rue de Babylone apartment in 1976, admitting, "It was very hard for me to leave Yves."

Left alone for the first time, an increasingly reclusive Saint Laurent was devasted by what he saw as abandonment and betrayal. In reality, the two men remained inextricably bound, both in a loving and loyal friendship and in their business dealings, with Bergé continuing to control the phenomenal success of the global empire they had built up together, while still protecting its most valuable asset.

THEATRE, BALLET
AND CINEMA

THE IRRESISTIBLE ALLURE OF THE STAGE

"If I wasn't a couturier I would have probably devoted myself to the theatre. The theatre's spell has appeared as a livelier, more radiant refuge than reality."

YVES SAINT LAURENT, 1959
(MUSÉE YVES SAINT LAURENT PARIS)

Throughout his life, Yves Saint Laurent complained bitterly that the fashion noose that weighed so heavily around his shoulders was a constant torment, even going so far as to tell a British journalist in 1977: "I hate fashion, I don't have any fun doing it. A show terrifies me."

If fate hadn't propelled a teenage Saint Laurent directly into the gilded environment of Christian Dior's salon, he may well have followed an alternative childhood dream and achieved comparable success in the magical world of entertainment – an early family trip to the theatre in 1950 had unleashed a passion that would stay with him for the rest of his life. Following this formative

OPPOSITE: Yves Saint Laurent with his friend, the choreographer Roland Petit, discussing costumes for Zizi Jeanmaire's Paris show *La Revue*.

RIGHT: Zizi Jeanmaire in one of the many spectacular cabaret costumes designed specifically for her by Yves Saint Laurent.

experience of theatrical illusion, the teenager would spend hours alone at home, making cardboard characters wearing costumes he had designed himself, to perform in his "Illustre Petit Théâtre", a delightful miniature theatre he had constructed to put on plays for his sisters, Michèle and Brigitte. An adolescent Yves also spent time absorbed in literature, immersing himself in the poetic nostalgia of Marcel Proust, a discovery that would influence many future decisions. At the height of his fame it is thought Saint Laurent would book into hotels using the pseudonym Monsieur Swann (the protagonist of Proust's *À La Recherche du Temps Perdu/ In Search of Lost Time*) so as not to be recognized, and in 1983, he and Pierre Bergé purchased Château Gabriel, a lavish retreat in Normandy, where Bergé would deliver weekend guests by helicopter. Every guest room was identified with a brass door plaque naming a Proustian character.

The archives at the Musée Yves Saint Laurent Paris include many accomplished illustrations for costumes and stage sets that Saint Laurent produced at home in the early fifties for imaginary productions such as Jean Cocteau's *L'Aigle à Deux Têtes (The Eagle with Two Heads),* but his first professional commission came in 1956 when he was working as an assistant at Dior. Saint Laurent was approached to design the sets and costumes for *Le Bal des Têtes*, a flamboyant dressing-up ball that required attendees to wear an extravagant showstopper headdress. Hosted by the prominent aristocrat Baron Alexis de Rede, with a guest list that included every high society *grande dame* in Paris, this early invitation into the beau monde introduced the young couturier to many influential people, such as Hélène de Rothschild, Comtesse Jacqueline de Ribes and the Duchess of Windsor, as well as the acclaimed choreographer Roland Petit and his wife, the dancer Renée "Zizi" Jeanmaire. The couple became lifelong friends of the designer and they would go on to have many successful professional collaborations. The first came in 1959 with the ballet *Cyrano de Bergerac* at the Théâtre de l'Alhambra, with Saint Laurent designing all the sets and costumes and dressing the female lead, Roxanne, in layers of flouncy taffeta.

Though working nonstop in a demanding industry that required constant cyclical invention, Saint Laurent was a great lover of art and opera and took on many other projects during his 40-year career, creating costumes and sets for the theatre, ballet and cinema and winning many awards along the way. He worked with directors Claude Régy, Jean-Louis Barrault, Luis Buñuel, François Truffaut and dressed French stars of stage and screen Arletty, Jeanne Moreau, Isabelle Adjani and Catherine Deneuve, who remained a lifelong friend. The fantasy element of performance allowed him to indulge his imaginative creativity in a way that was often impossible within the commercial constraints of fashion, although visually, there were occasional signs of convergence between the disciplines. Most notably for Petit's ballet *Notre-Dame de Paris*, performed at The Palais Garnier, Opéra national de Paris, in December 1965, where the costumes for Phoebus were reminiscent of the Mondrian-inspired dresses he had first presented at his haute couture show earlier that year.

With the lithe body of a ballerina and lamp-post legs that went on forever, Zizi Jeanmaire was the perfect foil to pull off Saint Laurent's more outlandish showgirl costumes. Fusing burlesque tropes of feathers and sequins with a stylish aesthetic of elegance, the costumes he created for *Le Champagne Rosé*, a frothy pink confection of twinkling ostrich feathers, worn in her music hall show *Spectacle Zizi Jeanmaire* in 1963, perfectly exemplified the spirit of Parisian glamour. For *La Revue* at the Casino de Paris in 1970 the costumes became even more luxurious, with swathes of lavish fur, exotic palm tree plumes and topless dancers wearing thigh-high sparkly boots.

In 1965, Saint Laurent was introduced to Margot Fonteyn and Rudolf Nureyev, both of whom would become good friends, with the designer creating outfits for Fonteyn in both a professional and personal capacity. At her final benefit gala in 1990 the ballerina chose to bow out wearing a colourful YSL beaded couture dress.

Saint Laurent created costumes for many leading ladies of the cinema, starting with the wardrobe of Italian movie star Claudia Cardinale in *The Pink Panther*, a 1963 Hollywood comedy directed by Blake Edwards, but his most acclaimed cinematic collaboration came in 1967 with the wardrobe of Catherine Deneuve in *Belle de Jour*. Directed by the Spanish surrealist Luis Buñuel, 23-year-old Deneuve plays the bored housewife

OPPOSITE: Costumes for the principal dancers Roland Petit and Claire Mott in the 1965 ballet *Notre-Dame de Paris*.

protagonist Séverine Serizy, who enlivens her dull bourgeois lifestyle by spending her afternoons working in a high-class brothel. The neutral colour palette of modest costumes – the military vinyl trench coat with textural knitted sleeves, black shirt dress with demure white satin collar and cuffs and low patent pilgrim pumps with a silver buckle (produced by the shoemaker Roger Vivier) – became an integral part of the film's success and went on to become some of Saint Laurent's most iconic fashion staples.

Belle de Jour kick-started a long-standing friendship and the designer created costumes for Deneuve in François Truffaut's *La Sirène du Mississippi* (*Mississippi Mermaid*) in 1969, Jean-Pierre Melville's *Un Flic* (*A Cop*) in 1972 and Tony Scott's erotic vampire movie *The Hunger* starring David Bowie and Susan Sarandon in 1983.

In the mid-seventies at the height of fashion's obsession with the retro glam of 1920s and 30s Hollywood, Saint Laurent dressed Anny Duperey in a series of figure-hugging satin evening gowns and extravagant fox-fur shawls for her part as Arlette in Alain Resnais' biographical drama *Stavisky*. Having to create for both historical and futuristic projects on stage or through the medium of film gave him the freedom to invent a parallel universe that usefully counterbalanced the different demands of his considerable artistic output, something he readily acknowledged.

When in 1977 Pierre Bergé acquired and renovated the Théâtre de l'Athénée, and the following year staged the Cocteau play, *L'Aigle à Deux Têtes*, Saint Laurent was finally able to realize his childhood ambition, designing the sets and costumes for the romantic drama and receiving rave reviews for his resolute modernism and style.

OPPOSITE: Catherine Deneuve in her breakthrough role of Severine Serizy in Luis Buñuel's 1967 film *Belle de Jour*. Deneuve always acknowledged the importance of Saint Laurent's clothes in the film, describing the style as "timeless".

THE ICONIC PERFUMES

MODERN SCENTS

That a couture house could substantially boost both annual
income and brand recognition with sales of a successful
perfume had been well documented by the time Yves Saint
Laurent diversified into this market.

*T*he early Parisian couturier Paul Poiret (1879–1944) had
been subsidizing his bespoke fashion with the profits
from a branded fragrance since 1910 and it was more
than 40 years since Mademoiselle Chanel, for whom Saint
Laurent had the utmost respect, had created the blueprint
for Chanel No 5, the world's best-selling perfume. When US
cosmetics giant Charles of The Ritz (who had bought out J.
Mack Robinson's original investment in the Yves Saint Laurent
fashion house) got in touch with Pierre Bergé with a proposal to
oversee the production and marketing of a perfume bearing Yves
Saint Laurent's name in return for a royalty fee of 5 per cent, the
businessman was eager to strike a deal.

In spring 1964, Saint Laurent launched his first perfume using
simply his initial "*Y*" (pronounced "ee-grec" in French) stencilled
in gold on a square-cut modern bottle designed by Pierre Dinard.

OPPOSITE: The first perfume launched in 1964, simply named *Y*.

The light fragrance was created by Jean Amic of Roure perfumers using tuberose and ylang-ylang as mid notes and sandalwood, patchouli and oak moss as base notes. By the time an opportunity arose to expand the range, Charles of The Ritz had been sold to an American pharmaceutical group, Squibb-Beechnut, who agreed a deal to return the couture house to Saint Laurent and Bergé, while taking control of all new perfumes and agreeing a royalty payment. Saint Laurent wanted to create a fragrance targeted directly at the young women who were loyal fans of his ready-to-wear collections and in 1971, the company launched *Rive Gauche*, created by Jacques Polge, best known for his role as head perfumer at Les Parfums Chanel and considered to be one of the greatest "noses" of the twentieth century. With a name that was already recognizable as a result of the international success of the boutiques, marketing the product in an aluminium canister painted with silver, black and blue stripes (unlike any other perfume packaging of the time) and an advertising slogan that teased "Rive Gauche is not for self-effacing women", the fragrance resonated with a ready-made audience of independent women. Later that same year, the designer posed naked for the promotional campaign shot by his friend, the photographer Jeanloup Sieff, to launch his first menswear eau de toilette, *Pour Homme*. Though much in keeping with the zeitgeist of the time (the free loving hippies at Woodstock and the musical *Hair*) the figurehead of a luxury brand posing nude to sell his own products caused a terrific scandal and consequently huge publicity for the house and the fragrance. *Pour Homme* was a fresh and aromatic blend of bergamot and lemon verbena combined with base notes of amber and sandalwood to create a distinctly citrusy aroma.

Opium was promoted in Europe to coincide with the Opéras-Ballets Russes collection in 1977, but to celebrate the official

OPPOSITE: Marketed to reflect the design ethos of the ready-to-wear boutiques of the same name, *Rive Gauche* launched in 1971 and was presented in an ultra-modern striped tubular canister.

Parfums

YVESSAINTLAURENT

Paris

rive gauche

PREVIOUS PAGE:
American photographer Helmut Newton captured Texan model, Jerry Hall in a seductive mood at Yves Saint Laurent's Rue de Babylone apartment for the *Opium* campaign in 1977.

ABOVE: A rare image of Yves Saint Laurent smiling, at the extravagant launch party for *Opium* held on a Chinese junk in Manhattan's East Harbour.

arrival in America the following year, the Squibb Corporation threw a decadent party for Saint Laurent widely perceived as the "fashion event of the decade". The publicity stunt that cost an estimated $300,000 provided entertainment for 800 VIP guests on a spectacular Chinese junk called the *Peking*, moored in central Manhattan's East Harbour. Smiling like a superstar, the designer was surrounded all night by a handful of A-list friends (Diana Vreeland, Halston, Cher, Diane von Furstenberg) and a posse of perfectly groomed models, glittering in high-end couture. The fragrance, which had taken many years of research to produce, was an unusual blend of patchouli, myrrh and vanilla, presented in a unique bottle designed to look like an inro (a Japanese box with several compartments worn by the Samurai, fastened with a cord and closed with a netsuke, a small carved ornament of ivory or wood, to keep their spices, salt and herbal medicines).

RIGHT: Presented in a red lacquer bottle designed to look like a Japanese inro box, *Opium* was an immediate bestseller.

The original Chinese "lacquer" packaging with gold lettering was suitably sophisticated, but the name *Opium* caused immediate outrage. Saint Laurent was accused of glamorizing drug use and the provocative advertising campaign shot by Helmut Newton and featuring American model Jerry Hall languishing seductively on a bed of cushions beneath the strapline, "*Opium*, for those who are addicted to Yves Saint Laurent" did little to detract from the charge. Having invested so heavily in the marketing campaign, Squibb were reluctant to respond to the criticism and rode out the protests, explaining that the name was evocative of the romance and mystery of the East. The ensuing press coverage boosted sales and *Opium* became an instant hit, with the initial stock selling out on both sides of the Atlantic.

RIGHT: Model Mounia Orosemane with Yves Saint Laurent, at the launch of *Paris,* at the Hotel Intercontinental in 1983.

Rudolf Nureyev, a close friend of Saint Laurent, seemed the perfect choice to dance for an invited audience of 1,200 guests for the launch of a new men's fragrance, *Kouros,* at the Opéra Comique in 1981. The fragrance concept played heavily on themes of Adonis as the word itself is the term given to the erotic nude sculptures that first appeared in Ancient Greece. The press release for *Kouros* read: "He is handsome like a God. He is handsome like a man. He is the Absolute, the eternal beauty, the miracle, the revelation of the Divine, true and simple grandeur". Renowned for his monstrous ego and divine body, Nureyev danced flawlessly and when the performance was over, Saint Laurent surprised the audience by thanking his friend with a passionate mouth-to-mouth kiss.

Next came *Paris*, launched at the couture fashion show at the Hotel Intercontinental in 1983. At the runway finale, Mounia Orosemane, one of Saint Laurent's favourite models, strutted down the catwalk in a short shift wedding dress covered in birds-of-paradise plumes, clutching an oversized bottle of the new fragrance to present to the audience. *Paris* represented Saint Laurent's love letter to his city; the floral fragrance was tinged with the nostalgia of garden roses and the advertising campaign utilized the most iconic of Parisian landmarks, the Eiffel Tower, as a backdrop. As with previous perfumes, the name was controversial and the Paris City Council objected, ensuring publicity that only helped to boost sales, with *Paris* quickly joining *Opium* to become one of the top 10 bestsellers.

Jazz, an eau de toilette for men, was launched in 1988 with a stylish monotone advertising campaign featuring the cut-out silhouettes of jazz musicians harking back to Paris in the 1920s, one of the most decadent periods of French history. Saint Laurent's next perfume sold itself with the strapline "A Tribute to the Women Who Sparkle" and was packaged in a bottle designed to resemble a classic champagne cork. Launched in 1993 and called simply *Champagne*, the full-bodied perfume created by Sophia Grojsman (also responsible for *Paris*) was subject to legal scrutiny before it had even arrived in-store. Faced with a lawsuit from the Comité Interprofessionel du vin de Champagne (CIVC) for contravening the use of the word "champagne", which can only be used for a specific type of sparkling wine grown in one region, Saint Laurent was forced to rethink. *Champagne* was re-named as *Yves Saint Laurent* and then later in 1996, the perfume name was changed again to *Yvresse*.

ACCESSORIES AND JEWELLERY

ADORNED AND BEJEWELLED

"I like a dress to be simple and an accessory to be crazy."

YVES SAINT LAURENT
(MUSÉE YVES SAINT LAURENT PARIS)

S aint Laurent was a perfectionist. His early career with
Christian Dior had instilled in him an understanding
of the importance of a finished look – a signature hat,
the right shoes, a discreet necklace – all of these accessories
conveyed the formality of 1950s society expressed through haute
couture fashion.

As an instigator of radical change, he was responsible for
sweeping away the conventional codes of couture while still
believing the overall expression of modernity he was creating
required the requisite details of jewellery, scarves, gloves and
hats to complete his vision and pull the whole look together.
At show time he could be found backstage changing last-
minute details, finding different earrings for a model to wear

OPPOSITE: Yves Saint Laurent trying out different jewellery on a model in
preparation for the Christian Dior Autumn/Winter haute couture show in 1959.

ABOVE: Bespoke
body jewellery
created by the artist
Claude Lalanne, for
Yves Saint Laurent's
Autumn/Winter 1969
collection.

with their outfit or swapping a handbag, demonstrating a
passion for visual perfection that never waned. Early examples
of his incredibly imaginative experiments with jewellery were
produced in collaboration with friends, the artists François-
Xavier and his wife, Claude Lalanne, to whom he had been
introduced at the end of the 1950s through a mutual friend,
Anne-Marie Muñoz.

On a visit to their studio, Saint Laurent had seen sculptural casts of torsos and chests which Claude Lalanne had made using a method called galvanoplasty. His imagination was fired, and for the Autumn/Winter haute couture collection of 1969, the sculptor made gold-plated metal castings from the body of the statuesque model Veruschka, which Saint Laurent incorporated into two stunning evening dresses made from diaphanous chiffon. Taking inspiration from the natural world, Lalanne continued to create statement jewellery for her friend until the early eighties, most notably the gilt bronze torque of the designer's own lips in 1970, intricate wisteria belts that wrapped decoratively around simple fluid gowns in 1971 and a spectacular range of headdresses in 1981.

An eternal theme of "love" permeated Saint Laurent's work, evident in the unique greetings cards he produced annually for friends, collaborators and clients from 1970 onward. The leitmotif for the house was a famous crystal brooch in the shape of an asymmetrical heart made of smoke-grey diamante encrusted with rubies and pearls. The oversized jewel, 12 by 8 cm (5 x 3½ in), was created by costume jeweller Roger Scemama for the first collection Saint Laurent produced under his own name in 1962. Initially worn as a statement necklace with a demure short evening dress, the piece became a good-luck talisman and was retained from one collection to the next, with other versions of the heart endlessly reinvented from 1979 onward in a myriad of materials, from wood to rock crystal.

On the day of the catwalk show the original heart necklace was delivered in a shoebox to Saint Laurent, who would decide who would be lucky enough to wear it – a tradition that became a hotly anticipated ritual in every show. Like Chanel, who detested precious gemstones and created a

trend for costume jewellery, Saint Laurent declared early on his preference for "*bijoux de fantaisie*", explaining at his first interview after winning the International Wool Secretariat prize in 1954, "I want to make daring accessories, 'couture' jewels that are so much more spiritual than real ones."

In the early seventies Paloma Picasso – who was making jewellery from beads bought at flea markets – was encouraged by Saint Laurent to make pieces for him, but it was Loulou de la Falaise, who joined in 1972, who would become a real asset to the company, dreaming up magical ideas in unorthodox materials that the artisan ateliers would skilfully turn into reality. At the beginning of a collection, Saint Laurent would set the theme and de la Falaise would immediately start the process of sketching out her own ideas, often juxtaposing strange materials like straw, plastic, glass or pebbles into her designs and working with the design team in the studio. With such madly inventive pieces becoming an integral part of the YSL style, the importance of jewellery escalated to the point that by 1990, the couture accessories were sold separately from the clothes in their own boutique on the rue du Faubourg Saint-Honoré. Saint Laurent was generous in acknowledging Loulou's input into his business, saying in 1984, "She is the real star among us, she strikes gold time after time with wonderful pieces of jewellery." The company utilized a wide range of specialist ateliers employing craftsmen who were experts in their own field to produce all of Saint Laurent's creative pieces. Robert Goossens, who had worked directly for Chanel and Balenciaga, produced rock crystal and gilt bronze, while Roger Scemama worked with wood, Augustine Gripoix produced *verre nacré* pieces, a mixture of poured glass and mother of pearl that set like pearl, and François Lesage created exquisite embroidery pieces.

PREVIOUS PAGE:
Sculpted torso and
breast imprints taken
from the model
Veruschka's body
were made in
galvanized copper by
Claude Lalanne, for
Yves Saint Laurent's
vibrant chiffon gowns.

RIGHT: Veronica Webb
on the catwalk in the
early 1990s, swathed
in gold jewellery, an
amber cuff and an
elaborate headdress.

LEFT: The famous heart created in 1962 by Roger Scemama became a house talisman that appeared in every catwalk show.

OPPOSITE: The butterfly motif, seen here as part of a decorative headpiece, was a recurring theme of nature, utilized as decoration on belts, earrings and brooches.

LEFT: Statement
accessories used to
offset the mannish
cut of the trouser suit,
Spring/Summer 1990
collection.

The Saint Laurent aesthetic played provocatively with colour and texture. The designer loathed the idea of coordinated accessories and often deliberately used contrasting materials and clashing shades to create impact. Hats made in-house were always an integral addition to the overall image.

"ONE CAN NEVER OVERSTATE THE IMPORTANCE OF ACCESSORIES."

YVES SAINT LAURENT, 1977, FRENCH ELLE

The conical "Chinese"-inspired hats for the Imperial China Autumn/Winter 1977 haute couture collection stunned for their simplistic shape executed in lavish brocade and fur fabrics, the fedora tipped perfectly across one eye became synonymous with the silhouette of his masculine trouser suits and many examples of the turban, either sleek and chic or wildly decorative, became a House staple throughout his career. Saint Laurent was experimental in both shoe and bag design, using a wide range of materials, including snakeskin, vinyl, plastic, velvet and the very best-quality leather and suedes.

Initially, shoes were made at Saint Laurent's own in-house workshops and later produced under licence. Quality was paramount, but he was also insistent that the flow of an outfit should not be interfered with by ill-conceived footwear. As such, everything he produced from the golden Cossack boots for the Opéra-Ballets Russes collection to the flat leather mules worn with his first pair of sailor pants was superbly crafted but extremely elegant.

ABOVE: Backstage
Loulou de la Falaise
puts the finishing
touches to Laetitia
Casta's outfit in
Yves Saint Laurent's
final show, January
2002.

By 1977, with the success of the company growing
exponentially, Pierre Bergé set up lucrative deals around
the globe to license the YSL name to numerous accessory
manufacturers. Saint Laurent agreed to sign his name to over
35 products, including scarves, jewellery, furs, sunglasses,
bed linen, shoes, umbrellas and even cigarettes, all of which
boosted the YSL brand while allowing the designer himself
to concentrate on what he did best.

RIGHT: Decorative
earrings made up
from strings of fake
pearls, as Yves Saint
Laurent was known
to favour costume
jewellery.

GLOBAL
INSPIRATION

INSPIRATIONAL JOURNEYS AROUND THE WORLD

"If you don't have the power of imagination, you don't have anything."

YVES SAINT LAURENT, 1978, WOMEN'S WEAR DAILY

*A*s a successful young designer, Saint Laurent's revelation in 1968 that black was his favourite colour in response to the Proust Questionnaire, a set of 35 questions made famous by Marcel Proust and frequently used in interviews, came as no great surprise, given that much of his ground-breaking androgynous style depended on a subdued palette.

His modernist clean-cut lines of Summer 1975 featured 35 black designs from a collection of 74 outfits.

But Saint Laurent was a provocateur who liked to shock and his next, totally unpredicted, move unleashed a storm of superlatives. With an explosion of stunning theatricality performed to a sweeping operatic soundtrack, he revealed a new aesthetic that rejected his signature pared-down masculinity in

OPPOSITE: A luxurious take on traditional costumes inspired by the Ballet Russes for the Autumn/Winter ready-to-wear collection in 1976.

ABOVE: Models in the Rive Gauche boutique wearing ready-to-wear pieces from the Opéras-Ballets Russes collection.

favour of dazzling fantasy. His winter 1976 Opéras-Ballets Russes collection captivated his audience, who were delighted by a parade of luxurious Russian peasant dresses, Cossack coats trimmed with mink, extravagant "babushka" gypsy skirts, jewel-coloured velvet bodices and gold lamé boots. The flamboyant presentation staged for the first time on a raised catwalk at the Hotel Inter-Continental in Paris received universal praise, with *The New York Times* proclaiming it "a revolutionary collection that will change the course of fashion" and the 40-year-old designer himself later conceding, "Perhaps it wasn't the best collection, but it was certainly the most beautiful." Inspired by the vast shelves of travel and art books pored over in his studio, he was continually drawn to the romantic themes of art and beauty from a bygone era. He explained to *Le Monde* in 1983 that his fantasy interpretations of a place were best explored by reading illustrated books from the safety of his own sofa: "my best journeys are in my imagination."

Time spent at his newly acquired pretty pink mansion Dar Es Saada la Zahia, "The House of Happiness in Serenity", located near the gorgeous Jardin Majorelle in Marrakesh, exposed Saint Laurent to a daily atmosphere of vibrant colour and sensuality. The traditional Moroccan dress of harem pants, tunics and hooded *djellabas* (long, loose-fitting robes with decorative embroidery worn by the locals in the medina) proved influential in his work, although subsequent "imaginary journeys" to investigate folkloric codes of Spain, China, India and Japan were just as impactful.

Twice a year he would stay for several weeks in Morocco, producing hundreds of preliminary sketches that included details of accessories and jewellery as the starting point for each collection. Saint Laurent drew quickly with a Staedtler 2B Graphite pencil or felt tip pens, but the demands on him to produce four shows a year (Spring/Summer and Autumn/Winter for haute couture and prêt-à-porter) continued to take their toll on his physical and mental wellbeing. His output for the Opéras-Ballets Russes show was prolific and Loulou de la Falaise spoke of his "total frenzy" when he returned to Paris with "4,000 beautiful drawings".

Preparation for a show followed a well-rehearsed system established over many years, which began by narrowing down hundreds of original research sketches into a workable, cohesive collection. Individual outfits were assigned to the specific *chefs d'atelier*, who would use their unique technical skill sets of dressmaking or tailoring to produce a "toile". This first fabric interpretation of the design made in ecru cotton and worn by the mannequin cabine (the fit model) would provide a realistic idea of what the final silhouette would look like. From the bright daylight studio on the second floor at Avenue Marceau the couturier and his collaborative team, which for 30 years included Anne-Marie Muñoz and Loulou de la Falaise, would inspect the toile

from every angle using the mirrored wall at the end of the studio to gain a different perspective.

After three or four toile fittings, the garment was ready to be made up in the sumptuous collection of fabrics ordered specifically for that season, many of them commissioned from Abraham, a Swiss silk company that Saint Laurent worked closely with. Rolls of satin, silk and mousseline filled every corner of the studio, with trimmings and fabrics for accessories chosen from sample books bursting with magnificent swatches of colour and texture. Having worked alongside Christian Dior, who relied heavily on stiffened interfacing to create shape, Saint Laurent banned it from his workrooms, relying instead on complex cutting techniques to create an outfit that he demanded must feel light and unrestrictive to wear.

From his inaugural collection in 1962, the designer was meticulous about keeping a factual record of every garment produced, something he continued to do until his resignation in 2002. In a book the team called "the bible" every item was included, from initial sketches assembled into a collection board named according to date and season, details of the *chef d'atelier*, fabric swatches, costs of materials, sales ledgers with details of customers purchases to photos of the model wearing the outfit.

The Opéras-Ballets Russes collection heralded a dramatic transformation in the overall aesthetic Saint Laurent presented, with every subsequent show becoming more staggeringly beautiful than the last. The Jamaican-born model and singer-songwriter Grace Jones opened the romantic Carmen collection inspired by an imaginary vision of Spain for Spring/Summer 1977. Paying homage to the Spanish artist Diego Velázquez, Saint Laurent had designed much of this show confined to his sick bed being treated for depression and addiction problems in the American Hospital of Paris in Neuilly-sur-Seine, but still succeeded in producing 280

OPPOSITE: Colourful embroidery and fringed shawls created for the Carmen collection, Spring/Summer 1977.

OPPOSITE: Gold Indian-inspired brocade and lavish embellishment for this "Shakespeare" wedding dress, from the Autumn/Winter 1980 collection.

RIGHT: Opulent fabrics and superb use of colour, showcased in Yves Saint Laurent's Imperial China collection, Autumn/Winter 1977.

outfits for a presentation that thrilled the audience for two and a half hours. Sexy velvet corsets, tiered layers of taffeta, fringed shawls, black lace mantillas and lacquered fans subverted the traditional iconography of the Flamenco dancer's wardrobe into something sensuously modern and gloriously colourful. A day after the show, Saint Laurent returned to hospital in another attempt to deal with his demons.

Tapping into unchartered cultural influences across the globe sparked new avenues of creativity in 1978 with the splendour of Imperial China, a collection commercially timed to coincide with the launch of Saint Laurent's new fragrance, *Opium*. Influenced by elements of traditional clothing, the designer created a fantasy interpretation of reality; the collection included wide-cut sleeves, asymmetric fastenings with embroidered tassels, short mandarin collars and millinery in the style of Asian conical hats, all made up in a stunning assortment of opulent gold brocades, jewel-coloured silks and the most extravagant mink-trimmed accessories.

Saint Laurent returned to the majesty of India in 1982, juxtaposing brilliant silk taffeta evening skirts with ornate turbans and intricate embroidery, having first presented Indian-inspired brocade coat dresses in 1962. Evidence of a Japanese influence then appeared in 1984 in the guise of short kimono-style jackets cut in a T shape, his use of oversized decorative bows in contrasting colours positioned on the backs of dresses, a stylish interpretation of the Japanese obi belt, the wide sash used to fasten a traditional kimono.

Saint Laurent was one of the first couturiers to celebrate diversity on the runway, working with black models such as Fidelia as early as 1962. From the seventies onward, his favourite house models included Mounia Orosemane, who said Saint Laurent had made her proud of the colour of her skin, Pat Cleveland, Iman, Rebecca Ayoko, Katoucha Niane and Naomi Campbell, who later credited the designer with getting her first French *Vogue* cover.

OPPOSITE: Long evening dress with contrasting oversized pink satin bow, from the Autumn/Winter 1983 collection.

THE LEGACY OF YVES

A NATIONAL ICON

"Fame bought him nothing but suffering and more suffering."

*PIERRE BERGÉ, 2010 (*L'AMOUR FOU*)*

From the early 1980s, Yves Saint Laurent began a long, drawn-out process of withdrawal from public scrutiny, living an increasingly isolated existence surrounded by spectacular art and antiques in one of his many elegant homes, with only his French bulldog, Moujik III, for company.

In 1980, he and Pierre Bergé bought and lovingly restored a large 1930s mansion in Marrakesh called Villa Oasis, owned originally by the French artist, Jacques Majorelle. The property and surrounding six acres of Jardin Majorelle, filled with exotic cacti and palm trees landscaped around private ponds, provided an oasis of calm for the troubled designer. In 1983, the couple also acquired Château Gabriel, a Normandy retreat near the coast in Deauville, which reportedly cost $5 million and took several years to renovate in a style inspired by Saint Laurent's favourite Proust novel, *À La Recherche du Temps Perdu*.

OPPOSITE: Villa Oasis bought in 1980 in Marrakesh, in the colourful setting of the Jardin Majorelle.

ABOVE: Yves Saint
Laurent provided a
spectacular opening
ceremony at the
1998 FIFA World Cup
finals at the Stade de
France, Saint-Denis
with a fashion show
featuring 300 models.

OPPOSITE: A vibrant
colour palette,
opulent prints and
luxurious fabrics
typified much of Saint
Laurent's later work.

At 47, Saint Laurent was universally acknowledged as the most
influential couturier of the twentieth century and as such was
the first living designer to be honoured with a retrospective of his
work at the Metropolitan Museum of Art's Costume Institute in
New York. Instigated and curated by Diana Vreeland, it featured
180 exhibits from over a 25-year period and opened with a
glittering $500-a-plate dinner for 800 VIP guests. The American
fashion expert told *The New York Times* that the exhibition
provided "an opportunity to show the work of a living genius."
The 1983 show at the Met attracted around a million visitors and
was followed by large-scale retrospectives in Beijing, staged in Paris
at the Musée des Arts de la Mode in 1986, before travelling to
Moscow, St Petersburg, Sydney and finally, Tokyo in 1990.

The success of the museum shows kick-started a trajectory that
changed Saint Laurent's oeuvre, latterly dominated by tribute
collections which often looked more like extravagant costume
exhibits than modern womenswear. He paid homage to his own

work by re-presenting updated themes on Mondrian, the trouser suit, Le Smoking, and Le Trench, as well as acknowledging the talent of other famous artists showing collections that celebrated Picasso, Matisse, Shakespeare, the surrealist poet Louis Aragon and the witty 1930s couturier, Elsa Schiaparelli.

In 1990, the designer creatively recognized all the figures he had admired in life, including Marilyn Monroe, Catherine Deneuve, Marcel Proust, Bernard Buffet and, of course, Christian Dior. These runway shows, though no less spectacular, were played out in front of a fidgety audience, who waited anxiously to see if an expressionless Saint Laurent was capable of making it onto the catwalk, with many fashion commentators feeling his once-visionary contributions to a contemporary wardrobe were now long behind him.

Apart from the obligatory end-of-show appearance a couple of times a year, sightings of Saint Laurent were rare, although he did turn up to receive the numerous accolades bestowed upon him. In 1985 he was made Chevalier de la Légion d'Honneur by President François Mitterrand, then in 1999 the Council of Fashion Designers of America (CFDA) honoured him with a Lifetime Achievement Award; he received Italy's prestigious Rosa d'Oro Prize for artists in 2001 and was recognized again by his own country in 2007 when President Nicolas Sarkozy awarded him the Grand Officier de la Légion d'Honneur.

By 1990 Saint Laurent was drinking heavily again and ill enough to try another stint in rehabilitation, recounting both his hospitalization and detoxification programme to *Le Figaro* the following year as an experience that "changed my character".

With his partner's ongoing deterioration, Pierre Bergé worked tirelessly on a strategy to build a long lasting legacy for the brand he had helped create, seizing every opportunity to elevate Saint Laurent's status from that of genius couturier to a French national icon.

OPPOSITE: Yves Saint Laurent with Laetitia Casta at the 18th annual CFDA America fashion awards in New York, 1999.

LEFT: A new museum dedicated to the life and work of Yves Saint Laurent opened in Marrakesh in October 2017.

For the 30th anniversary of the House in 1992, Bergé organized a gala event at the Opéra Bastille in Paris, where 100 models showcased three decades worth of iconic designs for 3,000 guests. The opening ceremony of the FIFA World Cup final in 1998 at the Stade de France in Paris featured a 15-minute Saint Laurent extravaganza, with 300 models from five continents strutting elegantly around the pitch to Ravel's *Bolero*, before floating seamlessly into the instantly recognizable YSL logo for the finale. The TV spectacular was watched by an estimated 1.7 billion viewers and made fashion history. Such was Saint Laurent's stature within France that his image was stamped onto the last franc coins produced before the introduction of the Euro in 2000.

Throughout their professional relationship he and Bergé understood their own roles perfectly, and it was Bergé who took control of all financial dealings, with the company having various owners over the years. In 1989 the YSL Group was successfully floated on the stock market with demand for shares far exceeding the offer. A few years later, in 1993, to safeguard against rising debts Bergé negotiated a £400 million transaction with the state-owned French pharmaceutical company Elf Sanofi, leaving both men exceedingly wealthy in a deal that surrendered the YSL perfume division, while they kept control of Yves Saint Laurent Couture. Five years later, Elf Sanofi sold to the Gucci Group, headed up by Domenico De Sole and Tom Ford, with an agreement that they would oversee the ready-to-wear and perfume divisions, with Saint Laurent happily in charge of haute couture until his retirement.

An emotional Saint Laurent held a press conference on 7 January 2002 in the salon at Avenue Marceau to announce his intention to retire from the profession he had given his life to. He spoke proudly of his achievements of the last 40 years and passionately about his commitment to haute couture:

RIGHT: Model
Claudia Schiffer in
an updated version
of the famous Le
Smoking, variations
of which appeared in
every catwalk show.

"I have always placed a respect for this profession above all else.
While not exactly an art, it nonetheless requires an artist for it to
exist." The designer also talked openly about his drink and drug
problems, placing them firmly in the past: "I have been through
sheer hell. I have known fear and the terrors of solitude. I have
known those fairweather friends we call tranquilizers and drugs. But
one day, I was able to come through all of that, dazzled yet sober."

A fortnight later came his grand finale at the Centre George
Pompidou, a two-hour show featuring a roll call of international
beauties, including Carla Bruni, Jerry Hall, Naomi Campbell
and Claudia Schiffer, who showcased a parade of 350 classic YSL
designs taken from the archives, alongside new pieces from his
Spring/Summer 2002 collection. The show ended with many
interpretations of his most iconic piece Le Smoking, as the

designer appeared to a standing ovation, with Catherine Deneuve and Laetitia Casta singing softly "*Ma plus belle historie d'amour, c'est vous"/My greatest love story is you*. When the last orders from the show had been made and delivered (all stitched with a special commemorative label) the couture house closed its doors forever, with only new ready-to-wear clothes designed by a creative director appointed by the Gucci Group permitted to bear the Yves Saint Laurent name.

Five years on from his retirement, on 1 June 2008, Yves Saint Laurent died of a brain tumour at his home in rue de Babylone, aged 71, with his lifelong friends, Pierre Bergé and Betty Catroux, by his side. His funeral, held at the seventeenth-century Église

BELOW: The rue de Babylone apartment where Yves Saint Laurent and Pierre Bergé lived, with an extraordinary collection of priceless art and antiques that were put up for auction after his death.

ABOVE: The final applause on the catwalk at the farewell haute couture show in January 2002 at the Centre Pompidou, Paris, flanked by Catherine Deneuve and Laetitia Casta.

Saint-Roch on rue Saint-Honoré (known as the artists' church), was a grand affair attended by French President Nicolas Sarkozy and First Lady Carla Bruni-Sarkozy alongside a host of fashion elites and his mother Lucienne and sisters, Brigitte and Michéle. Bergé spoke movingly of his longstanding soulmate, with whom he had recently entered into a formal civil union, and the designer's ashes were later taken to be scattered in the beautiful Jardin Majorelle in Marrakesh, where a memorial plaque was erected that simply reads "Yves Saint Laurent – French couturier".

With Yves gone, Bergé continued his work to cement an unshakable legacy for the exceptional man he called "an anarchist", who "remained subversive throughout his career." The Fondation Pierre Bergé – Yves Saint Laurent, which preserved thousands of haute couture garments, accessories and sketches, was established in 2002 and opened to the public in 2004 in the Avenue Marceau couture house, with plans for it to be turned into a permanent museum, alongside an equally impressive newly-build museum in Marrakesh. Geographically and architecturally, these monuments represented the flip sides of Saint Laurent's professional and private persona, but both would be dedicated to the heritage of the couturier, providing permanent exhibitions as well as curated experiences for paying visitors, while also acknowledging the vital role that Bergé played in the designer's international success.

One year after Saint Laurent's death, in what was dubbed "the sale of the century", Bergé put the extraordinary private collection of furniture, paintings, objets d'art and sculpture that the couple had amassed over a 40-year period under the hammer to fund his ambitious plans for the posterity of Yves Saint Laurent. The record-breaking three-day sale, which listed over 800 items, raised more than €375 million. Highlights included works by Piet Mondrian, Pablo Picasso, Edvard Munch, Paul Cézanne, Edgar Degas, Henri Matisse and Marcel Duchamp. Without a hint of nostalgia, Bergé also sold off Château Gabriel, a decision that sealed the final chapter of their complex journey together, with proceeds from the sales of Saint Laurent's personal homes and possessions used to secure his oeuvre within fashion history.

Pierre Bergé died in September 2017, aged 86, a month before he could witness the conclusion of his long-standing mission to pay tribute to the life and work of his partner. In October 2017, two YSL museums opened in Paris and Marrakesh, celebrating and consolidating the outstanding contribution Yves Saint Laurent, the most influential designer of the twentieth century, had made to contemporary fashion.

INDEX

Captions are listed in italics on the page they appear

À La Recherche du Temps Perdu 94, 143
Abraham 134
Aigle à Deux Têtes, L' 95, 99
Algeria 13
amber cuff *121*
American Hospital of Paris 134
Amic, Jean 104
Amour Fou, L' 88, 143
Amour, L' (film) 74
Arroyo, Eduardo 54
Avedon, Richard 25
Avenue Marceau 133, 150, *154*, 155
aviator suit *67*
Ayoko, Rebecca 138

"babushka" gypsy skirts 132
Bal des Têtes, Le 95
Balengiaca, Cristóbal 18, 28, 29, 120
Ballet Russes 8, 44
Balmain, Pierre 28
Bardot, Brigitte *63*
Belle du Jour 96, 99, *99*
belt 117
Bérard, Christian 15, 74
Berenson, Marisa *74*, 76
Bergé, Pierre 29, 31, 32, 50, 71, *72*, 88, 89, 94, 95, 99, 103, 104, 126, 143, 147, 150, *152*, 153, *153*, 154, 155
"bijoux de fantaisie" 120
Bohan, Marc 24, 32
Bolero 150
Bousquet, Marie-Louise 31

Boussac, Marcel 23, 28, 32
Bowles, Hamish 50
Braque, Georges *43*
Bricard, Mitzah 29
brocade *137*
Bruni, Carla 152, 154
Buffet, Bernard 31, *154*
Buñuel, Luis 99, *99*
Burgess, Anthony 73
butterfly motif *122*

Campbell, Naomi *76*, 138, 152
Cardinale, Claudia 96
Carré, Madame Marguerite *28*, 29
Cassandre 37
Casta, Laetitia *127*, *147*, 152, 153, *155*
Catroux, Betty 50, *50*, 72, 88, *89*, 153
Catroux, François 72, 88
Centre George Pompidou, Paris 152, *155*
CFDA America Fashion Awards *147*
Champagne fragrance 111, (*see also Yvesse*)
Champagne, Rosé, Le 96
Chanel No 5 103
Chanel, Coco 8, 31, 49, 56, 103, 117, 120
Charles of the Ritz 103, 104
Château Gabriel 94–5, 143, 155
Chevalier de la Legion d'Honneur 147
"Chinese"-inspired hats 125
CIVC (comité Interprofessionel du vin de Champagne) 111
Cleveland, Pat 138

Collections
Autumn/Winter 1959 *115*, 117
Autumn/Winter 1965 37, 38–9
Autumn/Winter 1966 *40*
Autumn/Winter 1977 125, *137*
Autumn/Winter 1980 *137*
Autumn/Winter 1983 *138*
Bambara 62, 66
Beat 31, *31*, *32*
Carmen *134*
"Forties" 74
Imperial China *137*, 138
"Liberation" 76
Longue 31
Opéras-Ballets Russes 8, 44, 104, 105, 125, 132, *132*, 133, 134, 135
Pop Art 73
Prêt-à-Porter *52*
"Scandal" 76, *76*, 80, *85*
Spring/Summer 1967 *64*
Spring/Summer 1988 *43*, 44
Spring/Summer 1990 *124*
Spring/Summer 2002 152
Spring/Summer 1977 134, *134*
Spring/Summer 2002 *76*
Summer 1975 131
Cossack boots 125
Cossack coats 132
Courrèges 38, 39
Cyrano de Bergerac 95

Dar Es Saadda la Zahia 133
de Bascher, Jacques 88
de Brunhoff, Michel 19
de la Falaise, Loulou 50, *74*, 76, 86, *86*, 88, *89*, 120, 133

De Rede, Baron Alexis 95
Deauville 143
Deneuve, Catherine *52*, 54, 96, 99, *99*, *152*, 153, *155*
dependency on drink and drugs 88, 147
Dinard, Pierre 103
Dior, Christian 7, 18, 19, 24, *24*, 26, 28, 29, 134
Dior, House of 23–6, 28–9, *28*, 31, 32, 37, 74, 93
djellabas 133
Doutreleau, Victoire 26
Douvier, Guy 24
Dovima 25
Dupercy, Anny 99

Echo d'Oran, L' 19
École de la Chambre Syndicale de la Couture Parisienne 19
École des femmes, L' 15
Église Saint-Roch 153–4
Elf Sanofi 150
Elle 79, 125
embroidery pieces 120
extreme tailoring *81*

fabrics *144*
fedoras 125
Fidelia 138
FIFA World Cup *144*, 150
Figaro, Le 15, 147
Fondation Pierre Bergé *76*, *85*, 154
Fonteyn, Margot 96
François-Xavier 116

galvanised copper *120*
galvanoplasty 117
Getty Jr, Paul 71
Getty, Talitha 71
Gilot, Françoise 74
gilt bronze 120

Givenchy, Hubert de 15, 18, 19, 28
Globe, the 14
gold jewellery *121*
gold lamé boots 132
Goosens, Robert 120
Grand Officier de la Legion d'Honneur 147
Great American Nude series *40*, 44
Gréco, Juliette 31
greetings cards 117
Gripoix, Augustine 120
Grojsman, Sophia 111
Gucci Group 150, 153

Hall, Jerry *108*, 109, 152
Harper's Bazaar 23
hats 125
headdress *121*
"Heart" necklace *122*
Heybey, Isabelle 54
House of Lesage 44, *44*
House of Racine 39

"Illustre Petit Théatre" 94
Iman 138
India 138
inro 108, *109*
International Herald Tribune 79
International Wool Secretariat competition 1954 18–19, *18*, 74, 120

Jagger, Mick 80, *85*
Jagger, Bianca 80, *85*
Japan 138
Jardin Majorelle 133, 143, *143*, 154, 155
Jazz 111
Jeanmaire, Zizi *93*, *94*, 95, 96, *152*
Jones, Grace 134

jumpsuit 66, *67*

Klossowski, Thadée 72
Kouros 110

Lagerfeld, Karl *18*, 74, 88
Lalanne, Claude 116, *116*, 117, *120*
Lelong, Lucien 52
Lesage, François 120
Lifetime Achievement Awards (CFDA) 147
"Ligne Mondrian" 41

Ma plus belle histoire d'amour, c'est vous 153
Macias, Bianca Pérez-Mora 80, *85 see also* Jagger, Bianca
Manet, Edouard 80
Marrakesh 62, 71, 72, *73*, 133, 143, *143*, *149*, 154, 155
Mathieu-Saint-Laurent, Brigitte (sister) 13, 94, 154
Mathieu-Saint-Laurent, Charles (father) 13, 19
Mathieu-Saint-Laurent, Lucienne (mother) 13, *14*, 19, 26, 39, 74–6, 154
Mathieu-Saint-Laurent, Michèle (sister) 13, 94, 154
Metropolitan Museum of Art Costume Institute 144
Monde, Le 132
Mondrian, Piet 8, 37, *38*, 39, 41, 147
Mondrian, Piet: Life and Work 39
Morocco 13, 72, 133
Mott, Claire *96*
Moujik III 143
Muñoz, Anne-Marie 26, 37,

50, 115, 133
Musée des Arts de la Mode 144

necklace 117
"New Look" 23
New York Times, The 132, 144
Newton, Helmut *76, 108,* 109
Niane, Katoucha 138
Notre-Dame de Paris 96, *96*
Nureyev, Rudolf 71, 96, 110, 111

Olympia 80
Opéra Bastille 150, *152*
Opium 104, 108–9, *108, 109,* 111, 138
Oran 13, *18,* 29, 76
Orosemane, Mounia *110,* 111, 138

Paris 18, 19, 25, 26, 29, 32, 41, 52, *52, 55,* 62, 71, 72, *72,* 73, *73,* 74, *76, 85,* 86, 111, 132, 133, 144, 150, *152,* 155, *155*
Paris (perfume) *110,* 111
Paris Match 86
Paris-Presse-L'intransigeant 29
Petit, Roland *93,* 95, 96, *96*
Picasso, Paloma 74, *74,* 76, 120
Pink Panther, The 96
Poiret, Paul 103
Polge, Jacques 104
Poliakoff, Serge 39
Pop Art cocktail dresses 41
Pop Art movement 44
Pour Homme 86, 104
prints *144*
Proust, Marcel 15, 94, 131, 143

Proust Questionnaire 131

Quant, Mary 38

Ravel, Frederic 150
Rawsthorn, Alice 72
Renée, Great-Aunt 13
Revue, La 93, 96
Rive Gauche (perfume) 104, *104*
Rive Gauche, London *50,* 55
Rive Gauche, New York 55, *61,* 66
Rive Gauche, Paris 52–6, *52, 55*
Robinson, J. Mack 32
rock crystal 120
Rosa d'Oro Prize 147
Ross Diana *61*
Rouet, Jacques 29
Roure perfumers 104
Route, Jacques 26
Rubartelli, Franco 66.
rue de Babylone 89, *108,* 153, *153*
rue de Tournon 32, 55–6, *55*
rue du Faubourg Saint-Honoré 120
rue Saint-Honoré 154
rue Spontini 32, 76, 80
rue Vauban 32
Russian peasant dresses 132

"Saharienne" safari jacket 56, 66
Saint Laurent, Yves Accessories 115, 117, 125
Saint Laurent, Yves Fragrances 86, 103, 150
Saint Laurent, Yves House of 32, *52,* 54, 56, 150
Saint Laurent, Yves Jewellery 115, *116,* 117, 120
Saint Laurent, Yves 7–8, *7,*

13–15, *13,* 18–19, 23–6, *23, 24,* 37–9, 49–50, *49, 50,* 52, 54–6, *56,* 62, 66, 71–4, *72, 73,* 76, 79–81, *85,* 86, *86,* 88–9, 93–96, *93, 94,* 99, 103–04, 108–111, *108, 110,* 115–17, *115, 116,* 120, *121,* 125–6, *127,* 131–3, 135, *137,* 138
Saint Laurent, Yves museum (*Musée Yves Saint Laurent*) 95, 115, *149,* 155,
Saint Laurent, Yves retirement 151–2
Yves Saint Laurent (biography) 72
Saint Tropez 80, *85*
Saint, Clara 50, 72
Sánchez, Fernando 72
Sarkozy, Nicolas 154,
Scemama, Roger 117, 120, *122*
Schiaparelli, Elsa 147
Schiffer, Claudia *151,* 152
Scuphor, Michael 39
"see through dress" 62
"Shakespeare" wedding dress *137*
shawls *134*
Sheppard, Eugenia 79
shoes 125
Sieff, Jeanloup 86, 104
"Smoking, Le" *58,* 62, 147, *151,* 153
Snow, Carmel 23, 24
Soirée "de Paris" 25
Spectacle Zizi Jeanmaire 96
Squibb-Beechnut Corporation 104, 108, 109
statement accessories *124*

Théatre de l'Athénée 99

Time 26
Toile 133, 134
torque 117
"Trapeze" line *26*, 29
Trench, Le 147
Trompe-l'oeil pop art dresses
    40, 41, 44
trouser suit 8, 49, *52*, 54, 56,
    56, 62, *63*, 66, 80, *124*,
    125, 147,
Trouville 14
Turbeville, Deborah *86*

Van Gogh, Vincent 44, *44*

Velázquez, Diego 134
velvet bodices 132
verre nacre 120
Veruschka 66, 117, *120*
Villa Oasis 143, *143*
Vionnet, Madeleine 52
Vivier, Roger *52*, 99,
Vogue 19, 66, 86, *86*, 138,
Vreeland, Diana 144

Warhol, Andy 71, *72*, 73, 74
Webb, Veronica *121*
Wesselmann, Tom *44*, 44
Wilbaux, Madame Marianne

13
Women's Wear Daily 54, 80,
    131

Y (perfume) 103, *103*
Yvesse fragrance (briefly *Yves
    Saint Laurent*) 111

Zehnmacker, Madame
    Raymonde *28*, 29

RESOURCES

Benaim, Laurence, *Yves Saint Laurent: A
    Biography*, Rizzoli International Publications
    Inc, 2019
Berge, Pierre, *Yves Saint Laurent, Fashion
    Memoir*, Thames and Hudson 1997
Drake, Alicia, *The Beautiful Fall: Fashion,
    Genius and Glorious Excess in 1970s Paris*,
    Bloomsbury, 2006
Duras, Marguerite (introduction) *Yves Saint
    Laurent, Images of Design 1958–1988*, Ebury
    Press, 1988
Fraser-Cavassoni, Natasha, *Vogue on Yves Saint
    Laurent*, Abrams Image, 2015
Mauries, Patrick, *Yves Saint Laurent: Accessories*,
    Phaidon Press Ltd, 2017
Muller, Florence, *Yves Saint Laurent: The
    Perfection of Style*, Skira Rizzoli Publications,
    2016
Ormen, Catherine, *All About Yves*, Laurence
    King Publishing, 2017
Palomo- Lovinski, Noel, *The World's Most
    Influential Fashion Designers: Hidden
    Connections and Lasting Legacies of Fashion's
    Iconic Creators*, BES Publishing, 2010

Petkanas, Christopher, *Loulou and Yves*,
    St.Martins Press, 2018
Rawsthorn, Alice, *Yves Saint Laurent: A
    Biography*, Harper Collins, 1996
Samuel, Aurelie, *Yves Saint Lauren, Dreams of
    the Orient*, Thames and Hudson, 2018
Vreeland, Diana (ed) *Yves Saint Laurent, The
    Metropolitan Museum of Art New York*,
    Thames and Hudson, 1984

L'amour fou, Director Pierre Thoretton, 2010
Yves Saint Laurent: The Last Collections, Director
    Olivier Meyrou, 2019

anothermag.com
guardian.com
museeyslparis.com
nytimes.com
numero.com
telegraph.com
wwd.com

CREDITS

The publishers would like to thank the following sources for their kind permission to reproduce the pictures in this book.

The Advertising Archives: 106-107

Alamy: BNA Photographic: 38; /Everett Collection Inc 63, 98; /Trinity Mirror/Mirrorpix 40

Bridgeman Images: AGIP: 75; /Marion Kalter 126

Getty Images: Adoc-photos/Corbis 92; /AFP 36, 58, 114; /Apic 102; /Archive Photos 27; / Michel Arnaud/CORBIS 121; / Pierre Boulat 8; /Jean-Claude Deutsch/Paris Match 78, 82-83; / Thomas Coex/AFP 144; /Conde Nast 89; /Ron Galella 108; /Bertrand Guay/AFP 76, 85; /CBS Photo Archive 48; /Jean-Philippe Charbonnier/Gamma-Rapho 31; /John Cowan/Conde Nast 70; /Loomis Dean/The LIFE Picture Collection 24; /Michel Dufour/WireImage 72, 124, 151; / Hubert Fanthomme/Paris Match 44; /Ian Forsyth 43; /Horst P. Horst/Condé Nast 73; /Hulton-Deutsch Collection/CORBIS 9; /Keystone Press: 97; /Keystone-France/Gamma-Keystone 14, 18, 33; /Reg Lancaster/Express 52, 66; /Manuel Litran/Paris Match 116, 118-119; / Jean-Luc Luyssen/Gamma-Rapho 153; /KMazur/WireImage 146; /Duane Michals/Conde Nast 6; /Jeff Morgan 04 105; /Jean-Pierre Muller/AFP 154; /Alain Nogues/Sygma 53, 55; /Thierry Orban/ Sygma 122, 123; /Francois Pages/Paris Match 16-17; /Paul Stephen Pearson/Fairfax Media 109; /Bill Ray/Life Magazine/The LIFE Picture Collection 57, 59; /J Michel Renaudeau/Gamma-Rapho 142; /Jack Robinson/Conde Nast; 60-61; /Bertrand Rindoff Petroff 44, 110, 136, 152; / Popperfoto 22, 28; /Jean-Claude Sauer/Paris Match 132; /Fadel Senna/AFP 148-149; /Daniel Simon/Gamma-Rapho 139; /Staff 81; /Simon/Stevens/Gamma-Rapho 77; /Deborah Turbeville/ Conde Nast 87; /Pierre Vauthey/Sygma 42, 130, 134, 137, 145; /Roger Viollet 94

Shutterstock: Associated Newspapers 84; /AP 30, 51, 64, 64; /Mediapunch 12; /Steve Wood 127

Every effort has been made to acknowledge correctly and contact the source and/or copyright holder of each picture and Welbeck Publishing apologises for any unintentional errors or omissions, which will be corrected in future editions of this book.

LITTLE BOOK OF

Schiaparelli

LITTLE BOOK OF

Schiaparelli

EMMA BAXTER-WRIGHT

WELBECK

To Dusty the Fashionista

First published by Carlton Books Limited in 2012. This
edition published in 2024 by Welbeck. An Imprint of
HEADLINE PUBLISHING GROUP LIMITED

2

Design and layout © Carlton Books Limited 2012
Text © 2012, 2020 Emma Baxter-Wright

Cataloguing in Publication Data is available from
the British Library

ISBN: 978-1-78739-828-3

Printed in China

Headline's policy is to use papers that are natural,
renewable and recyclable products and made from wood
grown in well-managed forests and other controlled
sources. The logging and manufacturing processes are
expected to conform to the environmental regulations
of the country of origin.

HEADLINE PUBLISHING GROUP LIMITED
An Hachette UK Company, Carmelite House
50 Victoria Embankment, London EC4Y 0DZ

The authorised representative in the EEA is Hachette
Ireland, 8 Castlecourt Centre, Castleknock Road,
Castleknock, Dublin 15, D15 YF6A, Ireland

www.headline.co.uk
www.hachette.co.uk

Contents

Introduction   6

The Early Years   8

Launch of "Pour Le Sport"   18

The House of Schiaparelli   26

The Collections   50

Fashion and Art   70

Hollywood Glamour   88

The War Years and Beyond   98

Accessories   116

Fragrances by Schiaparelli   138

A Revival for the Twenty-First Century   152

Index   168

Resources   172

Acknowledgements   174

Opposite Black-on-pink printed
evening gown, fitted to the body
and flared from the knee; worn
with full-length, black evening
gloves and a cropped faille bolero.
The turban, shown here unbound,
and the bolero were key pieces
for Schiaparelli.

Introduction

When Elsa Schiaparelli arrived on planet fashion, she smashed down the walls of convention and watched the world fall in love with her. In the most brilliantly, dramatic style she set out to challenge our perception of what fashion could be, if only we dared abandon the commonplace and instead allowed her strangely imaginative vision to entertain us. A tiny Italian dynamo with an unspeakably difficult name, she joked that nobody would know how to pronounce it properly S-k-e-e-a-p-a-r-elly – but she *knew* that everybody would understand what the name stood for. A complex hybrid of contradictions – an aristocratic Italian living in Paris, who was hugely influenced by the cultural modernity of 1920s New York – she never ceased to cause a commotion with her inventive spirit. Elsa craved colour, loved laughter and insisted on only two rules in her workroom: that the word "impossible" should be banned and also "creation" – a word she found completely pretentious. Throughout the 1930s Schiaparelli caused a riotous sensation, season after season, with each collection more daring, more ambitious and more memorable than the former. She fell in step with the Surrealists living in Paris and was one of the first couturiers to collaborate with contemporary artists. Visual irony, textural contradictions and elaborate details were frequently employed to question the function of gender in the most defiant style. Yves Saint Laurent famously said Schiaparelli "didn't want to please, she wanted to dominate", and of that there is no question. She was the most innovative of couturiers, disciplined, shy, unpredictable and relentlessly pushing new forms and ideas. The genius forerunner of every modern designer, she found a way to successfully combine eccentricity with functionality, to provoke and shock us in the most beautiful way.

Opposite In this portrait of Schiaparelli, taken in 1932 by leading fashion photographer George Hoyningen-Huene, she is wearing one of her own designs. The white evening dress had quilted pocket details and was worn with a white coq feather boa.

The Early Years

In her autobiography *Shocking Life*, Schiaparelli's own recollection of childhood appears to rollercoaster endlessly between disappointments, the first of which was that she turned out to be a girl when her parents were desperately hoping for a boy, and a constant stream of practical jokes. Born in 1890 at the Palazzo Corsini in Rome, her early life was undoubtedly one of privilege and status. Brought up in a loving and honourable family, the second of two girls, born to an aristocratic Neapolitan mother and an academic father, who was an expert on Oriental Studies and taught at the University of Rome, there was little in her family background to suggest a creative career in haute couture lay ahead.

She claims to have been an ugly-looking child and often felt criticized by her mother, who continually made disparaging comments about her appearance while simultaneously praising her sister for her classical Greek beauty. Allowing her childish imagination free reign, Elsa thought to beautify herself by planting soil and flower seeds all over her face, including in her mouth and ears, believing a beautiful floral face would sprout. On this occasion there was no punishment, just more disappointment that no flowers grew to transform her into a great beauty. At the Convent of the Lucchesi in Rome, she prepared for her first communion in a state of panic, overcome by the mystical atmosphere of ceremonial ritual. Determined to accuse herself of the greatest sins possible, in order to allow herself to be absolved and so transcend to heaven faster, she whispered to the priest, "Yes, Father, I have fornicated," at which point she fell theatrically to the floor in a dead faint. It was the first documented account of many such dramatic entrances that lay ahead.

Opposite Portrait of Elsa with her dog, taken at the start of her career in Vienna, circa 1926.

Elsa's strait-laced family seemed resigned to her acts of lunacy, which played a significant role in family life. Once, after an earthquake had destroyed a large part of Sicily and the country was in mourning, large open trucks trundled slowly through the city, allowing survivors to contribute to a relief fund by simply throwing any items of surplus clothing onto them. Alone at the time, Elsa rushed through the family home gathering up armfuls of clothes and linen, then joyously threw them down from the windows onto the passing lorries, convinced of her own generosity. On another occasion she threw herself out of a window with an umbrella, believing it would act as a parachute. It didn't, but she fell into a heap of manure unscathed! The quirkiness of these childhood anecdotes reveal an early penchant for humour that lay the foundations for the grown-up couturier's desire to endlessly amuse with her creativity.

Elsa's unpredictable behaviour disrupted her formal education as her family moved her to different institutions to maintain an element of control. As a teenager her wildly imaginative poems about love, loss and sorrow were published in a small volume called *Arethusa* and the controversial work, which was considered to be a disgraceful taint on the ultra-conservative Schiaparelli family, resulted in another punishment that saw her packed off to a convent in Switzerland. Angry and unhappy in the hostile environment, Elsa went on hunger strike until her kindly father capitulated and came to collect her home.

To escape the amorous attentions of an ugly Russian suitor, Elsa took a job in London as a nanny, travelling via Paris to attend her first society ball. With nothing appropriate to wear she visited Galeries Lafayette and bought four yards of dark blue crepe de chine and two yards of orange silk, which she wrapped around her and pinned into place. Her outrageous attire caused a small sensation and was noted as the start of many such extraordinary appearances. She called it her "first couturier's

Opposite Theatricality and an element of shock were themes that Schiaparelli often explored in fashion, and she was certainly her own best advertisement for her designs. Here, she wears outrageous fancy dress for a ball given by Jacques Fath at the Château de Courbeville, near Chessy in France, in August 1952.

failure". In London, Elsa, who had briefly studied philosophy at the University of Rome, spent her time visiting libraries and attending lectures. At one of these she met a lecturer in theosophy who was half Breton French on his father's side and half Swiss French on his mother's side. He was in his early thirties and his name was Compte William de Wendt de Kerlor. Within 24 hours of meeting each other the couple had decided to get married.

London, New York, Paris

Despite opposition from her family, who rushed to intervene, the wedding took place at a registry office, with little grandeur and no white wedding dress. The year was 1914 and Elsa was 23 years old. On returning from the simple ceremony to the small mews house they were renting, the new Comtesse de Kerlor discovered all seven mirrors in the house had been smashed. The mystery was unresolved, but as Elsa remarked, "it was a sinister beginning". With the First World War imminent, life in London became increasingly impossible for the young European couple, who escaped to a small flat on the seafront in Nice. Precise details of these first few years of married life in the South of France remain unclear, but Elsa's husband became increasingly absent, acting like a "drifting cloud in the sky" and leaving her waiting for days at a time for him to return. Although Elsa writes in her autobiography that she did not want to leave Nice, William wanted to go to America and so in 1919 they arrived in New York City. That year Elsa gave birth to her only child – a girl, named Maria Luisa Yvonne Radha de Wendt de Kerlor, who was quickly nicknamed "Gogo". While Elsa responded immediately to the modernity of New York, her husband – who never felt psychologically strong enough to cope with the pressure of the

Opposite Elsa Schiaparelli (right), walking with a friend in London in 1935. She is wearing culottes of her own design.

city – succumbed to the charms of many other women, including the dancer Isadora Duncan, and abandoned his family soon after the birth of his daughter. Nearly 30, alone and broke in a foreign city, with a newborn baby to take care of, a proud and independent Elsa almost hit rock bottom. The death of her father at this time, together with the disintegration of her marriage, acted as a catalyst to shape the future direction of Elsa's life. She knew that she would not re-marry and never again would she be dependent on any man to provide for her. The desire to stand alone and live independently ultimately led to the invention of her alter ego "Schiap", who would later find international success as the creator of so many of the avant-garde ideas that still have resonance today.

On the Atlantic crossing from France to America, Elsa and William had met Gabriella Picabia, ex-wife of the French modernist artist Francis Picabia, who together with Man Ray (Emmanuel Radnitzky) were significant contributors to both the Dada and Surrealist art movements. Fortuitously the two were destined to meet again in New York and the older French woman, whom Elsa described as "a woman of great intelligence and a great heart" not only gave support as a friend but also provided some childcare for Gogo, allowing Elsa time to search for work. More importantly perhaps she also introduced the designer to an interesting circle of artistic friends, which included the photographers Alfred Stieglitz, Baron de Meyer, Edward Steichen, Marcel Duchamp and Man Ray, many of whom were destined through their own artistic practice to have great influence on Schiaparelli.

Living in cramped accommodation in Greenwich Village, a haven for artistic and literary types, Elsa developed a great friendship with another strong woman who was to prove instrumental in shaping her future. Blanche Hayes was a young American woman who had been married to a wealthy lawyer, but was now, like Elsa, seeking a divorce. When Elsa made the shocking discovery that at 15 months Gogo could only "walk like a crab" and was diagnosed with infantile paralysis, it was Blanche who calmly suggested a solution. They were to travel together to Paris, which was much cheaper than New York, where they would stay as her guests and seek medical expertise to help Gogo. They sailed in June 1922, and in Paris Elsa started divorce proceedings against her absent husband and also renewed her passport in her original name of Mlle Schiaparelli.

This trip to Paris was to change her life, as she recalled in 1954: "If I have become what I am, I owe it to two distinct things – poverty and Paris. Poverty forced me to work, and Paris gave me a liking for it."

In Paris, Elsa struggled financially, surviving on small handouts from her mother, and scouring the flea markets and auction houses in

search of beautiful items that could be sold on through sympathetic antique dealers. Her friendship with Gaby Picabia was reignited, which connected her to the Parisian group of artists and poets still operating loosely under the Dada collective. Tristan Tzara, Francis Picabia and Jean Cocteau all congregated at a small den of debauchery called *Le Boeuf sur le Toit,* to which Elsa was introduced by Man Ray. There she found le tout Paris, many of whom would figure prominently in her life. Among them were Pablo Picasso, Nancy Cunard, Gabrielle "Coco" Chanel, Erik Satie, Mrs Reginald (Daisy) Fellowes and the Prince of Wales.

Living alone in two rooms on two floors of the Rue de l'Universite, the hand of fate intervened when Elsa met the French couturier Paul Poiret, a man whom she greatly admired – calling him the "Leonardo of

Fashion". Poiret was revolutionary in his influence on women's fashion, designing successive collections that experimented with silhouette, colour, print and extravagant fabrics. An innovative visionary, he was one of the first fashion designers to collaborate with an artist, working with the young Raoul Dufy, who created printed textiles for Poiret's clothing. Elsa had never before set foot in a *maison de couture* and in her autobiography *Shocking Life* she describes her first meeting with Poiret:

> While my friend was choosing lovely dresses, I gazed around moonstruck.
> Silently I tried things on, and became so enthusiastic that I forgot where I was. I put on a coat of large loose cut that could have been made today. This coat was made of upholstery velvet – black with big vivid stripes, lined with bright blue crepe de chine.
> "Why don't you buy it *mademoiselle*? It might have been made for you."
> The great Poiret himself was looking at me. I felt the impact of our personalities.
> "I cannot buy it," I said. "It is certainly too expensive, and when could I wear it?"
> "Don't worry about money," said Poiret, "and *you* could wear anything anywhere."

So began a great friendship of excellent food, cheap white wine and wonderful conversation. Poiret was terrifically kind to Elsa and gave her a fabulous wardrobe of extravagant clothes to wear. While this generosity enabled her to become a fashion leader, it also lit the fuse to ignite her own passion for creating fashion, something Poiret encouraged.

Launch of "Pour le Sport"

With Gogo safely packed off to a school in Lausanne, Elsa had time yet again to consider her own future. She did not know at this point how her own terrific accumulation of energy would find a way to express itself, although she was starting to think that perhaps instead of painting or sculpture (both of which she was fairly accomplished in), that she could perhaps invent dresses or costumes. Highly creative and even in the early days always conceptual in her thinking, Schiaparelli's approach to dress designing was something she perceived not as a profession but always as an Art. In her recollection she,

> found that it was a most difficult and unsatisfying art, because as soon as a dress is born it has already become a thing of the past. Once you have created it, the dress no longer belongs to you. A dress cannot just hang like a painting on the wall, or like a book remain in tact and live a long and sheltered life.

Fashion had started to change in a radical new direction. Poiret's elaborate grandeur was out of step with post-war women as a new emphasis had been placed on youth, simplicity and a growing appreciation of sporting activities. Gabrielle Chanel capitalized on this youthful spirit, designing specifically for the modern woman, who with her bobbed hair and narrow slim-line body was known as *la Garçonne*. The emphasis on sporty, wearable clothes that allowed a woman to move her body without uncomfortable restriction owed much to Chanel's choice of fabric. She introduced lightweight silk jersey and pioneered the use of machine knits, for dresses, twinsets and sweaters, all in a neutral colour palette. In fact it

Opposite Schiaparelli's early designs were highly influenced by sporting activities. This 1928 knitted two-piece swimsuit, consisting of a black-and-white striped vest and black flannel shorts with side opening, worn with matching striped socks, appealed to a new generation of modern women, as it was both comfortable and practical.

was the simple sweater, which became such a symbol of modernity for fashionable women of the 1920s that kickstarted Elsa's career and became forever associated with the designer. Dissatisfied with the way she herself looked in the modern sports clothes, Schiaparelli designed the first handmade sweater specifically for herself. Choosing the bold colour combination of black and white, she was complimented by many friends and acquaintances when she first wore it. A wealthy friend of Blanche Hayes, a Mrs Hartley, agreed to sponsor Elsa in a small collection of sports clothes, and from a small dress house called Maison Lambal, situated near Place Vendôme, her first collection appeared. These interchangeable separates, of knitted jackets and crepe de chine skirts, received a favourable response from both the public and the press. In January 1926, *Women's Wear Daily* reviewed Maison Lambal's stylish garments: "The collection, although not large, is carefully conceived and executed. Each mode maintains individuality and reveals interest. They are all simple and direct with very fine detail work and pleasing colour combinations."

Although the financial backer backed out at this point, the capsule collections continued with the help of French businessman Monsieur Kahn, who had associations with Galeries Lafayette and Madeleine Vionnet.

Above The famous trompe-l'oeil sweater caused a sensation when Schiaparelli wore it to lunch in 1927. The final version, achieved after several less-successful attempts, was much copied and became one of the most famous designs of Schiaparelli's career.

Opposite Schiaparelli's early collections were heavily based on knitwear and she used it for everything from socks to swimsuits. This winter sports outfit from 1934 includes matching gloves, scarf and Peruvian *chullo*, a traditional hood with long earflaps.

The first few pieces were called Display No. 1 and were laid out on tables, piece by piece, in Schiaparelli's small apartment. Taking design inspiration from Futurism and Cubism, Elsa's aesthetic reflected the stark strong lines and bold patterns and colours of those contemporary art movements. In April 1927 a smart American friend visiting Elsa in Paris wore a sweater that caught the designer's eye. Although much has been made of Elsa's first handmade trompe-l'oeil sweaters, in *Shocking Life* she reveals that she never learnt to knit, and that "the art of clicking two little metal needles together has always been a mystery". The Armenian refugee who had actually made the sweater lived nearby. When approached by the designer and asked to copy her drawings of a simple white butterfly bow tied around the neck of a fitted black sweater she enthusiastically agreed to give it a go. It took three attempts to get right, but the third sweater caused a sensation when Elsa wore it to a grand luncheon. Feminine and decorative, it was very different to the woollen clothes that Chanel was making.

A buyer from the New York store, Strauss, recognized how striking the sweater was and immediately placed an order for 40 sweaters and 40 skirts. Thrilled with the response, Elsa agreed, even though she had absolutely no idea where the skirts would come from and what they would look like. But true to her word, the order was shipped on time and the New York store paid for the work within three weeks. Buoyed up by her success, Elsa wanted bigger premises. She found a small garret at No. 4 rue de la Paix, where she could both live and work, from which her first modest collections of shantung seaside pyjamas, bathing suits, frocks and tailored jackets with geometric patterns were shown. By the end of the decade garments for watching sports in were the strongest influence on fashion and Schiaparelli, inspired by Charles Lindbergh's flight across the Atlantic, designed flying suits for women as well as clothes for skiing and suits for tennis and golf. Her wrap-around skirts first arrived in 1928, as did the divided skirt which caused such a stir at Wimbledon in 1931, when the Spanish player Lili de Alvarez arrived in an outfit that had been specially made for her by Schiaparelli.

All the clothes were simply laid out on tables and it was from these three attic rooms in January 1928 that an official sign appeared above the door on the street. In black and white it simply said – Schiaparelli – and underneath "Pour le Sport".

Above The Spanish tennis player Lili de Alvarez caused uproar when she appeared at Wimbledon in 1931 in an ensemble that had been specially created for her by Schiaparelli. The divided skirt (known as "culottes") was another Schiaparelli invention, designed with practicality in mind.

Overleaf left Wrap-around skirts and dresses were a Schiaparelli innovation, repeated years later by Diane von Furstenberg. These beach dresses consisted of four half-dresses, each with one armhole and a tie that passed through a slit on the other side; each side was in contrasting shades of silk.

This page An easy all-in-one sports suit made from pink wool in 1940. Featuring the trademark Schiaparelli button detail, the divided culotte skirt had a slightly gathered hem.

The House of Schiaparelli

"She slapped Paris. She smacked it. She tortured it.
She bewitched it. And it fell madly in love with her."

Yves Saint Laurent

Elsa Schiaparelli acknowledged that ignorance and courage were the qualities that drove her early success in rue de la Paix and as the garret became increasingly crowded, her designs became more daring. Speaking of herself in the third person (as she often did in her autobiography), she stated: "Schiap herself did not know anything about dressmaking" and it is this lack of formal training that she used brilliantly to her advantage. From the start she felt that clothes should be constructed architecturally and that the body should be thought of as a frame, as in a building. With this basis she found a way throughout her career to produce clothes that could empower women. She became increasingly experimental with the colours and designs, trompe-l'oeil ties appeared, as did scarves, slung low around the hips and then tied with a real tie at one side. Sometimes she drew African-inspired designs or magical symbols influenced by the tribesman in the French Congo, and tattoos that mimicked a sailor's chest with pierced hearts and snakes. Nothing had ever been seen like the Skeleton sweater, which so shocked the fashion press. Graphically stark, it consisted of a black sweater with white knitted lines resembling the thorax and ribcage, and it gave the women who were brave enough to wear it the appearance of being seen through an X-ray machine. Her knitwear expanded to include the most extraordinary collection of clothes, some of which seem totally at odds with the elasticity of the fabric: sandals, stockings, bathing suits, bonnets and skirts, as well as a knitted turban, which proved so popular she had to copy the design in cotton.

Opposite In January 1935 Schiap moved her business to 21 Place Vendôme. From here the House of Schiaparelli really took off as the boutique was on the ground floor, allowing customers to walk away with her prêt-à-porter clothes and matching accessories.

Expansion into Eveningwear

According to Schiaparelli, the first evening gown she produced turned out "to be the most successful dress of my career". Consisting of a long simple sheath dress made of black crepe de chine and a jacket in white crepe de chine with long sashes that crossed over the back and tied at the front, the silhouette was stark and the use of colour dramatic. The outfit created a sensation and was copied worldwide, something the designer took as a massive compliment to her newsworthy status within the fashion world. In 1930 she created a tiny knitted cap like a tube, which hugged the contours of the skull and immediately caused a furore when worn by the actress Ina Claire. An American manufacturer copied the newly named "Mad Cap", and made millions from mass production, which resulted in Schiap destroying her own stock and insisting the sales girls never mention it again. It was inevitable that her constant outpouring of creativity would be seized upon and copied by the rag trade; Schiap found it both flattering and infuriating in equal measure, but was unable to control it.

Opposite Strong use of colour and a languid silhouette often defined Schiaparelli's eveningwear. Two views of this sleeveless gown in shades of nasturtium show the deep V back and ribbon-tied bow at the front. The optional crepe satin cape covers bare arms and also has a large bow to mirror the waist.

Above Black and gold was a favourite combination, as shown in these two dresses from 1936. The model on the left wears a black satin sleeveless gown with bands of rippled gold ribbon at the hem. On the right, a simple sheath worn over satin pyjamas features gold inlaid braid.

Opposite Superb cutting ensured the most simplistic of shapes would create a dramatic entrance. This strapless dress from 1937 has a fitted waist and a front slit from the knee to reveal satin-ribboned ballerina pumps. An extravagant train flips elegantly over the wearer's arm.

Right Schiaparelli often chose to cover her evening gowns with either a short cape, mini bolero or, as shown here, a much longer, more flamboyant draped cape. Both sheath dress and cape are made from shades of gold lamé, which shimmers beautifully as the light catches in the drapes and folds of the design, circa 1936.

Opposite Schiaparelli often embellished her eveningwear with tiny mirrored paillettes, which dazzled as the wearer moved. The decorative panels shown on this detail of a black *marocain* evening jacket were designed in the shape of lamb chops, while the four buttons were purely decorative.

Overleaf left Schiaparelli loved to experiment with unusual fabrics and this evening coat and stole from 1938 are made of hand-sewn gilt braid that has been plaited into strips and sewn onto a chiffon foundation. Strong architectural lines of broad shoulders and tapered waist are favoured over a feminine silhouette.

Overleaf right A Chinese-influenced dramatic evening cape made from flame orange quilted taffeta, with a neat high neckline and 23 buttons. The Eastern influence extends to the cut of the grey satin gown, with its gored hemline that gently flares out to imitate the shape of a pagoda roof.

Despite the economic crash of the early 1930s, Schiaparelli continued to expand her business, and was able to provide women a moment of fashionable escape, at a time of sombre depression. Never afraid to experiment with line and detail, she constantly offered sensational clothes in bright colours and unusual fabrics. She invented a trousered evening gown and dictated slacks for dining out in. She put sequins on a mannish dinner jacket and produced suits and coats that echoed the skyscraper silhouettes of New York with straight vertical lines, barely a nod to the waist and broad squared-off shoulders achieved through padding. Influenced by menswear she produced Cossack jacket-coats and silk cloaks that owed something to those of the Venetian Doges. Heavy embroidery was used on short capes and fox and astrakhan fur utilized for interesting scarves and removable collars, all topped off with doll-sized hats. Schiaparelli's ongoing quest for originality had not gone unnoticed and regular features about her now appeared in mainstream press throughout the world. Janet Flanner's profile in *The New Yorker* in June 1932 produced the much-quoted line, "a frock from Schiaparelli ranks like a modern canvas" while *Time* magazine in 1934 declared, "Madame Schiaparelli is the one to whom the word 'genius' is most often applied."

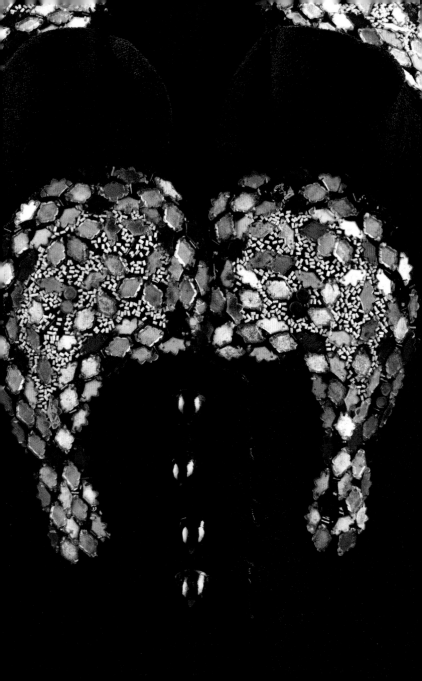

Opposite The three Schiaparelli suits in this illustration taken from a *Vogue* magazine of 1932 reflect the trend for broad shoulders and an architectural V shape that pulls into a slightly raised waist. Small tipped hats or Schiaparelli's signature knitted beret were the must-have accessories.

Right A streamlined suit made from fluid wool jersey in 1935 for a look that is softly tailored and elegant. The slim leather belt cuts over the jacket, drawing attention to the newly raised waistline. Gauntlet gloves were a Schiaparelli favourite at this time and the neat pull-on skull cap is a variation of the minicap she called the "Mad Cap".

Overleaf An illustration from the House of Schiaparelli catalogue shows part of the 1935 collection. While the smart daytime silhouette is still strongly architectural, as shown in the new hip-length box jacket and Tyrolean-type hat, eveningwear remained totally fluid and flowing in strong colours. Skirt lengths were variable for daywear and, as always, accessories played an integral role in the overall design concept. Schiaparelli's new poke bonnet (centre) was much copied.

Left and below Typical of Schiaparelli's structured silhouette at this time, this magenta silk crepe dinner suit from 1938 has a floor-length dress with nipped-in jacket. The sleeve head (inset below) is very full and carefully padded to create a broad horizontal shoulder line that contrasts with the narrow line of the body. Detailed cutting on the jacket pockets echoes the shape of the embroidered leaves on the sleeves, which are all hand-stitched using gelatin and metal sequins.

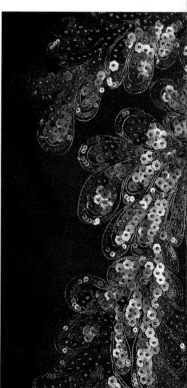

Invention in Materials

Novelty fabrics were endlessly adopted by the couturier, who had already used pigskin and ponyskin for trimmings, transparent plastic straps on a swimsuit and woven metallic thread into knits to produce a sparkly effect. Together with Jean Patou, she had embraced an elastic woollen fabric called "kasha" when it was first patented by Rodier as a material that appeared to hold the body and create a slimmer figure. Later, Schiaparelli was to use rayon, vinyl and cellophane. Collaborations with the textile manufacturer Colcombet, a pioneer of artificial fabrics, ensured she was always at the forefront of any new fabric developments. In 1932 she used a crinkled matt crepe – "tree bark" – for a whole collection and later used a rayon that resembled "oak-cork". Elsa invented waterproof taffeta and made a memorable *cape de verre* from a brittle spun synthetic known as Rhodophane, which really did resemble glass. She was also fond of paper straw for scarves and belts, monkey fur as a trimming and placed plastic zippers in the most unlikely places. The juxtaposition of the wrong type of fabric for the wrong purpose amused her and she often deliberately chose to work with materials that would cause controversy. She used Latex for gloves, oilskin for flying suits and transparent cellophane for evening bags. Bright colours, bold prints and an exaggerated line were consistently part of her signature look, whereas her rival Coco Chanel's success was based on the exact opposite: a neutral palette and simple, unstructured shapes.

Inspired by a trip to Copenhagen, where she saw women in the fish market with hats made of old newspaper. Schiaparelli produced a newsprint fabric made from journalistic cuttings about herself. Made up in all sorts of colours, in silk and cotton, the fabric was another audacious first as the designer capitalized on her own self-promotion, using it for blouses, scarves and hats, and creating another success story for the manufacturer Colcombet, who sold thousands of yards of the unusual print.

Overleaf Always keen to experiment, Schiaparelli often used animal fur and even plaited horsehair. Here, she covers the front of a fitted black sweater with monkey fur. The suede ankle boots, also trimmed with cascading monkey fur and part of the same 1938 collection, were made in collaboration with André Perugia.

No. 21 Place Vendôme

By the time she moved into her new premises at No. 21 Place Vendôme in January 1935, Elsa Schiaparelli was a fully-fledged star. A new design era came into being as her boundless creativity and fantastic imagination – what she called the "cascades of fireworks" – were forcefully unleashed in this new venture. Her success brought with it a daredevil approach: her indifference to what people thought gave her the freedom to totally express herself without fear. Here in the centre of sophisticated Paris, under the watchful gaze of Napoleon Bonaparte, she launched her first Schiaparelli Boutique.

The idea was revolutionary at the time and although it was soon copied by others, it was Schiap who first realized the potential of having a ground-floor shop where wealthy clients could simply walk in and buy off the peg. The prêt-à-porter concept was totally unique to Schiaparelli and it was not only garments the customer could try on and take away. The boutique stocked everything a fashionable woman could want, all in one place: interchangeable separates, evening sweaters, skirts, blouses and lingerie. The designer also offered an expanding range of accessories. Bags, shoes, scarves, fake jewellery and her range of perfumes were all displayed for women to pick up and buy. The new boutique, like many of her projects, challenged the existing conventions of a couture house. Her idea was derided by competitors, but Elsa of course was ahead of the game. Today we take it for granted that all the big fashion houses promote their brand through products such as sunglasses, hosiery and key rings, but in 1935 the concept was totally innovative.

Opposite This long brown crepe evening gown with gold braid trim provides a perfect example of the shock tactics for which Schiaparelli became famous. The dress, from 1936, is demure in some respects – high-necked and cut to the floor – but the designer has emphasized the breasts by placing two circular pads of gathered and ruched material on the outside, drawing the eye directly to the bosom in a provocative way for the time.

Overleaf left Although she loved colour, black was also a favourite with the designer, and a colour she often wore herself. The simplicity and versatility of this simple crepe dress provides a perfect backdrop for the stunning embroidery. A spray of perfect white lilies was made up from various sizes of pearls and sequins with metallic strip for the stems, all hand-stitched by the specialist embroidery company Lesage in 1940.

Overleaf right This summer dress from 1939 was worn by socialite Millicent Rogers, a devotee of Schiaparelli's designs. Made from crepe rayon, the pairs of embroidered keys reference the designer's fascination with heavenly themes (here, they represent Peter's "keys of the kingdom of heaven" received from Christ). The low-scoop neckline and puff sleeves are constructed from pearl bead lattice work, studded with jewels, and reference sixteenth-century decoration as seen on Catherine de Medici's clothing.

Colour

"Life-giving, like all the light and the birds and the fish in the world put together, a colour of China and Peru but not of the West."

Elsa Schiaparelli, on the colour she named "shocking pink"

Colour would always dominate Elsa Schiaparelli's vibrant life and it became something of a trademark for the House, from the introduction of ice blue through to the exotic shades she insisted on using at the tweed factories on the Isle of Skye: periwinkle, lettuce green, rose lavender and burnt orange. Elsa craved dynamic colours and tried to recreate them from the ceremonial garments she had seen in Rome as a child and the striking colours viewed later in the paintings of the Fauvist artists.

Endlessly experimenting and constantly pushing for something that commanded attention, the creation of Schiaparelli's most famous colour came after many attempts to find the right shade. In *Shocking Life* she recalls that she knew instinctively exactly what she wanted: "The colour flashed in front of my eyes. Bright, impossible, impudent, becoming, life-giving, like all the light and the birds, and the fish in the world put together, a colour of China and Peru, but not of the West – a shocking colour, pure and undiluted."

When her creative craftsman (the man responsible for baking so many of her buttons) Jean Clement added a streak of magenta to a pink he had already made – the explosive, shocking pink was born. Wowing Paris and the world, it would forever be associated with Schiaparelli.

Opposite This shocking pink dress is complemented by a dark plum, silk velvet evening jacket, embroidered by Lesage. From the winter 1937–38 collection, the detailed embellishment consists of silk and metallic threads with sequins.

"Fashion is born by small facts, trends or even politics, never by trying to make little pleats and furbelows, by trinkets, by clothes easy to copy, or by the shortening or lengthening of a skirt."

Elsa Schiaparelli

The Collections

From the mid-1930s on Elsa Schiaparelli showed each collection as a themed event comparable to a modern-day fashion show. She used dramatic lighting, music and dancing to present her shows, which owed much to theatrical performance and were not to be missed. Stop, Look and Listen was the first collection she presented from Place Vendôme and the title spoke volumes about Schiaparelli's intention to make the world sit up and take notice of her.

It included multicultural influences, which manifested themselves in the most diverse collection of clothes: tweeds from England for eveningwear, embroidered saris in heavy crepe, padlocks for suits, glass dresses, a black evening dress inspired by an Ethiopian warrior's tunic and buttons made from gold sovereigns and French Louis d'or, to mock the next French currency devaluation. She also used zips for the first time and although not the only couturier to experiment with this new invention, Schiap was certainly the most flamboyant, using them for decoration as well as practicality and putting them on everything from eveningwear to hats and gloves.

Fascinating ideas exploded into a series of grand themes, each one more daring than the last, and though not always entirely successful, they were certainly surprising, each an inventive whirlwind of wit and folly. The Eskimo collection, not surprisingly, made the body appear bulked up and it was not a huge hit with customers, although the suede-lined fur gloves certainly were.

Butterfly motifs provided endless variations on a theme for her Metamorphosis collection for spring/summer 1937, which proved much more successful. Examining every possible connotation of a summer garden, Schiaparelli created singing birds, buzzing bees and fluttering sequinned butterflies.

Opposite Schiaparelli in her studio in 1938, studying the charts for her new collection.

This page For her spring/summer collection of 1937, Schiaparelli devised a theme of "metamorphosis" – a Surrealist symbol for change, particularly from ugly to beautiful, something Schiaparelli empathized with. She felt her clothes transformed plain women into extraordinary creatures.

This page Schiaparelli often took inspiration from around the globe when designing and simply reinterpreted a traditional style she found. The Peruvian *chullo* (right), *montera* (below) of wool and braid, and armlets known as *punos*, which were lavishly embroidered and worn with evening gowns, were designed in 1937. Elements of the *tapadas Limeñas* (main pic), eighteenth-century women from Lima who covered their bodies with long skirts and hid their faces with long veils, also inspired her designs for this year.

Las Tapadas

The Covered Ones of eighteenth-century Peru

*"She alone could have given to a pink the nerve of a red ...
a neon pink, an unreal pink ... Shocking Pink!"* Yves Saint Laurent

Inspired by the elaborate showmanship of PT Barnum, the Circus collection of spring/summer 1938 was the most ambitious to date. Riotous, swaggering and splendidly over the top, Schiaparelli presented a cavalcade of dancers, acrobats and jugglers, jumping in and out of the windows, tumbling down the stairs and dancing madly in the dignified salon showrooms. There were bright satin boleros, fitted ringmaster jackets with oversize high collars, tights worn under long black narrow skirts, dazzling bejewelled bodices and Dalí's ripped chiffon Tear dress. Detailed embroidery depicted dancing horses, flying acrobats and pirouetting elephants; Schiaparelli also went wild for circus-themed accessories. Buttons shaped as candyfloss, peppermint sticks and jolly clowns competed with handbags shaped like balloons and ice-cream cone hats. Most importantly, not a single wealthy customer walked critically away from the show and Schiaparelli gained a lot of new fans.

Opposite and right Four acrobat buttons in cast metal leap from this bright pink fitted jacket by Schiaparelli; the buttons have a unique fastening as they are anchored with brass screws that slide into industrial hooks. The silk twill has a woven repeating pattern of rearing horses in two shades of blue with their saddles, manes and plumes picked out in metallic thread. Renowned jewellery designer Jean Schlumberger produced the accompanying buttons, as well as clown fur clips and costume jewellery, for the collection.

Opposite The Circus collection of 1938 was one of the most imaginative and successful themes for Schiaparelli. This blue printed silk evening dress is covered in larger-than-life drawings of carousel creatures, dancing horses and white rabbits, all designed by the artist Marcel Vertès. Colour clashes of pink, purple, yellow and orange present a childlike vision of the circus atmosphere.

Below Detail of a tailored wool jacket, designed for the Circus collection in 1938, with coloured glass and metal appliqués on the front. The four dancing horse buttons are made from cast metal and hand-painted. Behind the detailed appliqués there are concealed pockets, cut into the front of the jacket.

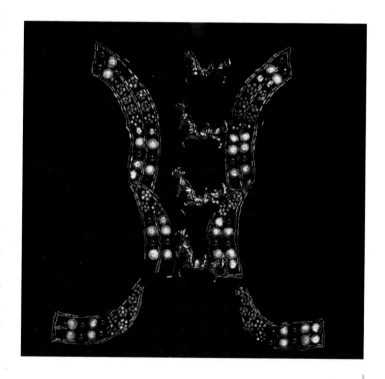

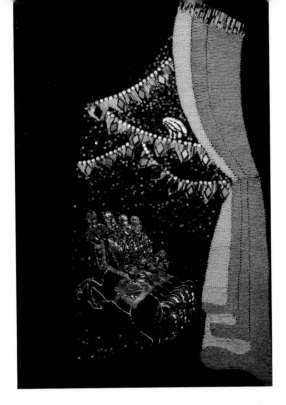

Above A detail from an embroidered jacket made of velvet, metallic thread, glass beads and rhinestones, designed by Schiaparelli for the Circus collection and executed by the House of Lesage – the perfect marriage of a visionary couturier and a master embroiderer. Several versions of jackets were made for the collection, including a lavishly decorated bolero with a row of dancing elephants, famously worn by the make-up guru Helena Rubinstein.

Opposite The stark black crepe Skeleton dress, a collaboration between Salvador Dalí and Schiaparelli for the Circus collection, used an ingenious form of trapunto quilting to create padded ribs, spine and leg bones. Most likely inspired by the Surrealist preoccupation with the human body, the skeleton motif has since been reincarnated in countless forms on the catwalk by designers such as Alexander McQueen, Christian Lacroix and Rodarte.

In April 1938 Schiaparelli showed the Pagan collection. Models were dressed as if they had fallen out of a Botticelli painting, with wreaths of delicate flowers embroidered onto simple classical gowns. Later she showed the Zodiac collection, which delved into astrological imagery. Rich dark velvets were studded with metal and rhinestones in the shape of the Great Bear constellation. Strong on dramatic colour, and lavish golden embroidery, the sun, moon and stars glittered on evening frocks and coats. Memorable from this collection is the Christian Bérard sketch of three women in evening dress, the central figure with her back turned to show the elaborate golden sun embroidered onto a hip-length silk cape.

Below The autumn 1938 Pagan collection featured ideas drawn from nature. This typically Surreal choker, which is made from gold grosgrain ribbon, decorated with purple velvet bows and hanging gilt pine cones, perfectly encapsulates Schiaparelli's desire to shock.

Opposite Made from silk crepe, the neckline and bodice of this black dress are decorated with creeping foliage interspersed with pretty pink flowers and falling petals. Beautifully executed in plastic and silk thread, the embroidery was produced by Lesage.

Left and above Before launching his own label in 1952, Hubert de Givenchy worked for Schiaparelli and this Harlequin costume was his first design for the fashion house. Worn for a fancy-dress ball in Venice, the playful ensemble consists of a satin patchwork jacket with detachable ruffles at the neck and wrists, plus cropped pants with laced ribbons at the hem.

Opposite A dramatic evening gown from 1939 cleverly creates a softness from the severity of the stripes with the inclusion of a shaped bustle. The bustle was constructed by folding two rectangular pieces of fabric in half, then pleating them back into the seam at the waistband.

Schiaparelli created the Music collection – jumping musical notes and bars scattered among embroidered musical instruments – for autumn 1937. Details and accessories always provided the opportunity for folly that so appealed to her, and she created bags shaped like an accordion and a suede belt that had a treble-clef buckle. One particularly striking evening dress, embroidered all over with metallic thread forming bars of music and exquisitely detailed tambourines and violins, had a belt with a working musical box as the buckle.

Schiaparelli's last great collection, the Commedia dell'Arte, was flooded with colour and presented to the strains of Scarlatti and Vivaldi. Drawing loosely on an improvisational comedy that toured Italy in the sixteenth century, the designers used actors' traditional costumes as a springboard to reinterpret costume into fashion. Tutu skirts and shocking pink hosiery were paraded playfully alongside the narrowest of suit silhouettes, while the wandering minstrels wore big bulky topcoats with sharply contrasting coloured linings. Pompoms, ruffles, masks and dramatic tricorn hats provided the fun element, but it was the wool harlequin coat with its dramatic use of colour and geometric design that stole the show. The inspirational colour blocking of Man Ray's celebrated painting *Le Beaux Temps*, 1939, was a source of influence for this collection.

From 1935-39 Schiaparelli was the designer to be seen in, but the outbreak of war broke the spell, and things were never quite as good again.

Previous pages Two variations of a white silk dress, printed with a freehand style interpretation of sheet music, using ribbons for bars and roses as notes. The dress on the right was seen at Elsa Maxwell's Red, White and Blue Ball of 1937.

Left Schiaparelli excelled in making inventive buttons that were shaped into every conceivable object except plain rounds. Here, plaster-cast buttons in the shape of a drum were used in her Music collection of 1937. Jean Clement, who worked in Schiaparelli's studio, was responsible for the production of most of her outlandish buttons and was often known to bake them in the oven.

Opposite Variations on a musical theme adorned all the clothes in the Music collection of 1937. Detailed embroidery from Lesage included sheet music motifs, with notes and instruments all in perfect detail. This purple chiffon gown is softly ruched across the shoulders and bodice, falls smoothly over the waist and hips to a fuller skirt with loose inverted gathers. The embroidered ribbon detailing that falls around the hips depicts hanging cymbals, a violin, horns and a piano keyboard.

Below These silk crepe gloves were made to match the evening gown featured on the previous page. They exhibit the detailed embroidery by Lesage, made with both metallic and silk threads, plus tiny seed pearls to decorate the tambourine.

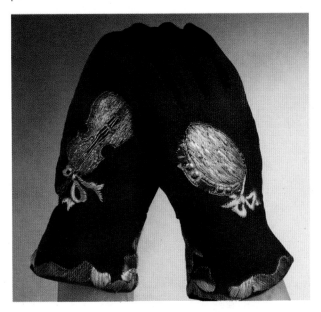

Opposite This famous illustration by Christian Bérard was shown in *Vogue* magazine in 1938, the year Schiaparelli created her Zodiac collection. The three evening ensembles were dramatic in colour and design. Rhinestones in the 12 signs of the zodiac shone out from a midnight blue velvet jacket, while the Medusa head in the shape of the sun, designed by Bérard, dazzled on the back of the shocking pink cape. Lesage produced the pink Phoebus cape design, in gold tweed and sequins.

Fashion and Art

"... that Italian artist who makes clothes."

Gabrielle "Coco" Chanel, on Elsa Schiaparelli

The first artistic group that Elsa Schiaparelli met socially in 1919 were part of the international Dada group who had converged on New York to escape First World War. Their art was diverse, shambolic, nihilistic and outrageous, but more importantly and perhaps what struck a chord with Schiaparelli, was the philosophy that united the various artists, poets and performers. Dada challenged the conventional notions of what art should be it took established convention and turned it on its head, appropriating found objects and printed literature and re-presenting both with either a political or ironic message. Nonsense, craziness and a desire to tease and shock were all Dada traits that could equally well refer to so many of the successful collections of Schiaparelli.

Many years later in Paris, it was another group of avant-garde artists, including Man Ray, Meret Oppenheim, Salvador Dalí and Jean Cocteau, whose artistic outpourings not only inspired Schiaparelli, but gave her a great sense that her own artistic creativity was understood. She claims her friendships with these talented artists not only provided a source of exhilaration and support, but lifted her "from the boring reality of merely making a dress to sell".

Schiaparelli was in the business of selling glamour and did so most successfully through her exuberant, humorous and often outrageous

Opposite Unsurprisingly this collaboration with Dalí, known as the Skeleton dress, met with public outrage when it was first shown as part of the Circus collection of 1938. Trapunto quilting is used to suggest rib and hip bones and the design was stitched in outline through two layers of silk crepe and then padded with cotton wadding to create the "bones" on the front.

Overleaf Schiaparelli, with a model, has the Lobster print dress, designed by Dalí, on her lap.

creations. She liked visual jokes and gags and her imaginative spirit produced work that sometimes relied heavily on the absurd. In this she had much in common with the Surrealist artists. Far from simply adopting some of the Surrealist ideas into her own work, Schiaparelli led the way in a dialogue that opened up the connections between art and fashion. She specifically commissioned artists like Christian Bérard, Jean Cocteau and Leonor Fini to design fabrics, buttons, scent bottles and advertisements. Like the Surrealists she deliberately set out to create optical illusion and to make the mind question the perception of reality.

Surrealism was creeping insidiously into the visual culture, particularly through the pages of woman's magazines such as *Vogue* and *Harper's Bazaar*, where illustration and photography captured the symbiotic relationship between fashion and art. The arrival of the first International

Surrealist Exhibition in London of June 1936 confirmed the relationship, as Salvador Dalí turned up wearing a deep-sea diving suit to deliver a speech. Confounding expectations, exploring visual irony with incongruous details or prints and disrupting the conventional meaning of fashion are all ideas that translate to Schiaparelli's oeuvre.

The legacy of Surrealist art is it developed ideas that connect the thinking of modern psychoanalysts with visually disruptive, sometimes distorted images. Visual and verbal imagery that is fantasy-based and delves into the subconscious confronted the viewer with a different sort of reality, causing an unsettling confusion. While the commerciality of creating fashion was considered far less worthy of theoretical analysis, the collaborative work between the Surrealist artists and Schiaparelli explored the boundaries and functions of dress in many different ways and it seems oversimplistic to presume Schiaparelli's contribution was simply a nod to the witticism of Surrealism to amuse her rich clients.

Elsa and Salvador

Schiaparelli's most memorable collaborations are with the Spanish artist Salvador Dalí, who throughout the late 1930s embraced popular culture, commerce and every aspect of contemporary fashion. The partnership was rewarding for both artists, as Schiaparelli was known for her love of shock tactics and for her willingness to challenge the conventions of beauty and gender stereotypes. The Surrealist Desk suits and coats were thought to be based on a 1936 Dalí painting *The Anthropomorphic Cabinet*, which showed a naked man seated on the floor, with a torso resembling a chest of drawers, all open to various degrees with bits of fabric spilling out. The tailored Desk suit, famously photographed by Cecil Beaton in a painted Surrealist landscape, has multiple boxy pockets all over the front of the jacket, with large drawer knobs where the buttons might be. A single pocket has a practical purpose, but multiple pockets? Deliberate confusion, as some are real and are some fake, an idea that may have less to do with practical jokes than with the designer choosing to subvert the function of fashion and cause disharmony.

The Surrealist theory of displacement is best exemplified in the extraordinary Shoe-Hat that Schiaparelli and Dalí created together. Although the idea is thought to have originated from an earlier photograph of Dalí standing with a shoe on his head (taken by his wife Gala), the upside-down hat, which balanced seductively over the forehead, was just one of many crazy millinery creations that Schiaparelli produced in the 1930s. Realistic objects of a television, a birdcage and even a lamb cutlet with a white frill over the bone were all appropriated into outrageous, but never foolish hats.

Controversy greeted the next two collaborations, with the organza Lobster dress (1937) and the Tear illusion dress (1938) both becoming iconic. The lobster was a recurring theme and already a Dalí favourite, having been seen in his painting from 1935, *New York Dream – Man Finds Lobster in Place of Phone*, and used again, later, on the handset of his *Aphrodisiac Telephone* made for Edward James. Dalí's famous lobster print appeared as the focus of attention, positioned provocatively on a simple white evening dress with little other decoration to distract.

Opposite In spring 1937, Schiaparelli asked Dalí to design a lobster as decoration for a white organdy evening gown, which was interpreted into a fabric print by the leading silk designer Sache. From 1934, Dalí began incorporating lobsters into his work, including *New York Dream – Man Finds Lobster in Place of Phone* and the mixed-media *Aphrodisiac Telephone* (1936). The Lobster dress was made famous when it appeared in *Vogue,* modelled by Wallis Simpson.

The juxtaposition of innocent white floaty dress and a blood-red, super-sized lobster placed strategically between the thighs, left little to the imagination. Dalí's work often dealt with themes connecting sexuality and consumption, and here Schiaparelli aligns herself with the same ideas, executed not through painting but through the creation of a couture dress. The dress was shocking; it subverted questions of taste and played on the displacement of an object in an overtly sexual way. Elsa did not mention the dress in her autobiography, but after it was worn by Wallis Simpson, and photographs of her wearing it circulated throughout the world, the Lobster dress became one of Schiaparelli's most famous designs.

The Tear dress was presented as part of Schiaparelli's Circus collection of 1938 and may have been inspired by an earlier work of Dalí's: *Three Young Surrealist Women Holding in their Arms the Skins of an Orchestra*. The floor-length gown, which was made from pale

blue silk crepe (since faded to white), gives the appearance – using a painterly trompe-l'oeil effect – of torn and shredded pieces of fabric that have been ripped from the dress and left to hang in ugly tears. But the ravaged print causes confusion. Is it designed to resemble flayed animal fur on the inside, or are the colours suggestive of bruised flesh? Perhaps the print was designed to show that the dress was worn inside out, revealing the "right side" of the fabric only on the hanging rips. To further disorient the viewer and extend the puzzle of reality versus illusion, the matching headscarf had real three-dimensional tears sewn onto the fabric. Uneasy contrasts between the function of the beautiful evening gown and the shredded fabric confound on many levels. The rips give the illusion of exposure and possibly vulnerability, while the "torn" fabric suggests a level of violence, juxtaposing luxurious wealth with rags and poverty. It may even have been a sombre portend of the imminent war ahead.

"In difficult times fashion is always outrageous."

Elsa Schiaparelli

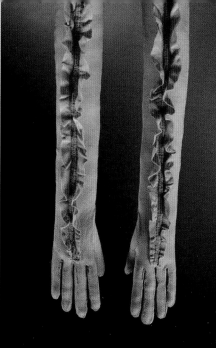

Opposite and detail above The Tears dress of 1938, inspired directly from a Dalí painting that showed a figure in ripped skintight clothing disturbingly suggestive of flayed flesh, is a mourning gown and veil designed by Schiaparelli just prior to the Second World War. This fabric, itself created by Dalí, looked as if it had been savagely and repeatedly torn, but is in fact printed with the rips carefully cut out and lined in pink and magenta. Images of fur incongruously lining the rips of the printed dress, add a bestial tone to the work.

Above Designed to be worn with the Tears dress, opposite, the strong pink of these gloves would have complemented the pink and magenta print of the dress. Schiaparelli had a knack for using unusual details and trimmings to make the everyday item appear extraordinary. Here, instead of a traditional glove leather, a stretchy pink crepe fabric was used, precluding the need for buttons or fastenings. The dramatic shirred ruffles, running the length of each glove, provide an additional unexpected touch.

Above Surreal fashion shot taken by Cecil Beaton in 1936. It shows two of Schiaparelli's Desk suits, designed with multiple pockets positioned all over the jacket, some of which were real, others fake. Real drawer knobs were used in place of buttons.

Right *The Burning Giraffe,* 1937, by Salvador Dalí was just one of many works where he explored the idea of a set of drawers spilling open from the body. These were thought to be secrets that could only be opened through psychoanalysis and represented the inner subconscious.

Above and opposite In 1937, Schiaparelli collaborated with Jean Cocteau on two long evening coats made from silk jersey. They differ slightly in final execution, but both display the talented draughtsmanship of Cocteau and the brilliant finesse of Lesage, who translated the idea into reality. Ambiguity comes from the two profile faces with pouting lips, which can also be viewed as a classic urn, topped with silk roses. The collaboration excels due to Schiaparelli's precision cutting of the coat.

Jean Cocteau

In 1937 Schiaparelli collaborated with her close friend the artist Jean
Cocteau (who also produced work for Chanel) on a complex design for
an evening jacket. Cocteau, who (among other talents) was a hugely gifted
draughtsman, drew the profile of a female face on the front shoulder
of an asymmetrical jacket, her head thrown backward with a mane of
golden hair cascading down the sleeve. A disembodied hand, which
was a favourite Surrealist motif, appeared at the front waist,
clutching a cellophane handkerchief, and Cocteau's perfect
freestyle line drawing was beautifully embroidered in
pale pink for the skin and detailed gold stitching for the
hair, all executed by the Maison Lesage. The result was
beautiful and unsettling, as Schiaparelli had chosen to
upturn convention by choosing coarse grey linen
as the basis for this elaborately embroidered
evening jacket. Cocteau was also responsible for
another memorable design that appeared on
the back of a long fitted, silk jersey evening coat in
1937. Creating the shape of a classic urn by positioning
two symmetrical female profiles facing each other, with
pursed red lips almost touching, the vase itself was filled
with pink silk roses, whose tight petals were wrapped
around each other to give a three-dimensional effect.
The beauty is in the collaboration between designer, artist
and a young François Lesage, who executed the exquisite
embroidery, as each is allowed to excel in their contribution
to the finished product. For Schiaparelli these complex
collaborative clothes always needed precision lines and she
provided a perfect blank canvas to showcase the Cocteau
design. The vase is positioned to sit precisely at the
small of the back, the narrowest part of the coat. The
long embroidered lines representing the column
that the vase rests on fall elegantly down over
slim hips, simply reinforcing the elegant line
of the silhouette.

Opposite and above A fashion
drawing by Jean Cocteau of 1937
shows his design for Schiaparelli's
fitted jacket and long skirt, beautifully
realized by Lesage in gilded metallic
thread, tiny beads and paillettes.
The woman's hand carrying a
cellophane handkerchief, which
appears prominently on the front,
was a common Surrealist motif.

Above Schiaparelli had a wide circle of artistic friends and her work was often influenced or inspired by their output. Man Ray's painting *Les Beaux Temps,* produced in 1939, resonates with the strong use of colour blocking that she utilized in her patchwork garments from her most successful collection, the Commedia dell'Arte.

This page This patchwork harlequin coat from the Commedia dell'Arte was made up of graduated geometric triangles of red, blue, black, white and yellow felt. Increasing the size of the pattern from small triangles around the neck, shoulders and waist to a gradually larger pattern around the hem was an inspirational way to trick the eye into shaping the body.

Hollywood Glamour

"Never fit a dress to the body but train the body to fit the dress."
Elsa Schiaparelli

The 1930s were the heyday of scandalous Hollywood movie stars and rich society women, who divided their time between fashionable resorts such as Cannes, St Moritz and Venice; they were also Schiaparelli devotees and regular visitors to the salon at Place Vendôme. Even in the early days Elsa Schiaparelli had worked her magic on a young Katharine Hepburn, who went on to claim in the press that this transformation had been the turning point in her career. A superb silhouette was a Schiaparelli trademark and while daytime looks were meticulously fitted and groomed, evening dresses were, in complete contrast, unspeakably seductive and languid. Those who could afford it wanted Schiaparelli to provide both.

At the height of her success the smartest seats in the salon were reserved for royalty, leaders of society and the wives of presidents. Actresses like Claudette Colbert, Myrna Loy, Norma Shearer, Merle Oberon and Vivien Leigh flocked to see the new collections. Greta Garbo was a customer, as was Marlene Dietrich, and then later Joan Crawford and Lauren Bacall. Perhaps her most famous client, however, was Wallis Simpson, who was regarded as *the* most fashionable women of her time. Her angular frame and strong face provided a perfect canvas for Schiaparelli, who had a fondness for *les jolies laides* and took pleasure in empowering the plainest of women through statement dressing. She contributed to Mrs Simpson's wedding trousseau, providing a black crepe day dress printed with little white turtles, a blue evening dress with yellow butterfly print repeated on the lapels of a blue tweed jacket, and a variation of the white organza lobster dress created with Dalí (see page 75).

Left Model wearing an outfit Schiaparelli designed for Wallis Simpson in 1937, that was to be worn after her marriage to the Duke of Windsor.

Schiaparelli had become the couturier whose clothes women wanted to be seen in; her aristocratic background ensured she was socially accepted within these circles and she turned out to be the best endorsement of her own style. Gala Dalí was a fan, as was Nancy Cunard, wealthy heiress and close friend of the Surrealists who often appeared in Schiaparelli. The Honourable Mrs Daisy Fellowes, one of Schiaparelli's best clients, shocked everyone when she turned up in leopard-print pyjamas when everyone else was wearing floaty tea dresses. She was also the only person thought to have worn the Shoe-Hat with the swagger and confidence it deserved.

The mystique of Hollywood in the 1930s and Schiaparelli's love of the dramatic produced a perfect marriage. Her clothes created high drama, with or without a movie star, and her influence on existing costume designers in Hollywood such as Gilbert Adrian and Edith Head was immense. Schiap designed the costumes for several films, starting in 1933 with the movie *Topaze*, which starred Myrna Loy, and going on to famously dress the voluptuous Mae West in *Every Day's a Holiday* in 1937.

She is also credited with being the costume designer for several British films in the 1930s, dressing Margaret Lockwood and Anna Neagle for *The Beloved Vagabond* and *Limelight*. Her last big production as a costume designer was the John Huston film *Moulin Rouge* (1952), starring Zsa Zsa Gabor, which was filmed in London and Paris.

Previous left and right Publicity poster and a promotional still from the 1937 film *Every Day's a Holiday* starring Mae West. Schiaparelli was brought on board to design the costumes despite the fact that the famously buxom and curvaceous West could not have been further from the strong-shouldered, narrow silhouette that was the designer's trademark. As West was not prepared to travel to Paris for fittings, the studio sent a life-size plaster torso of her hourglass figure to Schiaparelli, along with requirements for fabrics and colours.

Opposite The German film star Marlene Dietrich in the movie *Angel*, 1937. Both Dietrich and Greta Garbo were perfect muses for Schiaparelli – their masculine-type figures were perfectly suited to show off the classic Schiaparelli silhouette.

Right The Honourable Mrs Daisy Fellowes was a celebrated socialite of the 1930s, heiress to the Singer sewing machine fortune, an acclaimed beauty and a fashion icon. One of Schiaparelli's most loyal fans, she was thought to be able to carry off even the most shocking creations. Here, she wears a white Mandarin collared coat by Schiaparelli of 1935.

Above Photographed by Edward
Steichen in 1932, the indomitable
actress Joan Crawford wears an
unusual combination of dark
hyacinth-blue knitted woollen
dress with a structured, heavily
padded and quilted matelasse
crepe jacket by Schiaparelli.

Opposite Socialite Millicent Rogers
was a regular visitor to No. 21
Place Vendôme, where her slender
proportions provided a perfect frame
for Schiaparelli's sculptural pieces,
such as this classic black velvet suit
with detailed metallic braid edging,
worn with cross fleury brooches.

Opposite and above The
Hungarian actress Zsa Zsa
Gabor starred in the 1952
musical *Moulin Rouge,* directed
by John Huston. It was the last
film on which Elsa Schiaparelli
collaborated with her friend

Marcel Vertès, who was credited
as costume designer. Schiaparelli,
however, was certainly
responsible for producing the
extravagant outfits for the star and
the film won an Academy Award
for best costume design.

The War Years and Beyond

After the declaration of war, Schiaparelli sent Gogo to the United States, which she felt would be safer for her daughter. She carried on at the Place Vendôme with a depleted staff, her indomitable spirit and sense of humour still intact. Her last collection was called the Cash and Carry collection. Everything was designed with big pockets, so that in the case of an emergency a woman could grab everything she needed and run, leaving her hands free. There was a woollen boiler suit intended to be placed at the side of the bed and quickly pulled on for a trip to the air raid shelter, as well as an ingenious camouflage dress. Designed to look like a day dress, the wearer simply had to pull a ribbon at the appropriate time and the piece, as if by magic, lengthened into a full-length evening gown.

Determined to carry on whatever it took, Schiaparelli discussed with Captain Edward Molyneux and Lucien Lelong, the head of the Syndicat de la Couture, the possibility of moving staff out of the ateliers in Paris to a safe house in Biarritz so they could continue working. But it was not to be, and when Mussolini allied himself with Hitler and declared war on France, Schiaparelli steeled herself for the trouble ahead and vowed to do all she could to help her adopted country.

Columbia Lecture Bureau offered Schiaparelli a series of lectures that were to be illustrated with her dresses. Both Lelong and Molyneux urged her to go to America to fulfil the contract, hoping it would also help trade between the countries. The tour was considered a success, despite the fact that the ship carrying the dresses was sunk and Schiaparelli was forced to appeal to the good nature of Bonwit

Left A model wearing Schiaparelli eveningwear shows only the outline of her back view, which provides us with the iconoclastic silhouette of the stamp of the designer. Broad shoulders, narrow to the small of the back, offset by a huge embroidered pink bow, extravagantly decorated with embroidery by Lesage. Shocking pink contrasted with black was a much-loved combination.

Teller to try and replicate what had been lost. After visiting 42 towns in eight weeks, the tour ended and Schiaparelli travelled back to Paris where she found the doors to Place Vendôme still open, although operating in much-reduced circumstances. Her return was short-lived however, as her personal situation became more precarious and she was urged once again to leave the country. In May 1941, after a 20-year absence, Schiaparelli was back in New York. Although it was not the city she remembered, she encountered many friends and began working for a relief agency with all the energy and passion previously used for her business.

Left The last collection Schiaparelli produced before the Second World War was called Cash and Carry (1939). Always concerned with practicality, these Schiaparelli pyjamas were made to keep women warm in the air-raid shelters. Easy to take on and off, they also and had several zippered pockets to keep valuables safe.

Opposite After the war Schiaparelli continued her business and produced collections that relied less on severe padding and tailoring, more on simplicity. This elegant duster coat with easy sloping shoulders exemplifies her Hurricane line from 1947.

Opposite New York model Shari Herbert, shown here wearing one of Schiaparelli's evening gowns from her 1949 collection. The skin-tight sheath dress has a central seam with soft gathering around the waist and hip areas. Made from grape-coloured taffeta, it is worn with a separate flesh-coloured boned bra, decorated with hanging tendrils of pearls and sequins that drip down over the dress.

Overleaf Single-breasted linen afternoon jacket with three-quarter length sleeves and "sleeping blue" velvet trim on the collar and pockets, circa 1940. Designed for daywear, the lavish embroidery of flowers and foliage in silk and metallic thread is used as decoration around the scalloped hem, sleeves and lapels. The two metal buttons are made from enamel and decorated with painted swans.

During the war years, when Schiaparelli was absent from Paris, the House at Place Vendôme had cautiously kept going, simply chugging along without fanfare or financial ruin. When finally the war ended and Madame Schiaparelli returned to her beloved Paris, she found familiar faces waiting to greet her. It was her intention to continue business where she left off, but times had changed. Materials were harder to get hold of, there was general unrest in the country and for the first time ever Schiap's instinct to provide simple dresses that were less constructed – in fact much softer and flatter with gently sloping shoulders – proved out of tune. A young Christian Dior had wowed Paris in 1947 with his New Look line and as Schiap said later, although the rusty wheels of her business were beginning to turn again, she soon "discovered the wheels no longer had their axles in the centre". When she attempted to revive the masculine look in August 1945, the frock coats were too reminiscent of those of German officers. Subsequent offerings of her Mummy silhouette, Dandy look and Hurricane line were also met with similarly lacklustre reviews. Future collections seemed too contrived and showy; nothing she attempted appeared to recapture the thrilling years of the 1920s and 1930s.

Opposite This lavishly embroidered dinner jacket in silk crepe was made for wearing in the evening and dates from 1940. Schiaparelli makes a feature of the two large pockets on the front, which are intricately decorated with gilded metallic thread by Lesage. She also uses distinctive embroidered gold buttons, as she hated plain round ones, and gold edging to define the collar and pocket flaps.

Schiaparelli showed her final collection in 1954. She accepted the closure of her business without bitterness and chose instead to spend her time with family and friends. Although she no longer designed clothes, she continued to have business interests, and travelled the world promoting her perfumes and accessories. Mostly though, she was happiest reading books and socializing with a loyal group of famous friends. Elsa divided her year between her two homes in Paris and Hammamet in Tunisia and spent much time with Gogo, her second husband Gino Cacciapuoti (an Italian, which thrilled Schiaparelli), and her two grandchildren Marisa and Berinthia. Schiaparelli died in her sleep at home in Paris on 13 November, 1973.

Shortly after her death, the company was sold to an American firm called Schiaparelli Inc, and during the 1980's and 1990's there were several unsuccessful attempts to relaunch the fashion house. In 2006 the company name and archive were acquired by Diego Della Valle, chief executive of Tod's group, with the intention of updating and reviving the Schiaparelli brand for a new generation.

Previous left Long evening dress of silk satin and rayon damask, circa 1948. This shimmery bronze gown has been printed with an intricate flower and foliage motif on a large scale, completely in contrast to the striped shoulder and breast panel. Spherical cutting and contrasting fabric is used to create the distinct breast cups that draw attention.

Previous right Evening dress from Paris, 1947. This dress is notable for its wide flat-boned cummerbund, championed by Schiaparelli as she tried out a variety of new silhouettes after the war.

Opposite The fabric print for this dress depicts fin-de-siècle gentlemen, with dandy moustaches. These cartoonish illustrations were all produced with the expertise of the silk printer Sache. The design from 1946 is called *Les Vieux Beaux* (The Old Beauties) and the dress features an unusually wide fluid collar that cuts over the shoulder to form a loose cap sleeve.

Overleaf Publicity still of Schiaparelli posing in the garden of her Paris home in August 1949. This photo was accompanied by a press release announcing her deal to manufacture coats and suits in New York.

This page Schiaparelli was one of the first designers to consider a total lifestyle for her customer. In addition to clothes and accessories, she turned her attention to lingerie. In the early 1950s she designed a range of quilted housecoats lined in shocking pink and also beautiful dressing gowns trimmed with extravagant mink and ermine collars. This mink-trimmed peignor dates from 1951.

Previous left In 1950 Schiaparelli launched her Pyramid line of coats. This included the big duster coat, typical of which was this loosely sweeping and unstructured garment. The style usually came with three-quarter-length sleeves that often had turnback cuffs. Launched at the same time, the Dolman Greatcoat was much praised for the secret pockets hidden in the sleeves.

Previous right A model poses in a black floral summer two-piece, with mini cape that sweeps across the shoulder and ties in a deep V at the front, 1952. The matching hat and gloves are also by Schiaparelli.

Left An early 1950s damask-lined grey flannel suit with pencil skirt. The jacket has widely curved lapels, large flap pockets and mother-of-pearl buttons.

Opposite In 1954 at the age of 63, Schiaparelli showed her last collection. The theme was free and elegant and the collection, which was called Fluid line, showed shoulders that practically drooped. This raspberry pink raincoat with its oversize and strangely-cut collar was one of Schiaparelli's final designs.

Accessories

From the beginning, accessories played an important role in Elsa
Schiaparelli's collections as she preferred to design an entire ensemble,
including shoes, hat, gloves and jewellery. By the 1930s, Schiap had built
a reputation for creating daring and innovative accessories, but it was her
hats that made the biggest impact, with such eccentric designs as the Lamb
Cutlet Hat, the Brain-Hat and the Shoe-Hat. She used bold colours and
unusual materials, often adapting everyday objects for her designs such as
airplane propellers, igloos and even a birdcage holding a canary. Famous
for her creative fashion sense and unorthodox free-thinking approach
to detail and decoration, her designs were not merely unconventional,
they were unworldly, such as a woven-grass brimmed hat decorated with
crawling pink and green flies and beetles for her Pagan collection. Many
of her millinery designs featured extravagant bouquets of flowers, brightly
coloured feathers or heaps of fruit. She also introduced a Victorian revival
in the form of the modern snood in 1935 and paved the way for a variety
of turbans, pillbox and veiled styles with her radical designs.

Schiaparelli's early jewellery was showy, whimsical and surreal, with
organic forms that seemed to owe their design more to the living form
than the inanimate. There were aspirins strung together as necklaces
and plastic beetles, bees and crickets. She was unique in her choice of
materials, too, using china, porcelain, aluminium, glass, crystal and
Plexiglas, as well as plastics.

Unfortunately, the licensing of her name to David Lisner coincided
with a loss of that imaginative vision in design, and later pieces were

Opposite Elsa Schiaparelli taking
tea in the mid-1950s in Paris. The
turban was one of her favoured
hat shapes because it was so
versatile and it allowed her to keep
reinventing the basic silhouette.
Made from pink and ivory striped
silk, with grosgrain ribbon and
net, the stiffened headband
provides sufficient rigidity to place
decorative costume jewellery
and a feather. This turban was
donated to the Philadelphia
Museum of Art.

typical of the period, incorporating the popular "watermelon" glass and Aurora Borealis rhinestones. Her 1930s designs are unsigned and very rare until later in the decade, when her name appeared in lowercase block letters and then in script after 1949.

Schiap's collaborations with Italian shoemaker André Perugia, who worked in the same rue de la Paix building as she did, led to such designs as the Monkey-Fur boots (see page 43) and suede shoes with elastic fastenings that could be pulled on or off without the need for buckles, laces or buttons – a revolutionary idea at the time. In another "first" for the couturier, she and Perugia are credited with designing the wedge shoe with a cork heel.

Accessories provided Schiap with the perfect opportunity to show off both her imaginative vision and her practical side. Picking up details that others may have overlooked, she produced stockings with designs painted on the back of the legs and suede smoking gloves with a safety match tucked in the back that could be lit on the wristband.

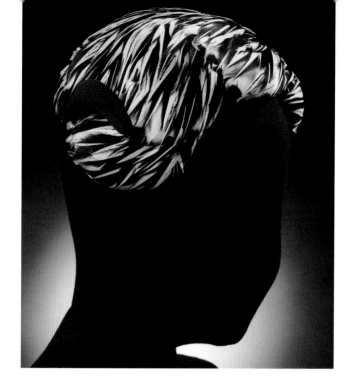

Opposite Schiap trying out hats on a model, circa 1951.

Overleaf left This black-and-pink wool felt Shoe-Hat from 1937 was perhaps her most whimsical design, inspired by a photograph of Dalí wearing his wife's slipper on his head. The shoe stands straight up, with the toe tilted over the wearer's forehead and the heel is in a shocking pink. This hat was worn by Singer sewing machine heiress and French *Vogue* editor Daisy Fellowes, among others.

Above The two main styles of hat during the 1950s were small skullcaps, suitable for a cocktail party or dinner, and wide "saucer" hats. This hat, designed by milliner Paulette Marchand (1900–84) for Schiaparelli, is constructed from intricately dyed game-bird feathers.

Overleaf right Schiaparelli, in Surrealistic mood, designed this red satin, visored evening cap with an elongated peephole for the eye. A diamond clip from Van Cleef & Arpels makes a unique eyebrow.

Above This hat, which was first shown in autumn/winter 1938, was part of Schiaparelli's Pagan collection, which used nature and the living world as its theme. Made from woven grass, the large brim was decorated with random bugs, flies and insects.

Opposite A nest of kingfisher and gull feathers appear perched on top of a soft mink brim in this extraordinary wool felt hat from 1938. Bird motifs often featured in Schiaparelli's work; she produced a birdcage hat and kept a birdcage to display accessories at her shop.

Overleaf left Portrait of Madame Schiaparelli by her friend and long-time collaborator, the Hungarian artist Marcel Vertès. Schiaparelli posed for *Harper's Bazaar* in 1938 in one of her new Oriental headdresses. The tiny pink fez sitting firmly on her crown was made from silk and decorated with embroidery, spangles and brightly coloured gemstones. Two silk scarves fell loosely from the fez to frame the face and wrap under the chin. Elsa's hand can be seen protruding from the scarf, adorned with multiple gold bracelets.

This page A 1938 illustration showing two similar hat designs from Schiaparelli. The Toy Hat was a puppet-sized hat, usually worn tipped forward onto the forehead. It is decorated below with a proportionately large pink hatband.

SCIAPARELLI acaba de lanzar estos dos modelos de sombreros inspirados en los de los monos de circo.

BALDRIGH
Paris 38.

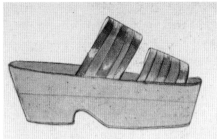

Striped kid straps on cork

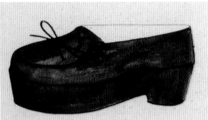

An elevated suede moccasin

Left, below and opposite

Schiaparelli always chose the best people to collaborate with when she needed to explore an area of expertise that she could not provide. Italian shoemaker André Perugia was one such person. Like the inventive couturier, Perugia was always experimenting and challenged preconceived notions of what a shoe should look like. For Schiaparelli he produced a shoe with a cork platform sole with striped kid straps (top left), a suede moccasin with a raised platform sole (centre) and two versions of a high-heeled satin sandal with kid-lined straps (below). He also designed summer shoes with a kinked ridged sole and thin ribbon laces that could be removed and re-tied as the customer wished (opposite).

a high and mighty sole

Satin lined with kid

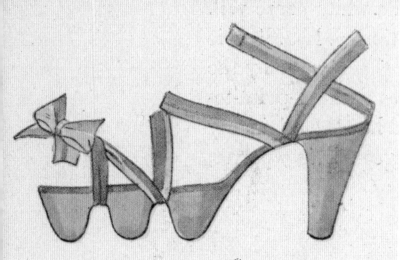

A kinked sole

Removable lacings

Opposite These silk satin ankle boots were also made by André Perugia for a specific collaboration with Schiaparelli in 1939–40. Made from leather and pink silk with a green and gold stripe, the flap opening is fastened with a row of tiny mother-of-pearl buttons.

Above The Duchess of Windsor was photographed wearing this ocelot fur pouch at Palm Beach in April 1950. It was on sale at the *Boutique des Ensembles Schiapsport* in 1949, and was made with a cylindrical base and a large leather heart-shaped panel, through which a metal loop was pushed to fasten it. The back of the pouch attaches to the fur-trimmed belt, which was fastened around the waist.

Above People expected Schiap to produce fantastical and amusing designs, and she rarely disappointed them. Her inventions were known as "Schiaparelli-isms", but not all were a huge success, like these sunglasses with fake eyelashes made from cellophane.

Opposite These black suede gloves with red snakeskin fingernails were made as accessories for the Surreal Desk suits, created in collaboration with Dalí in 1936. Schiaparelli produced two colourways: either in black or white, both with blood-red trim and nails.

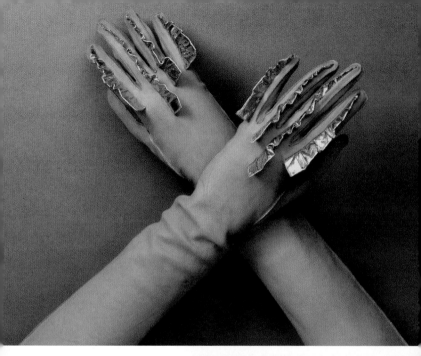

Above Touches of Surrealism were certainly evident on many of Schiaparelli's gloves. These elbow-length turquoise suede evening gloves from 1939 have gold kid ruffles running up the length of each finger, shaped in the form of the Italian *cornicello*, which is a small, gold, good luck charm used to protect the wearer from the evil-eye curse.

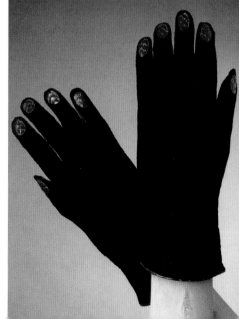

Opposite Schiaparelli often loved to distort the natural scale of things. Visually it shocked the senses to see a miniature hat or an oversize bow and here she created a super-size insect brooch, worn pinned to a black bouclé Shetland stole, 1952.

Overleaf A selection of ultra-modern bracelets and bangles from Schiaparelli, Boivin and Maggy Rouff from May 1935. The bold designs are graphic and architectural, from flat discs to chunky factory cogs.

Above At the beginning of her career Schiaparelli invented the name "junk jewellery" for her big ostentatious costume pieces, which she took care to position on the most severe clothes. Later she combined semiprecious stones with precious ones and started to work with Jean Schlumberger, who went on to become one of the world's most famous jewellers. This bracelet with three strings of coloured pearls, circa 1958, has a gilt metal clasp in the shape of a shell.

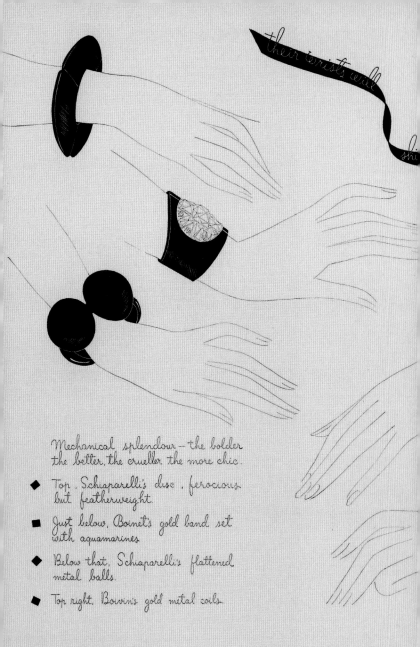

their wrists will

shi

Mechanical splendour — the bolder
the better, the crueller the more chic.

◆ Top. Schiaparelli's disc, ferocious
but featherweight.

■ Just below, Boivin's gold band set
with aquamarines

◆ Below that, Schiaparelli's flattened
metal balls.

■ Top right. Boivin's gold metal coils.

gold, massive, sculptured

light as air

- ◆ Agamemnon's wrists—hard bright gold bracelets worn with dead black Maggy Rouff.
- ◆ And left, Schiaparelli's golden factory cogs.

Opposite Tassels that swung around with the movement of the wearer were incorporated into a set of jewellery by Schiaparelli that comprised necklace, earrings and bracelet in 1953. The long streams of gold-coloured metal that fell from twisted swirling circles created a strong statement.

Above The tactile nature of bird feathers created jewellery that had a light textural quality but also moved easily when worn. This striking 1951 necklace was made from guinea fowl feathers that were mounted in clusters onto bright yellow taffeta balls, with matching dangling earrings.

Shocking
de
Schiaparelli

Fragrances by Schiaparelli

Elsa Schiaparelli was not the first couturier to expand into the
perfume market, as her great mentor Paul Poiret had, as early as 1911,
established a fledgling market for designer perfume, followed by
Patou and Chanel in the 1920s. It was 1928 by the time Schiaparelli
invaded the market with the first of many products, which over the
course of her career were to become extraordinarily successful and as
she said, "proved to be her salvation when hard times came". Crazily
superstitious, Schiaparelli had decided that all her perfumes needed a
name that started with the letter S, a small vanity perhaps that must
have seemed easy to accommodate at the launch of *Salut* in 1934 and
Soucis and *Schiap*, which quickly followed, but became increasingly
harder to continue as new fragrances were produced over a period of
20 years. Without consultation, it was the voluptuously sexy body of

Opposite A 1930s advertisement
for *Shocking* perfume. The top
notes are aldehydes, bergamot
and tarragon; middle notes are
honey, rose and jasmine; base
notes are cloves and civet.

Right An oriental floral fragrance
for women, *Shocking* by
Schiaparelli was launched in
1937. The bottle design, based
on the figure of Hollywood star
Mae West, was adopted by Jean
Paul Gaultier for his fragrance
for women in 1993.

Opposite American magazine illustration from the 1940s by Marcel Vertès. With the slogan "Colognes de Schiaparelli", it shows a girl juggling a variety of the celebrated perfumes and colognes available for both men and women at that time: *Shocking, Sleeping, Snuff* and *Salut*.

the movie star Mae West that provided the inspiration for Schiaparelli's most famous perfume, *Shocking*. Having previously measured the actress's body in preparation for costume fittings, Schiaparelli recalls, "She had sent me all the most intimate details of her famous figure, and for greater accuracy a plaster cast statue of herself quite naked in the pose of the Venus de Milo."

The naked woman's torso, which exemplified a perfect hourglass figure, remained in the studio and eventually became the inspiration for the *Shocking* perfume that came in a nakedly curvaceous body-shaped bottle. The young Italian Surrealist artist Leonor Fini designed the bottle, copying the actress's celebrated curves, but exaggerating broad Schiaparelli-type shoulders and an impossibly slim waist. A tape measure was draped around the neck, pulled together at the bosom to form a deep V-neck, and fastened with a mini button "S".

The perfume was launched with an explosion of shocking pink and, without any advertising campaign, it became an immediate bestseller. In 1938, *Sleeping* was launched in a hugely extravagant Baccarat crystal candlestick bottle, with a red glass lighted taper and a cone-shaped extinguisher to put over the top. Clever, witty, beautifully presented in strong turquoise and gold packaging, Schiaparelli's attention to detail never waned and she always found the best in the business to translate her visual ideas into commercial reality.

colognes

de

Shiaparelli

Schiaparelli's
Celebrated colognes:
Shocking · Sleeping
Snuff · Salut

Salut de Schiaparelli

Opposite and above Schiaparelli was one of the first couturiers to invade the perfume market and in the early 1930s she created three fragrances that were produced in England. *Salut* was put on sale in 1934; it was a light evening fragrance that hinted at lily-of-the-valley. The magazine illustration (opposite) shows an advert for *Salut de Schiaparelli* from the 1940s by Marcel Vertès, who was commissioned to produce nearly all the advertising imagery for Schiaparelli's perfumes. The unusual box (above), in which the perfume was presented, was made in cork by Jean-Michel Frank, an interior designer employed by Schiaparelli to decorate her shops and also her own apartment.

Fragrances and Launch Dates

1928	S
1930	Jealousy
1933	Flippant
1934	Salut
1934	Soucis
1934	Schiap
1936	Floraison
1937	Shocking
1937	Le Six
1938	Sleeping
1939	Snuff
1941	So Sweet
1943	Radiance
1946	Le Roy Soleil
1949	Zut
1949	Eau de Sante
1952	Succès Fou
1952	Sport
1957	Si
1959	Scent of Mystery
1976	Shocking You
1987	Arrogance
1992	Dance Arrogance
1998	Shocking Schiaparelli
1999	Exciting Arrogance

Opposite Faithful to her links with the Surrealists, and their obsession with dreams, *Sleeping* was meant to be a night-perfume to be spritzed before falling into bed. The scent was designed to "illuminate the subconscious and light the way to ecstasy," according to this ad, illustrated by Marcel Vertès. The turquoise blue of the packaging was also a new colour for Schiaparelli and was described as "sleeping blue".

Above The bottle for *Sleeping* depicted a candleholder with a red flame. It came in a box designed as a cone-shaped extinguisher.

Fit for a King...

a hundred-and-ten-percent he-man cologne for father...9.00 and 5.00 *prices*

also perfume, lotion, talc, soap, shave cream

Paying homage to René Magritte's famous Surreal painting *Use of Words* 1 (1929), which features a straightforward representation of an man's pipe with the words "*Ceci n'est pas un pipe*" written underneath, Schiaparelli launched a perfume for men called *Snuff* in 1939. Presented in a small cardboard box designed as a cigar box that opened to reveal a bed of straw and a man's crystal glass pipe filled with a dry, sober scent, the concept of a fragrance designed exclusively for the male market was yet another Schiaparelli first. The range continued with a collaboration with Dalí, who designed the elaborate bottle for *Le Roy Soleil*, based on a large golden clam shell that opened up to reveal the perfume inside.

Schiaparelli's imaginative series continued with many other perfumes, including *Succès Fou*, *Si*, *S* and *Zut*, which came in a bottle designed to complement the erotic *Shocking* torso, shaped instead to suggest the curvy lower half of a woman's body.

Opposite Marcel Vertès produced sketches for all the different products Schiaparelli needed to advertise, as she thought his spontaneous fresh style of illustration perfectly encapsulated her brands. This was a 1950s advertisement for *Snuff*, designed for the British market.

Below *Snuff* was launched in 1939, the first perfume designed exclusively for the male market. The bottle was shaped to form a man's smoking pipe, and it came beautifully wrapped up in a cigar box. The chypre scent was visible in the shaft of a crystal-glass pipe and the stopper was cork.

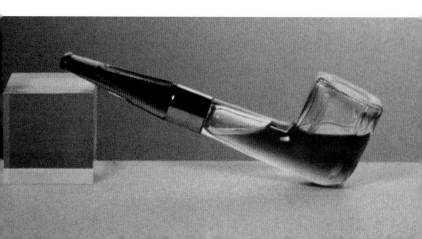

Schiaparelli's new perfume sensation ...100% imported from France

Above The perfume *Zut* was launched in 1949 and the bottle designed to complement the naked torso Schiaparelli had used years earlier for *Shocking*. It showed a woman's lower body standing immersed in a fluffy white cloud with stars.

Opposite The elaborate bottle for *Le Roy Soleil* was designed by Dalí in 1946. The sweet jasmine-smelling scent came in a bottle that represented the Sun King's face, presiding over a wavy blue sea with birds and fishes. Vertès produced the witty illustration.

This page In February 1947 *Vogue* magazine showed this double-page illustration of all the important perfumes of the era. Among the grand fashion houses of the day is Schiaparelli with her perfume *Shocking*, which outstripped all its competitors when launched.

JOY de PATOU

CALYPSO de RAULOUR

ANTILOPE de WEIL

BANDIT de ROBERT PIGUET

FEMME de MARCEL ROCHAS

LE CHIC DE MOLYNEUX

N° 7 D'ANNY BLATT

IMAGINATION de VIOLET

SOIR de PARIS de BO...

MUSE de COTY

PRÈS DU COEUR PIERRE DUNE

COEUR JOIE de NINA RICCI

ATTENTE VERLAYNE

PRÈS de VOUS de RIGAUD

TRANSPARENT D'HOUBIGANT

ESPOIR de PAGUIN

IRIS de JACQUES FATH

POLO TEN de KNIZE

CARAVANE de BIENAIMÉ

VŒU de NOËL de CARON

JONTHLÉGE de LE GALION

Le Bouquet.

A Revival for the Twenty-First Century

An exhibition held at New York's Costume Institute of The Metropolitan Museum of Art in 2012 did much to boost the fading reputation of Schiaparelli, highlighting the forgotten genius of a woman who was, after all, one of the most famous couturières in Paris between the 1920s and '50s. *Schiaparelli and Prada: Impossible Conversations* examined the work of two iconic Italian fashion designers, looking at the similarities and disparities of both women's creative output, how they engaged with contemporary artists, embraced the paradoxes of fashion and challenged the concept of beauty by popularizing "ugly" aesthetics. Showcasing Schiaparelli's unique modernity, with exhibits that included her surreal Shoe-Hat, black crêpe Skeleton Dress with padded ribs and spine, severe tailoring and exquisite use of embroidery, the successful exhibition reinforced her influence within contemporary fashion and reminded the public of her innovative embrace of Surrealist humour.

Opposite Blazing down the catwalk for Bertrand Guyon's collection for Autumn/Winter 2018, this Schiaparelli pink gown symbolizes the mix of tradition and innovation that has come to characterize the house's revival.

Overleaf left The Schiaparelli and Prada exhibition at New York's Metropolitan Museum of Art in 2012 reminded everyone that Schiaparelli, though a champion of colour, was not afraid to use black, as seen here in her suits from the late 1930s.

Overleaf right Outfits from the famous Circus collection from 1938 were on display at the Schiaparelli and Prada exhibition. Free-form, childlike drawings enliven a silk crepe evening gown with matching cape, with dancing horses and acrobat buttons used as detailing on the silk twill jacket.

In tribute to Elsa, the French couturier Christian Lacroix was asked to design a one-off haute couture collection for the House of Schiaparelli to honour the woman who had been so important in shaping his own career. Known throughout the late 1980s and 1990s for his exceptional use of clashing colour and his signature inclusion of giant oversized bows, Lacroix was a perfect choice to create a stunning, 18-piece collection in homage to the woman who had regularly shocked the world with her outlandish ideas. In July 2013 during the Paris couture presentations, Lacroix revealed his spectacular pieces (not for sale), shown on mannequins on a revolving carousel, in the magnificent setting of the Pavillon de Flore, part of the Palais du Louvre. Guests arrived through a recreated version of the bamboo cage that Jean-Michel Frank had originally designed for Schiaparelli's atelier, with electronic birdsong projected through a canopy of foliage and flowers. Not wanting simply to re-present the trademarks of Lobster print and Shoe-Hat for which Schiaparelli had become so famous, Lacroix looked elsewhere for inspiration, choosing instead to reference her flamboyant use of colour, love of circus motifs and exaggerated silhouettes. Lavish embroidery, oversized pockets, conical Pierrot pom-pom hats and clever juxtaposition of colour were evident in Lacroix's modern take on Schiaparelli, all of which served as a brand teaser, helping to raise the profile of the house in preparation for the appointment of a new design director later that year.

Opposite This spectacular evening dress in bold pink and black stripes, made from duchess satin, evokes the daring spirit of Schiaparelli at her best. It was designed by Christian Lacroix, with eye-catching details of rosette corsage and voluminous bustle.

Italian designer Marco Zanini was announced in October 2013 as the creative director of Schiaparelli, and clearly understood the significance of the complex challenge he was undertaking. While adhering to the spirit of Schiaparelli, he needed to create brand awareness for a name that was revered within the fashion world but which lacked the global profile of others in the luxury market. The challenge to ignite a label that had been dormant for so many years was a privilege, he told *Vogue*'s Lynn Yaeger, but also felt like "a total start up". His wildly creative imagination would be applauded, but Zanini was criticized for designs that played too literally in reflecting Schiaparelli's oeuvre and were considered unwearable, and his tenure was short-lived. Thirteen months later, the house announced the end of its collaboration with the designer.

They had already lined up a replacement, named the following year as Bertrand Guyon, an experienced fashion creative who had previously worked at Givenchy, Lacroix and Valentino. Guyon joined as design director at Schiaparelli in April 2015 and was credited with making the brand more accessible while still retaining elements of the daring innovation that was the trademarks of its founder. He launched the ready-to-wear line, was adept at reimagining the signatures of the house such as trompe l'oeil shadows and sunburst iconography, and steadily built up a significant celebrity fanbase. Guyon re-established a strong identity for the couture house, with intelligent collections that appealed to the fashion sensibilities of actors like Tilda Swinton and Cate Blanchett, who were happy to wear Schiaparelli on the red carpet.

Opposite Mannequins shown on a revolving carousel, wearing Christian Lacroix's unique collection designed to honour Schiaparelli, were presented in Paris during the couture collections in 2013.

Above This detail on a satin
evening gown references
Schiaparelli's acclaimed Circus
collection from 1938, reinterpreted
for the 2016 haute couture Autumn/
Winter show.

Opposite This updated reinvention,
in the form of an exaggerated
shoulder line, leopard skin prints
and pannier-like pockets, appeared
on the catwalk for Bertrand Guyon's
collection for Autumn/Winter 2018.

Left Designed by Daniel Roseberry to reflect her "strength and honour", Michelle Obama appeared in this acid yellow, haute couture gown at the American Portrait Gala. The statement dress, with fitted bodice and sweetheart neckline, is decorated with crystal bead overlay.

Opposite Appearing at the Venice Film Festival in 2018, Tilda Swinton chose a bias-cut gown with bold leopard-print type pattern, from the Autumn/Winter haute couture collection. Surreal, glove-like detailing on the sleeves and matching shoes completes the look.

Left Sunburst iconography, a recognized trope of the house, was made famous in Schiaparelli's Zodiac collection from 1938. It is referenced in a strikingly modern way for a new generation of fans in 2017.

So a statement issued by Schiaparelli, thanking Guyon "for his contribution to the haute couture activity of the House", surprised everyone when it was released in April 2019. A week later the company announced Daniel Roseberry as his successor, responsible for all collections and projects at the prestigious headquarters at the Place Vendôme. Having previously spent over a decade working for Thom Browne in Manhattan, the 33-year-old, Texan-born designer was the first American to head up an established French couture house. His debut collection came just two months later, where he showcased his vision for the brand, determined to focus on a modern take of Schiaparelli's individual spirit of irreverence and innovation, rather than get too heavily mired in the mythology of her iconography.

His assured start showcased a multitude of fantasy ideas, manipulated fabrics and prints, and utilized embroidery, feathers and gemstones in a collection that was notable for statement jewellery, exquisite tailoring and gravity-defying touches of artistic genius. It laid a bold foundation for what was to come and was heralded a great success by the fashion press. Speaking to Tim Blanks in September 2020, Roseberry explained his mission for the house was to "honour and embody Elsa Schiaparelli's ethos", insisting that to simply replicate what she did "would be a very arrogant disaster". Sketching original ideas on paper, then transferring them to a computer to construct an analogue digital collage, creates a modern chemistry for Roseberry, who feels this is a way to enrich his design process. Every stage of his creative procedure is beautifully documented on the official website and his Instagram postings, a conscious decision to enable his customers and fans to engage with his vision.

His ambition to push the Schiaparelli boundaries, and allow the world to feel part of his exciting journey to turn the house into one of the most influential of the twenty-first century, is well under way.

Opposite Excessive volume was showcased in the finale of Daniel Roseberry's debut show for Schiaparelli in 2020, in the form of this surreal, gravity-defying, rose pink, taffeta evening dress.

Above Lady Gaga in haute couture at Joe Biden's inauguration ceremony in January 2021. Her cashmere collarless jacket, designed to keep her vocal cords free, was decorated with a large gold dove holding an olive branch.

Index

Page numbers in *italic* refer to illustration captions.

accessories 44, 109, 116–37
    bags *129*
    belts *37*, 63, *129*
    gloves *5*, *20*, *37*, 51, *68*, *79*, *114*, 118, *130*, *131*
    scarves *20*, 27, 32, *123*
    sunglasses *130*
Adrian, Gilbert 90
advertisements, perfume *139*, *140*, *143*, *144*, *147*, *148*
Alvarez, Lili de 22, *23*
art movements
    Cubism 22
    Dadaism 14, 16, 71
    Fauvism 48
    Futurism 22
    Surrealism 7, 14, *52*, *58*, 71–81, *85*, *131*, 140, *144*, 147
art, works of *see* paintings
astrological motifs 60, *68*
autobiography *see* *Shocking Life*

Bacall, Lauren 89
Barnum, PT 55
Beaton, Cecil 73, *80*
Bérard, Christian 60, *68*, 72
Berenson, Marisa *15*, 109
Blanchett, Cate 159
Boivin *133*, *134*
boleros *5*, 55, *58*
Bonwit Teller 99–100
boots *41*, 118, *129*
bottles, perfume *139*, 140, *144*, 147, *147*, *148*, *150*
boxes, perfume *143*
bustles *62*
butterfly motifs 51, *52*, 89
buttons *25*, 48, 55, *55*, *57*, 66, *103*, *104*, *114*, *129*, 159

Cacciapuoti, Gino 109
capes and wraps *31*, 32, *32*, 60, *68*, *114*
Casares, María *17*
Cash and Carry collection 99, *100*
celebrities associated with Schiaparelli 88–97
Chanel, Gabrielle "Coco" 16, 19, 22, 41, 71, 84, 139
Circus collection 54–9, *71*, 76, *153*, *160*
Claire, Ina 28
Clement, Jean 48, *66*
coats 32, *82*, *87*, *93*, *100*, *109*, *114*
Cocteau, Jean 16, 71, 72, *82*, 84, *85*
Colbert, Claudette 89
Colcombet 41
collars 32, 55, *104*, *109*, *111*, *114*
collections
    Cash and Carry 99, *100*
    Circus 54–9, *71*, 76
    Commedia dell'Arte 63, *86*, *87*
    early 18–25
    Eskimo 51
    Metamorphosis 51, *52*
    Music 63–8
    Pagan 60, 117, *122*
    Stop Look and Listen 51
    Zodiac 60, *68*
    post-war *100*, 103, *103*, 109, *114*
colours 48–9
    see also shocking pink *and* sleeping blue
Commedia dell'Arte collection 63, *86*, *87*
costume design *17*, 90, *93*, *97*
Crawford, Joan 89, *94*
culottes *13*, 22, *23*, *25*
cummerbunds 109
Cunard, Nancy 16, 90

Dalí, Gala 90
Dalí, Salvador 55, *58*, 71, *71*, 73–83, 89, *119*, 147, *148*
Dandy look 103

Della Valle Group 109
Desk suit 73, *80*, *130*
Dietrich, Marlene 89, *93*
Dior, Christian 103
dresses 66, 89, *94*, 99
    wrap *23*
    see also eveningwear
dressing gowns *111*
Duchamp, Marcel 15
Dufy, Raoul 17
Duncan, Isadora 14

Edward, Prince of Wales 16
embellishments *57*
    metallic threads *48*, 63, *85*, *104*, *159*
    paillettes *32*, *85*
    pearls *44*, *103*
    rhinestones *58*, *68*, *159*
    sequins 32, *40*, *44*, *48*, *103*, *159*
embroidery 32, *44*, 55, *58*, *60*, 63, 66, *68*, 84, 99, *103*, *123*, *159*
Eskimo collection 51
eveningwear *5*, *7*, 28–40, *44*, *48*, *57*, 60, *60*, *62*, 63, 66, *82*, 84, 99, *99*, *103*, *104*, 109
    Lobster dress *71*, 74, *74*, 89
    Skeleton dress *58*, *71*

Tears dress 55, 74, *76*, 76–7, *79*

fabrics
    fur 32, *41*, *111*, *122*, *129*
    novelty *31*, *32*, 41–2
    printed *57*, *74*, *79*, 89, *109*
fancy-dress *10*, *62*
Fath, Jacques *10*
feathers *7*, *119*, *122*, *137*
Fellowes, Daisy 16, 90, *93*, *119*
films *see* costume design
Fini, Leonor 72, 140
Flanner, Janet 32
Fluid line 109, *114*
footwear *see* boots *and* shoes
fragrances *see* perfumes
Frank, Jean-Michel *143*, 156
Furstenberg, Diane von *23*

Gabor, Zsa Zsa 90, *97*
Galeries Lafayette 20
Garbo, Greta 89
Gaultier, Jean-Paul 109, *139*
Givenchy, Hubert de *62*
Guyon, Bertrand *153*, 159, *160*, 165

harlequin designs *62*, 63, *87*

Harper's Bazaar 72, *123*
Hartley, Mrs 20
hats 20, 32, *37*, *53*, 74, *114*, 117, *119*, *122–3*, *125*
    Mad Cap 28, *37*
    Shoe-Hat 74, 90, 117, *119*
    turban *5*, 27, *117*
Hayes, Blanche 15, 20
Head, Edith 90
Hepburn, Katherine 89
Herbert, Shari *103*
hosiery *see* stockings
housecoats *111*
Hoyningen-Huene, George *7*
Hurricane line *100*, 103
Huston, John 90, *97*

jackets 20, 32, *32*, *37*, *40*, *48*, 55, *57*, *58*, *62*, *68*, 84, *85*, *94*, *103*, *104*, *159*
James, Edward 74
jewellery *94*, *60*, *117*–18, *119*, *123*, *133*, *137*

Kahn, Monsieur 20
knitwear 20, *20*, 22, 27

Lacroix, Christian *58*, 156, *159*
lecture tours 99–100
Leigh, Vivien 89
Lelong, Lucien 99
Lesage, François 84

Lesage, House of *44*, *58*, *60*, *66*, *68*, *82*, *84*, *85*, *99*, *104*, *159*
Lindbergh, Charles 22
lingerie *111*
Lisner, David 117
Lobster dress *71*, 74, *74*, 89
Lockwood, Margaret 90
Loy, Myrna 89, 90

McQueen, Alexander *58*
Mad Cap 28
Magritte, René 147
Maison Lambal 20
Man Ray 14, 15, 16, 63, 71, *86*
Marchand, Paulette *119*
materials, invention in 41–2, 117
Maxwell, Elsa *66*
men, perfume for *see Snuff*
Metamorphosis collection 51, *52*
Metropolitan Museum of Art Costume Institute 153
Meyer, Baron de 15
millinery *see* hats
Molyneux, Edward 99
Mummy silhouette 103
Music collection 63–8

nature motifs 51, *52*, 60, *60*, 89, *103*, *109*, 117, *122*, *133*, *137*
Neagle, Anna 90
New Yorker, The 32

Obama, Michelle *162*
Oberon, Merle 89
Oppenheim, Meret 71

Pagan collection 60, 117, *122*
paintings
The Anthropomorphic Cabinet (Dalí) 73
Le Beaux Temps (Man Ray) 63, *86*
The Burning Giraffe (Dalí) *80*
New York Dream – Man Finds Lobster in Place of Phone (Dalí) 74, *74*
Three Young Surrealist Women Holding in their Arms the Skins of an Orchestra (Dalí) 76, *76*
Use of Words 1 (Magritte) 147
patchwork *62*, *86–7*
Patou, Jean 41, 139
perfumes 109, 138–49, *150*
Perkins, Berinthia *15*, 109
Perugia, André *41*, 118, *126*, *129*
Picabia, Francis 14, 16
Picabia, Gabrielle 14, 16
Picasso, Pablo 16
Place Vendôme, Paris *27*, 43–7, 51, *94*, 100, 103

pockets 73, *80*, *100*, *104*, *114*

Poiret, Paul 16–17, 19, 139
pyjamas 90, *100*
Pyramid line *114*

quilting *58*, *71*

Radnitzky, Emmanuel *see* Man Ray
Rhodophane 41
Rodarte *58*
Rodier 41
Rogers, Millicent *44*, *94*
Roi Soleil (perfume) 144, 147, *148*
Rouff, Maggy *133*, *135*
Roseberry, Daniel 162, 165, *167*
Rubinstein, Helena *58*

S (perfume) 144, 147
Sache 74, *109*
Saint Laurent, Yves 7, 27, 55
Salut (perfume) 39, *143*, 144
Sartres, Jean-Paul *17*
Satie, Erik 16
Schiap 139, 144
Schiaparelli, Elsa 7, *9*, *10*, *51*, *71*, *119*, *123*
autobiography *9*, 17, 22, 27, 48, 76
in London 13, *13*
in New York 13– 15, 71, 100

in Paris 15–49, 70–87, 99, 100, *109*, *117*
personal life
  birth 9
  childhood 9–10
  education 10
  marriage 13–14
  family 9, 10, 13, 15, *15*, 19, 99, 109
  later life 109
  death 109
quotations 32, 48, 50, 71, 78, 89
Schiaparelli, Gogo 13, 15, 19, 99, 109
Schiaparelli, House of 26, *27*, 43–7, *94*
  collaborations 17, *17*, 70–87, *123*, *126*, *129*, 147
  collections 50–69, *71*, *76*, *86–7*, 99, *100*, 103, *103*, 109, *114*, 117, *122*
  war years and closure 63, 99–100, 103, 109
Schiaparelli Inc. 109
Schlumberger, Jean *55*, *133*
separates *see* culottes; jackets; skirts *and* trousers
Shearer, Norma 89
Shocking (perfume) *139*, 140, 144, *150*

Shocking Life 9, 17, 22, 27, 48, 76
shocking pink 48, *48*, 55, *68*, *99*, *111*, *119*, *140*
Shoe-Hat 74, 90, 117, *119*
shoes
  evening *31*
  platform *126*
  sandals *126*
  wedge 118
Si (perfume) 144, 147
silhouette *33*, *37*, 89, *93*, *99*, 103
Simpson, Wallis *74*, *76*, 89, *89*
  see also Wallis, Duchess of Windsor
Skeleton dress *58*, *71*
Skeleton sweater 27
skirts 20, 22, 27, 55, *114*
Sleeping (perfume) 140, 144, *144*
sleeping blue *144*
Snuff (perfume) 144, 147, *147*
Soucis (perfume) 139, 144
sports clothes 18–25
Steichen, Edward 15, *94*
Stieglitz, Alfred 15
stockings 27, 118
Stop Look and Listen collection 51
Strauss store 22
Succès Fou (perfume) 144, 147

suits 32, *37*, *94*, *109*, *114*, *153*
  Desk suit *73*, *80*, *130*
Surrealism 7, 14, *52*,| *58*, 71–81, *85*, *131*, 140, *144*, 147
Swinton, Tilda 159, *162*

Tears dress 55, 74, *76*, *76–7*, *79*
Time magazine 32
trompe-l'oeil *20*, 22, 27, 77
trousers 32
Tzara, Tristan 16

Van Cleef & Arpels *119*
Vertès, Marcel *57*, *97*, *123*, *140*, *143*, *144*, *147*, *148*
Vionnet, Madeleine 20
Vogue magazine *37*, *68*, *72*, *74*, *119*, *150*

Wallis, Duchess of Windsor *129 see also* Simpson, Wallis
Wendt de Kerlor, William de 13–14
West, Mae 90, *93*, *139*, 140
Women's Wear Daily 20

Zanini, Marco 159
zips 51, *100*
Zodiac collection 60, *68*, *164*
Zut (perfume) 144, *148*

Resources

Further Reading

Baudot, François, *Elsa Schiaparelli: Fashion Memoir*, Thames and Hudson, 1997

Baudot, François, *Fashion and Surrealism*, Assouline Publishing, 2001

Blum, Dilys E, *Shocking! The Art and Fashion of Elsa Schiaparelli*, Yale University Press, 2003

Laubner, Ellie, *Collectible Fashion of the Turbulent Thirties*, Schiffer Publishing, 1999

Mackrell, Alice, *Art and Fashion*, Batsford Ltd, 2005

Martin, John, *Fashion and Surrealism*, Thames and Hudson, 1989

Schiaparelli, Elsa, *Shocking Life The Autobiography of Elsa Schiaparelli*, V&A Publications, 2007

White, Palmer, *Elsa Schiaparelli: Empress of Paris Fashion*, Aurum Press, 1986

Collections

Due to the fragility and sensitivity to light, many fashion collections are rotating or on view through special exhibition only. Please see the individual websites for further information.

Phoenix Art Museum
Arizona Costume Institute
McDowell Road and Central Avenue
1625 North Central Avenue
Phoenix, AZ 85004, USA
www.arizonacostumeinstitute.com

The Metropolitan Museum of Art
The Costume Institute
1000 Fifth Avenue
New York, New York 10028-0198, USA
www.metmuseum.org
Many items are part of the the Brooklyn Museum Costume Collection (www.brooklynmuseum.org).

Philadelphia Museum of Art
Costume and Textiles Collection
Main Building
26th Street and the Benjamin Franklin Parkway
Philadelphia, PA 19130, USA
www.philamuseum.org

The Victoria & Albert Museum
Fashion: Level 1
Cromwell Road
London SW7 2RL, UK
www.vam.ac.uk

Acknowledgements

Picture Credits

The publishers would like to thank the following sources for their kind permission to reproduce the pictures in this book.

Key: t=Top, b=Bottom, c=Centre, l=Left and r=Right

Akg Images: /Archives CDA/Guillot: 144
Image Courtesy of The Advertising Archives: 138, 141, 142, 145, 146, 148
Bridgeman Images: /Kunstmuseum, Basel, Switzerland /© Salvador Dalí, Fundació Gala-Salvador Dalí, DACS, 2011: 81, /Philadelphia Museum of Art, Pennsylvania, PA, USA /Gift of Mme Elsa Schiaparelli, 1969: 20, 42, 43, 47, 49, 52, 56, 61, 63, 67, 68, 83, 104, 105, 106, 108, 123, 128, 131t, 131b, /Philadelphia Museum of Art, Pennsylvania, PA, USA /Gift of Mrs Rodolphe Meyer de Schauensee: 64, /Private Collection /Archives Charmet: 150–151, /Private Collection /Photo © Christie's Images /© Man Ray Trust/ADAGP, Paris and DACS, London 2011: 86
Getty Images: 92, 96, /Bettmann: 3, 26, 88, 110, 121, /Stephane Cardinale - Corbis/Corbis via Getty Images 152, 160, 163, 164, 166, /Condé Nast Archive: 6, 18, 29, 36, 38–39, 80, 93, 94, 95, 98, 132, 143, /Julio Donoso/Sygma: 58, / Jonathan Ernst-Pool 167; /Gamma-Keystone: 10, /Francois Guillot/AFP 158, /Julien Hekimian 157, /Hulton Archive: 8, 12, 100, /Genevieve Naylor: 16, 101, 112, 113, /Philadelphia Museum of Art: 74, 75, 78, 85, 87, /Simon Russell 155, /Underwood & Underwood: 23, /Roger Viollet: 30, 107, /Peter White 161, /Paul Zimmerman/ WireImage 154, /Time & Life Pictures: 50, 102, 111, 118, 130
Kerry Taylor Auctions: 114, 115, 129
Mary Evans Picture Library: 125, /National Magazines: 1, 2, 4, 24, 25, 28, 35, 53br, 53tr, 53bl, 65, 84, 120, 124, 126–127, 134–135, /Retrograph Collection: 149
Collection of Phoenix Art Museum, Gift of Mrs John Hammond. Photo by Ken Howie: 40l & 40r
Picture Desk/The Kobal Collection: /Paramount: 91
Shutterstock: /GTV Archive: 97, /Paul Morigi/Invision/AP 162

SuperStock: /© Salvador Dalí, Fundació Gala-Salvador Dalí, DACS, 2011: 76–77
Topfoto.co.uk: 137, 147, /L. Degrâces et P. Ladet /Galliera /Roger-Violet:
31, 69,
Ronald Grant Archive: 90, /ullstein bild: 21, /Roger Viollet: 14, 37, 72, 116
Victoria & Albert Museum/V&A Images – All rights Reserved: 33, 34, 42,
45, 46, 54, 55, 57, 59, 60, 62l, 62r, 66, 70, 79l, 79r, 82, 119, 122, 133,
160, 176

Author Acknowledgements

Thanks go to the superb collections from the Victoria & Albert
Museum, the Philadelphia Museum of Art, the Metropolitan
Museum of Art, the Arizona Costume Institute at the Phoenix
Art Museum and Kerry Taylor Auctions. Special thanks to my
fabulous editor Lisa Dyer and all the team at Carlton Books.

Overleaf Detail of the embroidery
on a plum silk velvet jacket that
was made as part of a suit in 1937.
Lesage produced the exquisite
work with silk and metallic threads,
rhinestones and tiny sequins. The
bright pink floret-shaped buttons
are functional as well as decorative
and are made from metal.

LITTLE BOOK OF

Christian
Louboutin

Darla-Jane Gilroy is programme director in the School of Design and Technology at London College of Fashion. She was previously course leader of the Cordwainers Footwear and Accessories BA and senior tutor in footwear and accessories at the Royal College of Art, and as a fashion designer her work has been exhibited in the V&A. She lives in London.

First published in 2021 by Welbeck
An Imprint of HEADLINE PUBLISHING GROUP

13

Cataloguing in Publication Data is available from the British Library
ISBN 978-1-78739-739-2

Printed and bound in China

Headline's policy is to use papers that are natural, renewable and recyclable products and made from wood grown in well-managed forests and other controlled sources. The logging and manufacturing processes are expected to conform to the environmental regulations of the country of origin.

HEADLINE PUBLISHING GROUP
An Hachette UK Company
Carmelite House
50 Victoria Embankment
London EC4Y 0DZ

www.headline.co.uk
www.hachette.co.uk

LITTLE BOOK OF

Christian
Louboutin

The story of the iconic shoe designer

DARLA-JANE GILROY

WELBECK

CONTENTS

A Legend 06

Early Life 18

Birth of a Brand 20

The Red Sole 40

Career Highlights 52

Signature Styles for Women 78

The Sneaker Revolution 94

Something for the Boys 104

Collaborations 118

Celebrity Success 134

Index 156

Credits 160

A Legend

GLOBAL RENOWN

"Most people see shoes as an accessory to walk in,
however some shoes are made for running …
and some shoes are made for sex."
Christian Louboutin, designmuseum.org

Christian Louboutin is a Paris-based luxury footwear
designer known for the edgy design, distinctive materials,
delicate embellishments and perilously high heels of his shoes.
His work is inspired by his eclectic and nomadic lifestyle,
drawing creative ideas while on travels between his homes in
Portugal, Egypt and France. Lifelong passions for horticulture,
punk rock and architecture also inspire his work, in which
he uses colour and texture – with an intriguing mixture of
discretion and enthusiasm – to create well-crafted, original

OPPOSITE Christian Louboutin does his greatest creative work in the
mornings, drawing hundreds of design sketches for each season as the
first step in his creative process, before selecting his best designs to put
together into themed collections for Spring/Summer or Autumn/Winter.

shoes. A shy renaissance man, Louboutin is an accomplished tap dancer and trapeze artist in addition to being one of the world's premier designers of luxury footwear.

Louboutin's global reputation for exquisite design and quality means he needs little introduction, even to those with scant fashion knowledge. He is one of the few designers who maintains creative control and ownership of his business: since 1991, he has been the creative visionary behind the Louboutin footwear empire. The resulting liberty this gives him to respond to, and direct, the fashion landscape around him is critical. "The most important thing is freedom. So why would you give away something so important if you don't need to?" he said to the *Belfast Telegraph*.

Christian Louboutin's footwear is favoured by the world's most stylish women, and his creations have been worn by everyone from Princess Caroline of Monaco, Queen Máxima of the Netherlands and the Duchess of Cambridge to Rihanna, Madonna, Gwyneth Paltrow, Jennifer Lopez and Sarah Jessica Parker.

Louboutin helped to fuel the noughties obsession with designer shoes and "It" bags with his trademark lipstick-red soles. This signature detail makes the brand instantly distinguishable; that the cult shoes are synonymous with luxury and celebrity doesn't hurt either. Louboutin's footwear places the focus firmly on the feet, elevating any outfit.

Every pair of Louboutin shoes are made in a factory in Italy, which employs highly skilled artisans using traditional shoemaking techniques consisting of up to 30 manufacturing

ABOVE Louboutin's shoes are constructed around "lasts", made from wood or plastic, in the shape of a foot. Before the "upper" is formed around the last, an "insole" is attached to the bottom of the last. Stiff material at the heel and toe is placed inside the upper to help retain the shoe's shape. Finally, a heel and sole are attached.

processes. They use the best leathers and precious fabrics, like cashmere and silk grosgrain, that are then cut into pattern pieces, sewn together and crafted to bring the designer's dynamic drawings to life.

Each year, Louboutin sketches an average of 600 designs and produces over 1,000,000 pairs of shoes in his factory. The top part of the shoe, or the "upper", can be made of as many as 12

BELOW Once design drawings are finalized, each style is made into a pattern of individual pieces that are hand cut for every part of the shoe and ready to be stitched together.

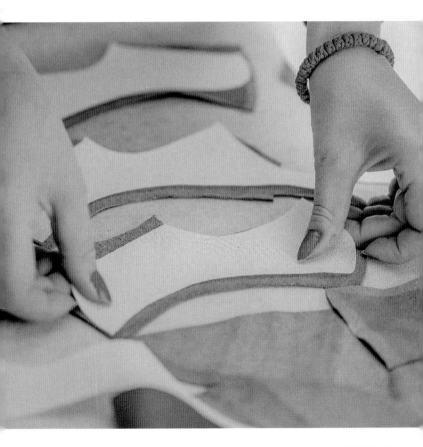

different materials, so sewing it together requires every stitch, just a few millimetres apart, to be incredibly precise in order to do justice to the intricate designs. To create the permanent shape of the shoe, the upper is formed around a wooden "last" shape representing the shape of a foot. Louboutin's father was a carpenter, which may account for his passion for the craft of shoemaking and expert knowledge of wooden last-making. Each last is individual to a specific design, and used to achieve a perfect fit.

> "I've always loved the shape of lasts – the concave
> and convex, the yin and the yang."
> Christian Louboutin, coolhunting.com.

BELOW Every style and size of shoe needs to be made on a pair of lasts to produce a left and right shoe and have a distinctive toe shape. In Louboutin's case, the shoes do not reflect the natural shape of a human foot, but add a touch of fashion through pointed, round or almond toe-shaped lasts.

RIGHT Even Louboutin's lasts are red. Each pair has a set of unique characteristics that replicate a particular toe shape and fit to make the shoe comfortable to wear.

ABOVE Christian Louboutin has luxurious boutiques in over 35 countries worldwide that showcase his collections in boudoir-style intimate spaces, featuring bold details like his signature crimson carpets, pictured here in 2015 at his Greater Manchester store in the UK.

Heels are then added, along with the famous red sole, and each shoe is polished and inspected to make sure it will form a perfect pair of shoes that meet Louboutin's exacting standards.

The shoes sell in some of the most exclusive shops in the world and through the designer's own branded stores in over 35 countries, and in cities including Paris, London, New York and Moscow. Louboutin has resisted lucrative offers to dilute his brand through high street collaborations. Of this decision, he told the *Evening Standard*, "You can do a low-budget line with a beautiful design. My problem is that I am really obsessed with quality." While it's true that the brand's shoes are costly – some of the most expensive pairs sell for £4,200 ($6,000) – but they are exquisitely made through a marriage of design and craftsmanship. Customers gain an entrée into the exclusive club of Louboutin with their purchase; demand for the shoes outstrips production, giving them a high resale value and consequently emphasizing the soundness of the investment.

In addition to the famous red soles, Louboutin shoes are also known for their impossibly high heels. The designer was quoted in *The Sunday Times* as saying, "One has to suffer to be beautiful." This may be true of some of his dominatrix-inspired museum pieces, but as an intern working with showgirls at

BELOW Christian Louboutin at a reception in 2010 at The Corner boutique in Berlin. He is holding a transparent shoe decorated with strass crystals in front of an array of styles, including stiletto-heeled pumps, wedge heels, boots and ankle-strap shoes.

BELOW TOP The
stitching of the top,
or upper, of a shoe is a
delicate process that
requires accuracy to
match pattern pieces
together, forming an
upper that fits exactly
onto the last.

the Folies Bergère music hall, he was sent to buy meat to
cushion the toes of the dancers' shoes, so is well versed in ways
to build comfort and wearability into his shoes. Louboutin
manufactures his women's shoes up to EU size 42 (UK size
9 and US size 12), because of the cross-gender demand for
his heels, and produces his sneaker ranges in smaller sizes for
the same reason, supporting the development of a new, more
inclusive approach to gendered products.

Though less well known, men's
shoes, flat ballerina-style pumps and
handbags are included in the product
range. The brand has also embraced
the athleisure trend, creating
technical sneakers for the Spring/
Summer 2019 season. Casual shoe
ranges are already well established
and include loafers and slipper styles,
all with his unmistakable red sole.

Louboutin is a craftsman,
designer and pioneer with a strong
desire to create objects of beauty,
not merely add to a mountain of
meaningless items. "I think that this
is almost a duty; if you make a new
object, it should be beautiful because

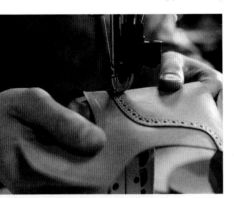

LEFT Louboutin's love of bold colour
combinations and his eye for quality are
reflected in his vibrant colour palettes and
the fine-quality leather skins he selects to
make his shoes.

there is so much crap. I'm not talking of fashion, I'm talking in general. It's important for the environment that if you add things, they should be beautiful," he told coolhunting.com. His sustainable view of design has led to "Loubi World", Christian Louboutin's collaboration with Korean gaming application Zepeto, which hosts virtual presentations of his new collections.

LEFT One of the world's most successful and well-known designers, Christian Louboutin has maintained his creative spark designing men's and women's footwear and accessories for over three decades .

Early Life

YOUNG &
CREATIVE

Christian Louboutin was born in Paris in 1963 and raised
in the bustling and diverse 12th arrondissement, situated
on the right bank of the River Seine. Both of his parents
originally came from Brittany – his father Roger was a
cabinetmaker, and his mother Irene was a homemaker.

He is the youngest of four children and has three sisters.
Louboutin credits them with being instrumental in
developing his appreciation for femininity and for nurturing his
interest in fashion.

In his teens, Louboutin started imagining ideas for footwear,
but a real passion for shoes was first ignited in 1976 when he
visited a Paris museum near his home, then called the Musée
des Arts Africains et Océaniens on the Avenue Daumesnil (the
collection of which is now in the Musée du quai Branly).

The museum contained a collection of extraordinary
sculptures and craft items from Mali, Ivory Coast, and Australasia

OPPOSITE Bas-relief sculptures on the façade of the Palais de la Porte
Dorée. Depicting the diverse people and flora and fauna of France's
colonial history, the sculptures inspired in Christian Louboutin a life-long
love and appreciation for craftsmanship.

in a grand Art Deco building. The building included valuable mosaics and beautiful, intricate wooden parquet floors. In the late 1950s and early 1960s, the fashionable "stiletto" heeled shoes of the day, named after a thin-bladed knife, were banned from the museum in case they damaged the surface of its ornate parquet floors. A simple pictograph sign was used to exclude visitors with stiletto heels, but by the 1970s stiletto heels were no longer fashionable and the sign made no sense to the 13-year-old Louboutin. However, the pictograph captured his curiosity. "I had never seen these kinds of shoes in the 70s," he recalled to *Footwear News*. "How could someone make a sign of a shoe that no longer existed to tell people not to wear them? I became obsessed."

Louboutin began drawing shoes, becoming increasingly aware of the world of fashion – which centred on Paris. He was expelled from school at the age of 16, but always claimed he was glad to leave as he felt so out of place and different from his peers. He then attended Académie d'Art Roederer to study drawing and decorative arts. During this period, he discovered the singer Cher, and is quoted in *Harper's Bazaar* as saying, "I come from another culture – mine is Cher." Around the same time, he also fell in love with the musical and cultural movement of punk rock. Both of these discoveries have had a lasting impact on him creatively, coming through in the gritty stud embellishments and theatricality of his shoes.

By the late 1970s, the young designer had become a regular on the Parisian club scene and appeared in the cult classic film *Race d'Ep*, which was translated into English as *The Homosexual Century*. He got himself noticed on the fashion scene by becoming part of the "Bande de Bandeaux" or the "Headband Gang". The Bande de Bandeaux were a group of avant-garde

LEFT Christian
Louboutin and
fellow "Bande de
Bandeaux" clubbers
attend the famous
Parisian nightclub Le
Palace, 1978.

fashionistas who frequented the legendary Parisian nightclub Le Palace. Le Palace was the French equivalent of New York's Studio 54: anyone who was anyone wanted to be seen there. The club's clientele included international celebrities like Andy Warhol, Mick and Bianca Jagger, Paloma Picasso, Jean Paul Gaultier, Loulou de la Falaise and Roland Barthes, who were all regulars. The 15-year-old Louboutin managed to talk his way into the opening of the club in 1978 and recalled in *The Face*, "I was there for the opening – Grace Jones was playing." The Bande de Bandeaux were welcomed by Fabrice Emaer, owner of Le Palace, who encouraged their individuality and outrageous dress. Louboutin claims he was there "pretty much every night" during the club's heyday from 1979 until 1981, making a new costume to wear each night.

Louboutin went on to work in the dressing rooms of the Folies Bergère, the famous cabaret music hall with a history of outrageous dance reviews stretching back to 1867. Their revues featured revealing costumes and extravagant headdresses, sets and special effects that appealed to his sense of drama and glamour. Louboutin was astonished at the ability of the showgirls to remain poised and sure-footed while wearing high heels and huge feather headdresses, and soon realized how strong his interest in footwear was.

After a period of travelling, Louboutin's fascination with world cultures grew, particularly with Egyptian culture. Years later, after his parents had both died, he would discover his own mixed ethnicity – his biological father had been an Egyptian, rather than the Parisian carpenter who had brought him up. His travels through India inspired him to put together a portfolio of creative ideas and intricate shoe designs and gave him the creative impetus to seek work as a designer.

Back in Paris in 1982, he took his portfolio to the top couture houses of the day. His efforts were rewarded when his talent was spotted by Charles Jourdan, a leading footwear designer of the period who offered him a job as a freelance designer and thus began his career. Louboutin's career went from strength to strength, as he worked for many of the most influential designers of the time, including Chanel, Yves Saint Laurent and Maud Frizon. In 1983, he started working for Christian Dior and in 1987, he met master shoe designer Roger Vivier, who had worked with Christian Dior in the 1950s. Vivier was credited as the inventor of the stiletto heel, whose image had intrigued the 13-year-old Louboutin at the Musée des Arts Africains et Océaniens. Louboutin knew Vivier's work well; Vivier admired Louboutin's talent. He offered the younger man an apprenticeship for the next two years, becoming his friend and mentor in the process. "Vivier taught me that the most important part of the shoe is the body and the heel. Like good bone structure, if you get that right, the rest is makeup," Louboutin later told *Newsweek*.

BELOW Punk-rock influences are a recurrent theme in Christian Louboutin's work, where he draws influences from spike studs, reflective materials like black patent leather and bright neon colours that are synonymous with punk.

Birth of
a Brand

BEGINNINGS OF AN ICON

For a period in the late 1980s, Christian Louboutin took
a career break from shoe designing and turned his
attention to horticulture.

Louboutin's flair for colour, texture and form was easily
translated into imaginative designs for landscaping gardens.
He regularly contributed his ideas to *Vogue*, but it was not
long before he returned to his greatest passion, shoe design,
and started to create his own collections. He readily admitted
that he "didn't have the patience to wait for a seedling to grow
five meters high". His first shoe was influenced by the tropical
aquarium in the basement of the Palais de la Porte Dorée, the
Art Deco museum which he frequently visited as a child. He
was fascinated by the exotic, iridescent fish in the aquarium,
prompting him to use fish-skin-patterned leather and create a
different silhouette for the shoe and heel of his "Mackerel" shoe
in 1987. The French word for "mackerel" (*"maquereau"*) is slang

OPPOSITE Christian Louboutin originally started designing his own
collections in 1991. He is pictured here with his collection for Spring/
Summer 2010.

for "pimp", which added a risqué sexual innuendo to this first shoe, a practice which has become a recurring theme of Louboutin's work.

Louboutin went on to launch his own company with the help of two friends in 1989. Two years later, on 21 November 1991, he opened a small eponymous boutique in Paris, on Rue Jean-Jacques Rousseau in the 1st arrondissement.

One of his first customers was Princess Caroline of Monaco, who wandered into his store one day. She was overheard gushing about Louboutin's shoes by a fashion journalist who also happened to be in the boutique at the same time. Thanks to the patronage of the Princess and the resulting press coverage, Louboutin's relationship with celebrity clients was cemented,

RIGHT Andy Warhol's Pop Art silkscreen print *Flowers* proved to be the creative motivation behind the "Pensée" (pansy) shoe, with its simple but effective graphic pansy design. It was worn by Christian Louboutin's first celebrity client, Princess Caroline of Monaco.

and he was firmly established as shoe designer to stars such as Diane von Furstenberg and Catherine Deneuve, who both became devotees of his stiletto heels. Soon, his stilettos were bought by the likes of Joan Collins and Madonna, to be followed by Gwyneth Paltrow, Jennifer Lopez, Nicki Minaj, Kim Kardashian and Christina Aguilera.

From the first store in Paris in 1991, Louboutin built a network of over 70 stores around the world, all boasting luxurious architectural design and bold façades. He opened his first of 15 American stores in New York in 1994, before opening stores in London (1997) and Moscow (2002), as well as stores in Jakarta, Las Vegas, Paris, Tokyo, and Singapore in the years following.

OPPOSITE The
inseparable "LOVE"
shoes were designed
in 1992, inspired by
the image of Princess
Diana sitting alone
and loveless during her
visit to the Taj Mahal
in India. Louboutin
wrote "LO" on one
foot and "VE" on the
other so the pair of
shoes spelled the word
"LOVE" when placed
together.

He added his legendary red soles in 1992 and has since said, "I wanted to create something that broke rules and made women feel confident and empowered."

Throughout the 1990s and early 2000s, Louboutin revived the stiletto heel by designing a range of extraordinarily high shoes embellished with bows, beads, feathers and studs, but he first attracted global attention for a beautifully crafted pair of quirky flat pumps he called "inseparables". This is a footwear-industry term for a single design that runs across the vamp (top) of a pair of shoes to create one complementary image, making each shoe "inseparable" from its partner. The Louboutin Inseparables became known as the "LOVE" shoes and are said to have been inspired by a photograph of Princess Diana that was taken in front of the Taj Mahal in India in 1992. In the documentary *Christian Louboutin: The World's Most Luxurious Shoes*, he recalled: "She was looking at her feet, and I thought she looked so sad, I thought it would be nice for her to have something to make her smile when she looked at her feet." Louboutin observed and set to work to create a pair of flat pumps. He drew a pair of shoes and placed "LO" on one foot and "VE" on the other so that when the feet were placed together to mirror Princess Diana's pose, the word "LOVE" would be spelled out.

The concept of the Inseparables continues to appear in Louboutin's collections to this day, but has been taken to a new level by the "Tattoo Parlors" located in his men's shops. Bespoke designs can be embroidered across a pair of loafers, sneakers or signature brogues that then take three months to be created by artisans in Italy and India. The service has been so popular that it is also available to women on flats, sneakers, ankle boots and pumps.

Louboutin has always resisted offers to license his name, but his creative ambitions have seen him expand his reach in fashion through brand extensions, the first of which came when he branched out into handbags in 2003. His bags boasted all the opulent embellishments, eye-catching hardware and expert craftsmanship of his shoes, and also featured crimson linings to mirror the soles of his shoes. Every Hollywood A-lister with a pair of Louboutin's red-soled shoes would now be able to carry his bags. His "Paloma" tote proved to be the best "grab and go" bag for running around town, and his "Rougissimie" was an instant red-carpet hit.

In 2011, he launched a line of men's shoes at a new exclusive store in Paris. There are different accounts given as to why Louboutin created a men's line. The first tells of a woman who asked Louboutin to create a bespoke pair of shoes in EU size 43.5 (UK size 10.5, US size 12.5) but she never collected them so he gave them to a friend's husband. The second account credits the singer MIKA for the idea of starting a men's line when he asked Louboutin to design all the shoes for his musical tour. Whatever the reason, Louboutin's eye for details, aesthetic, obsession with craftsmanship and with quality materials have made his men's line as desirable and durable as his women's range.

In order to grow his business but still retain creative control, Louboutin formed relationships with companies that have the expertise to develop and market new products that complement his footwear collections. Inevitably Louboutin turned his eye to creating his own cosmetics and partnered with Batallure Beauty LLC in 2012 to launch Christian Louboutin Beauté in July 2014. The new company presented a range of nail polishes exclusively

BELOW The "Espelio" has a platform wedge heel generously covered with metal fringing and a loosely knotted T-bar upper, made from specchio (mirrored) leather, that fastens around the ankle. It remains one of the most recognized Louboutin shoes because of its striking silhouette.

BELOW A display of lipsticks in 38 colour-matched shades to suit a range of skin tones, including Christian Louboutin's signature lacquer-red hue all packaged in his unique glass containers inspired by Babylonian architecture.

OPPOSITE Singer MIKA wearing black Oxfords with gold studs and brocade detailing at the 2010 BRIT Awards.

offering Rouge Louboutin, his signature red shade, at Saks Fifth Avenue in New York. Like his red soles, the products received attention for their provocative, sculptural packaging, which reflected the brand's characteristic wit and passion for innovation.

In 2015, he expanded his beauty brand to include a lipstick collection featuring 38 shades. Its packaging was inspired by Babylonian architecture and Middle Eastern antiquities. In 2016, Louboutin added fragrances – Bikini Questa Sera, Tornade Blonde and Trouble in Heaven – with bottles designed by Thomas Heatherwick.

In 2017, Louboutin introduced his limited edition collection of red-soled baby shoes in partnership with Gwyneth Paltrow's Goop brand. The Loubibaby collection featured scaled-down Mary-Jane style shoes in pink, red, blue, gold satin and nappa leather, each with a hand-tied bow that were every bit as refined as Louboutin's full-size offerings. He said to *Glamour* of the venture, "Gwyneth is a great partner in crime. When friendship meets work, the results are serious fun."

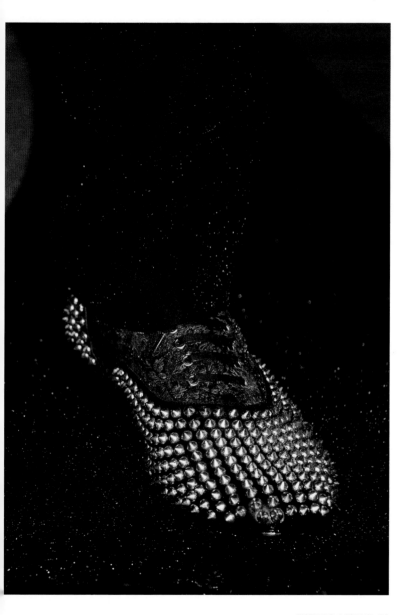

The Red
Sole

RED BOTTOMS

"In 1992, I incorporated the red sole into the design of
my shoes. This happened by accident as I felt that the shoes
lacked energy, so I applied red nail polish to the sole
of a shoe. This was such a success that it
became a permanent fixture."
– Christian Louboutin

The Christian Louboutin brand is instantly recognizable
around the world thanks to its signature red lacquer
soles – now universally understood to be a symbol of luxury
and elegance. However, the birth of the red sole came about by
accident. One afternoon, a prototype of a shoe inspired by Andy
Warhol's artwork *Flowers* arrived at the studio. Louboutin had
always wanted to make a shoe that referenced Warhol's work
and it arrived with a pink upper and heel adorned with a simple
blossom-shaped motif. While it looked similar to his initial
drawing, Louboutin said, "The shoe lacked energy." He noticed
an assistant painting her nails red, which inspired the idea
to paint the sole of the shoe red. Signifying love, passion and

OPPOSITE The red colour is applied to the soles of all Christian
Louboutin shoes using a special lacquering technique known only to his
manufacturers. It adds a perfect, glossy finish to the soles of the shoes,
which are then stamped with his logo and a size.

blood, red was used by Louboutin to create a visual shorthand to empower women, allowing them to break out of societal constraints while wearing his "forbidden shoe".

They have been immortalized in music, such is their cultural significance, including in The Game's "Red Bottoms". Louboutin red even has its own colour code, Pantone 18-1663 TPX.

The status of the red sole should not be underestimated; it is not just a colour but also an attention-grabbing device that draws our eyes to a neglected area of the shoe. The sole of a shoe had always been regarded as purely functional, and not a design or branding opportunity. The genius of Louboutin was to take this previously overlooked part of a shoe and make it not only visually dynamic but also commercially useful in communicating his brand. He has been so successful that today, it is arguable that no single shoe characteristic is as globally recognized as his red sole.

It has provided an ingenious way to unify all of Louboutin's many brand extensions through a single colour that reflects his reputation for opulence, luxury, quality and sexuality.

The lacquer red colour is used on all the soles of all Louboutin

BELOW The Pensée (pansy) shoe was originally designed in 1992. It is said to be the first shoe to have a painted red sole. It remains in Christian Louboutin's range today, reworked into new iterations.

OPPOSITE Influencer Kiwi Lee wears a pair of two-tone banana yellow and black suede "Pensée 85" sandals with a peep toe and a flower detail fastening at the side of the ankle.

OVERLEAF A powerful, repeated visual representation of the red sole, to create a display at the 2020 retrospective of Louboutin's decades of work in Paris.

shoes, men's and women's, the linings of handbags, the colour palettes for cosmetics and the packaging of fragrances. The colour has fuelled a red-sole addiction that sees collectors buy literally thousands of pairs at once. Louboutin claims men find them seductive, commenting, "Men are like bulls. They cannot resist the red sole."

The colour is not obtained by using tanning, the traditional process used to add colour to leather, but instead by using a delicate lacquering process known only to Louboutin's trusted manufacturers. The soles arrive at his factory protected by transparent film to avoid scratching and damage, and this film cover is only removed when the shoes are finished and finally boxed.

However, shoes are not only beautiful, aesthetically pleasing objects, they also have a function – to be worn. The lacquered soles, the herald of the Louboutin brand, will start to wear off as soon as the wearer steps onto a red carpet.

The Leather Spa, a repair facility in Long Island, New York, is known for its craft heritage, unparalleled attention to detail and artisanal expertise of more than 30 years. This state-of-the-art family-run company is known only to those who are lucky enough to own a pristine pair of Louboutin shoes. Each year, they restore the fortunes of thousands of pairs of iconic red-soled shoes, and in so doing, maintain the mystique of the Louboutin brand. They have become famous for helping to preserve, protect or refinish Louboutin soles and estimate that between 400 and 1,000 pairs of Louboutin shoes are refurbished there each month.

These dedicated luxury-leather specialists offer customers a range of different labour-intensive services. Soles can be coated in red rubber that will stay red when the shoes are worn, or customers can have their soles repainted using a delicate process that first sees the upper (top part of the shoe) completely covered for protection. The soles are then very gently sanded to restore the smooth finish to that of an unworn pair of shoes. Finally, four or five coats of red colouring, perfectly matching Louboutin red, are applied, with each coat drying for at least an hour between applications. Customers will have shoes repainted every two to three wears to safeguard their investment in such a prized status symbol and preserve the cachet of their Louboutin shoes.

LEFT The designer's brilliance has been to apply the red sole to a functional and highly visible part of the shoe to signify his brand and make it memorable to customers. The importance of the red sole is such that it now has social currency as well as status in the sphere of fashion, and "red bottoms" has become slang for Christian Louboutin's shoes.

BELOW The only thing better than a pair of red-soled shoes are signed red soles. These signed black calfskin high-heeled pumps with a decorative ribbon detail at the heel were displayed at Barneys department store in Beverly Hills, California in 2008.

With so much importance invested in the global success of his shoes, Christian Louboutin has had his share of imitators. For many years, the red sole has been the subject of litigation.

Christian Louboutin filed his first trademark application in 2001. His attempts to protect his distinctive sole as a registered trademark around the world initially had varying degrees of success. Rejected primarily because of the functional and utilitarian nature of the sole of a shoe – which had been considered essential to a shoe's function and not part of its design aesthetic – it was thus not entitled to trademark protection. In 2007, on his third attempt, Louboutin submitted

a drawing showing a high-heeled shoe, with a red sole clearly marked and the rest of the shoe as a dotted outline. The application described the claimed trademark as "a lacquered red sole on footwear". This time, he was successful and on 1 January 2008, the protection of his red-sole design element was secured in the United States.

The first case he brought was against fellow luxury brand Yves Saint Laurent in 2011. The court decided that a colour could not be a protectable trademark, but this decision was overturned on appeal because of a ruling in an earlier case of colour trademarking, which stated that each case should be determined on

an individual basis. The US Court of Appeals ruled in favour of Louboutin, recognizing the originality with which he had placed the colour red in a context that seemed unusual on a shoe. He then intentionally tied the colour to his products, creating an identifying mark firmly associated with his brand.

Since 1992, Louboutin has monopolized lacquer red soles on his footwear. He has established them as more than just a trademark of red soles on shoes, but a particular shade of red applied to a specific location on a shoe. The Louboutin red sole is not merely ornamental, but has come to symbolize the consistent high quality and design innovation the brand has built over 30 years. Courts around the world have agreed that the soles deserve the protection afforded to conventional trademarks, enabling the company to see off any pretenders to their luxury footwear throne.

Career Highlights

ACHIEVEMENTS AND LANDMARKS TO DATE

Louboutin's commercial success is undeniable. He topped the Luxury Institute's Luxury Brand Status Index for three years in a row, in 2007, 2008 and 2009, labelling his shoes as the most prestigious footwear for women.

L ouboutin became the most widely searched shoe brand online in 2011, and his footwear has graced the feet of celebrities, thought leaders and influencers for decades. Beyond financial success, his shoes have achieved cultural significance that is recognized through the bestowing of awards, the esteem of his peers and exhibitions of his work. Louboutin has received two Fashion Footwear Association of New York (FFANY) awards in 1996 and 2008 and *Footwear News* voted Louboutin Marketer of the Year in 2015 for his "hashtag Louboutin World" social media campaign featuring real customers. Also in 2015, Michael Waldman filmed a documentary for Channel 4

OPPOSITE "Let Me Tell You" (2012) lace-up ankle boot with letters stitched into the upper wrapped around a red platform sole and yellow spike heel displayed in a candy-striped hoop. Design Museum, London, UK, 2012.

BELOW Black
velvet shoes with
transparent straps
and a rhinestone YSL
logo, designed for
Yves Saint Laurent
to mark the fortieth
anniversary of his
luxury brand in 2002.
The shoes were
labelled "Christian
Louboutin for Yves
Saint Laurent Haute
Couture", and the
collaboration was
the only time Saint
Laurent worked with
another designer.

in the UK called *Christian Louboutin: The World's Most
Luxurious Shoes*. Filmed over a year, the behind-the-scenes
documentary gave an insight into Louboutin's creative energy
and determination that have cemented his importance in the
footwear world. Dr Valerie Steele, fashion historian, director
and chief curator of the Fashion Institute of Technology (FIT)
Museum in New York, has said of Louboutin: "Christian
Louboutin is one of the most famous shoe designers in history
and has had a tremendous impact on the fashion business
because he's become almost synonymous with sensuous,
luxurious shoes."

In 2002, Louboutin was asked to create a shoe for Yves
Saint Laurent's farewell haute-couture show. This was a defining
moment in Louboutin's career, marking the only time Saint
Laurent associated his name with that of another designer. The

shoe, named "Christian Louboutin for Yves Saint Laurent Haute Couture 1962–2002" was showcased in the finale of the Spring/ Summer 2002 catwalk show that celebrated 40 years of YSL.

In 2008, New York's prestigious Fashion Institute of Technology, one of the few museums in the world devoted to the art of fashion, mounted a retrospective of his work. *Sole Desire: The Shoes of Christian Louboutin,* in 2008, was the first exhibition devoted to Louboutin in recognition of his global influence as a shoe designer and his contributions to fashion. It celebrated the innovator by documenting a design style that exudes eroticism, recognizing his instinctive ability to respond to his clients' desires through footwear.

ABOVE "Daffodile" pump with a concealed platform, nude-coloured upper and 16-centimetre heel covered with black lace dotted with sequins, included in *The Showgirl* retrospective in 2012.

OPPOSITE Ivory leather, mid-calf-length boot with a lace laser-cut design in the upper, accented with silver spike studs at the heel and across the toe. The top of the boot is trimmed with ivory fur; this boot was included in *The Showgirl* retrospective 2012.

RIGHT Terracotta-coloured calfskin suede high-cut ankle boot (2008), with a central seam through the vamp, a concealed platform and upper, and a heel covered in gold spike studs. Design Museum, 2012.

Four years later in 2012, the Design Museum in London mounted the first UK showcase of Louboutin's work, highlighting his claim that "Every woman wants to be a showgirl." The exhibition was a theatrical experience to mark Louboutin's 20 years as a shoe designer. His glamorous, elegant and powerful footwear was explored through his creative inspirations, grouped together in the themes of transparency, travel, architecture, entertainment and handcraft, in order to capture his artistry.

BELOW As the first ever guest creator at Crazy Horse in Paris, Christian Louboutin created a range of shoes reflecting his love of musical hall, cabaret, and burlesque for a new tableau entitled "Feu" in 2012.

Louboutin released an exclusive capsule collection for the same 20-year anniversary. The collection of 20 shoes and six bags were all reinterpretations of classic Louboutin styles inspired by his love of cabaret, travel and architecture, which have become defining themes in his work. He also became the first guest creator at Crazy Horse to give a different interpretation to the iconic Parisian cabaret. Working with artists and choreographers he created four new original acts for their show, under the heading of "Feu" ("fire"). In the show, he added his vision and flair for theatricality, including a voodoo-inspired dance showing invisible hands caressing the dancer and leaving fluorescent handprints on her body. The show was filmed using 3D technology by director Bruno Hullin.

RIGHT *The Showgirl* retrospective exhibition at the Design Museum explored Christian Louboutin's background in theatre and interest in burlesque, cabaret and circus through a theatrically themed interior, using mirrored carousels surrounded by light bulbs, shown here housing his sheer mesh, strass crystal "Marale" ankle boot.

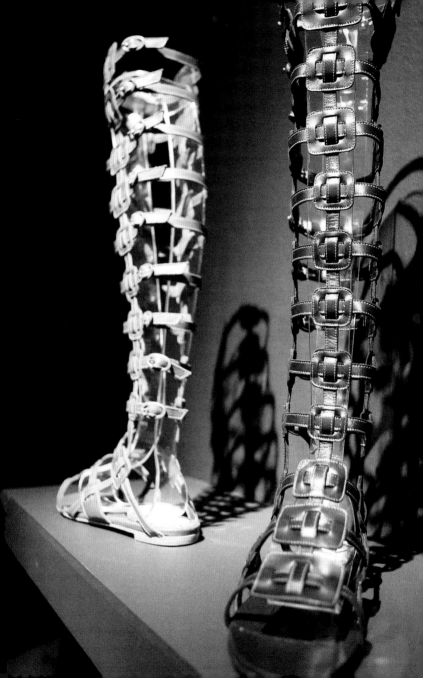

Louboutin was one of the first designers to explore diversity within the fashion industry. In 2013, his "Nudes" collection, originally conceived in 2008, recognized the multicultural nature of his global audiences. He created leather pumps and ballerina flats in a range of skin tones to celebrate different complexions, ranging from dark brown to light pink. Louboutin's "very simple idea" was realized in five skin tones and produced as a collection of inclusive and relevant footwear. Retailers around the world shared his vision for the Nudes collection, recognizing its groundbreaking and celebratory approach to different skin colours. The collection was so successful that it was later extended to seven skin tones in the Spring/Summer 2019 "NudesForAll" collection. Part of the proceeds from the sale of the shoes were subsequently donated to charity.

OPPOSITE Gladiator-style flat knee-length boots that fasten around the leg with a series of straps to contour the calf. Shown here in cream leather and olive green. Design Museum, 2012.

BELOW Blue satin mule-style backless shoe with long ankle ties and decorative feathers on the upper, infused with the glamour of the dancers at the Folies Bergère, on display in the Design Museum in London in 2012.

OVERLEAF A collage of "Nudes" pumps, platform sandals, ankle-strap high heels and transparent duffle bags that celebrate the diversity of skin tones displayed at L'Exhibitioniste in Paris in 2020.

In 2014, a selection of Christian Louboutin's "Fifi" pumps went on display at the Victoria and Albert Museum in London as one of the 12 initial exhibits in the museum's newest Rapid Response Collecting gallery, which is dedicated to a new style of instantaneous curation of work that engages with contemporary issues. In recognition of the success of Louboutin's Nudes, his classic Fifi pump was featured in five tones of nude, becoming a permanent exhibit within the Rapid Response Collecting gallery.

Shortly after, Louboutin designed "Malangeli" for Angelina Jolie's character in the Disney film *Maleficent*. The shoe was sold as a limited edition at selected Christian Louboutin boutiques around the world, and proceeds from the sales were donated to the SOS Children's Villages, a charity supported by Angelina Jolie.

Also in 2014, Louboutin created a design for an iconic handbag using the LVMH "Monogram" motif to celebrate 160 years of Louis Vuitton. In true Louboutin style, his exacting standards in design and craftsmanship created a stylish, studded tote bag accented with his famous lacquer red to highlight every detail.

The bag had a studded front pocket and sophisticated interior compartments, all outlined in red with a red calf-hair back panel. Louboutin also created a larger, "Shopping Trolley" version that included a Louis Vuitton logo clutch bag made of their "Damier" canvas.

In 2019, Christian Louboutin joined the prestigious list of designers to receive the Couture Council Award for Artistry of Fashion. This honour recognized Louboutin's artistry as a designer and the craftsmanship with which his shoes are made, honed by his perspective of valuing global artisanal work. This lens on craft techniques has allowed him to push his creative

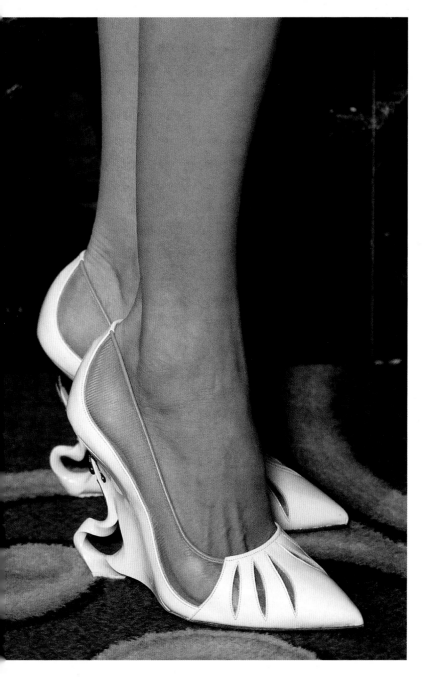

OPPOSITE Christian
Louboutin with
Belgian fashion
designer Diane von
Furstenberg at the
Couture Council
Luncheon where he
received the Couture
Council Award for
Artistry of Fashion
in 2019.

BELOW The ultimate
make-believe
shoe, made from a
transparent mesh
upper embellished
with gold strass
crystals, with
rhinoceros-esque
spike studs across the
toe and at the back
of the gold-snakeskin
platform heel.

boundaries, celebrate inclusivity and value exchanges of different
cultural ideas and techniques.

L'Exhibitioniste, perhaps the most comprehensive
retrospective of all Louboutin's exhibitions, was held at the Palais
de la Porte Dorée, his boyhood haunt in Paris, in 2020–21. It
was this museum that first sparked his curiosity about shoes
and began his lifelong love of the decorative arts. The exhibition
marked a homecoming for Louboutin, returning to his native
Paris as one of the world's most successful shoe designers.
Through an eclectic mix of his inspirations, evident love of Paris,
visual drama and cultural diversity, the show celebrated his work
but not in the way of a conventional retrospective. "It's not a
retrospective about my work. It celebrates collaboration but
not with other brands, rather it's an exchange of ideas with all
the people who have inspired me," Louboutin was reported as

ABOVE London based leather sculptors Whitaker and Malem were commissioned to create leather mannequins in different skin tones. The mannequins fused body and shoe together symbolising how they can become one and were shown as part of l'Exhibitioniste retrospective at Palais de la Porte Dorée, Paris in 2020.

saying in *Footwear News*. Louboutin has been heavily involved in restoring the Palais de Porte Dorée to its former glory.

The exhibition showcased over 400 pairs of his shoes and documented every remarkable moment of Louboutin's career. He assembled artists and artisans from around the world to create commissioned pieces for the show that underscored his love of decorative arts and crafts and respect for originality. Artwork, installations and moving images brought the Louboutin world to life, making his shoes more than just historical pieces. Stained-glass windows featuring his shoes were specially created by glassmaker Emmanuel Andrieux, working with La Maison du Vitrail. London-based leather sculptors Whitaker Malem produced a series of leather sculptures that amalgamated body and footwear using Louboutin's famous Nudes skin tones to symbolize the relationship between body and shoe.

BELOW Reflecting a more frivolous side to the brand, these pumps were first designed in 1994 and have heels inspired by Guinness cans, displayed at *L'Exhibitioniste* retrospective at Palais de la Porte Dorée in Paris in 2020.

BELOW A display of shoes that demonstrate the breadth of styles created by Christian Louboutin over his career. Palais de la Porte Dorée in Paris, 2020.

OVERLEAF A flamboyant neon circus-inspired sign marks the entrance to *The Showgirl*, an exhibition held at the Design Museum in London in 2012 to celebrate 20 years of the Christian Louboutin brand.

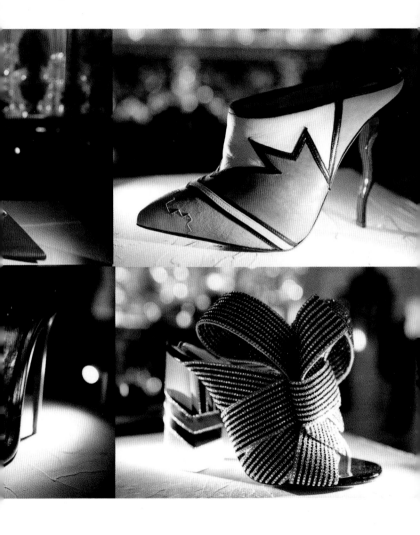

Signature
styles for
women

CLASSICS, KILLER HEELS & FAIRY TALES

The fact that Christian Louboutin's shoes range from classic, elegant high heels like his "Pigalle" pump to edgy, attention-grabbing contemporary footwear like his "Red Runner" sneakers has made him the footwear brand of choice for discerning shoe lovers. His shoes are an alluring mix of sex, glamour, craftsmanship and brand visibility.

Louboutin's design aesthetic can be remixed and reinvented to constantly refresh his collections, which has kept him fashion-relevant and able to speak to each new generation. An industry favourite since he first started designing, Louboutin has a loyal audience of A-listers, from Hollywood's biggest stars to fashion's leading influencers, and his popularity shows no sign of diminishing since he first stepped foot in the fashion spotlight in 1991.

OPPOSITE Black "So Kate" pointy pumps in suede, with 12-centimetre killer stiletto heels. This is the highest heel available by Louboutin, and is available in a range of colours and finishes.

CLASSICS

Louboutin's classic Pigalle pumps come in numerous iterations
and represent an investment in a shoe that is sophisticated
yet sexy. Louboutin described the Pigalle as the design that
encapsulates his career; it works equally well with a pair of
jeans, a day dress or a full-length evening gown. The Pigalle first
debuted in 2004. The 10-cm heel version comes in a range of
finishes, including the ever-popular glossy patent leather with a
classic pointed-toe silhouette and signature red-lacquered sole. It
has proved to be one of his most popular styles, along with the
So Kate pump style. The original Pigalle, the Pigalle Follies and
the So Kate are three of Louboutin's most coveted styles, and
they have become the mainstays of his classic-pump repertoire.
Although very similar, they sport subtle differences in toe length
and heel thickness.

ABOVE A pair of
"Pigalle Follies"
pumps with uppers
made from textured
iridescent leather,
snakeskin and clear
PVC create the illusion
of elongated legs. The
pumps have narrow
ankle straps and
fetish spiked studs at
the toe.

LEFT Actress Hilary
Duff puts confidence
in her stride in a pair
of classic black suede
"Pigalle" pumps with
unmistakable red soles
in New York in 2020.
This elegant shoe
is named after the
Pigalle district in Paris.

SANDALS

Louboutin's flair for design and ability to infuse his shoes with sex is not confined to his stiletto heels. He is equally adept at creating chic, sexy flat shoes and produces a range of sandals, mules and flats that suit the most exotic locations. His "Copte" flats have been popular for beach weddings and parties because of their balance of beach-chic aesthetic and wearability. They come in a range of colours, with a decorative detail across the instep of the foot and a brightly coloured foot bed. Like all Louboutin's shoes, the Copte flats reflect his exquisite standards of craftsmanship, boasting delicate, refined stitching and decorative logo-label details on the inside of the sandal.

KILLER HEELS

The So Kate pumps are the highest heels the brand offers, at 12 centimetres tall. Launched in 2013, So Kate caused a flurry of excitement when it debuted because of its elegant profile and ultra high heel. So Kate now comes in a range of colours, patterns and prints. A pump style like Louboutin's Pigalle and Pigalle Follies, the So Kate is more casual – definitely a "going-out-girl's shoe" that works well with a dressed-down wardrobe. Its stiletto heel and flattering pointed toe makes legs appear longer. So Kate has a longer toe box (the part of the shoe that encases the toes) than the Pigalle and the Pigalle Follies, which both reveal a bit more "toe cleavage" compared to the So Kate.

OPPOSITE Fashion blogger, model and entrepreneur Alexandra Lapp wears the perfect dress-down shoes, beige leather "So Kate" pumps teamed with casual trousers and a polo-neck top in Dusseldorf, Germany, in 2020.

BELOW Neon-pink patent leather "So Kate" pumps with distinctive pointed toes and 12-centimetre spike heels designed to emphasize the arch of the foot.

OPPOSITE Dita Von
Teese wears the nude
"Degrass" leather and
PVC pump, heavily
embellished with
strass crystals, at
her perfume launch
in 2017.

FAIRY TALES

The "Body Strass" is a sensual shoe that is a visual translation
of all the magic, glamour and drama of a fairy tale. It comes in
a killer heel or a refined flat pump. The higher version features
Louboutin's trademark stiletto heel, and both have a barely-
there body of transparent fishnet in nude or black adorned
with strass (a rhinestone made of brilliant glass) and edge-
finished with a delicate leather piping. A firm favourite on the
red carpet, this may not be an everyday shoe, but the Body
Strass has a touch of fairy-tale glamour that draws attention
whenever it makes an appearance.

STILETTOS

The "Bandy" makes a dramatic statement and comes in a range
of playful multicoloured decorative uppers or stunning black-
and-print versions that blend PVC and metallic calfskin leather.
An extravagant yet elegant accessory that becomes the focus
of any outfit, the Bandy is the perfect starting point for brand
loyalty. It's the ideal first shoe for a new Louboutin customer,
alongside one of the newest additions: the "Hot Chick" patent-
leather stiletto offered in vibrant colours. The Hot Chick pump
has a flattering distinctive scallop-top line that frames the foot
and gives the shoe a lighthearted, youthful feel but continues
Louboutin's love of uncompromising femininity combined with
a contemporary stiletto heel.

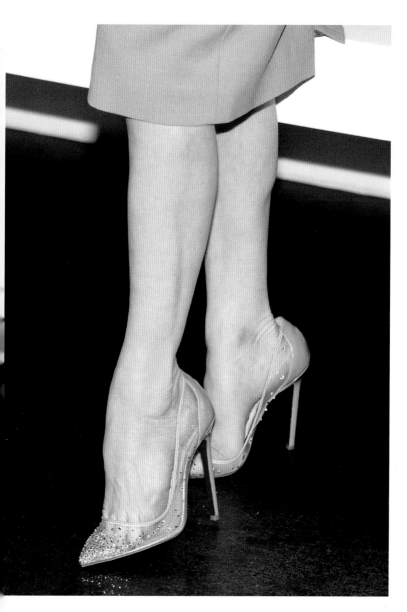

BOOTS

Louboutin's iconic boots set a new benchmark in leg adornment by making a very definite statement that screams for attention. The "Jennifer" boot, embodying a punk-rock aesthetic, is only for those fashion devotees with the attitude and confidence to carry them off. Made from soft and breathable perforated leather with a drawstring top that can be adjusted to create various silhouettes, the boots feature a provocative peep toe and come in an ankle-boot length as well.

OPPOSITE Singer-songwriter and actress Jennifer Lopez wearing one of the many iterations of the "Jennifer" boot – this one a set of pink suede spike-studded "Guerilla" booties – in London in 2013.

ABOVE Pale blue "Jennifer" slouchy boots made from soft perforated suede with leg ties, and red suede "Fifre Corset" ankle boots with elastic loop fastenings.

LEFT "Azimut" gladiator-style booties in black nappa leather, with open toes and intricately cut-away uppers, spotted at London Fashion Week Spring/Summer 2014.

ROMANCE

Christian Louboutin's expertise extends beyond his signature stilettos to a more romantic, easy but no less crafted range of open and peep-toe shoes, of which his "Rose Amelie" is one of his best-known styles. The Rose Amelie's soft, draped silhouette, with a simple ankle tie and a high block heel, offers a more playful version of his sandals that appeal to a global traveller who wants easy elegance no matter the setting. The Rose Amelie comes in suede, in a range of delicate pastel shades or in an edgier black leather with metallic-gold ankle tie.

PLATFORMS

One silhouette that has dominated Louboutin's portfolio of design is his "Bianca" pump. The Bianca is a shoe or boot in either graded black-to-red patent leather, studded finishes or nude leather. Our taste for platforms may wax and wane, but the Bianca, with its round toe, platform and 12-centimetre heel provides an alternative to his classic stiletto spikes. The Bianca has spawned countless imitations, but the designer has reinvented the popular shoe in the form of the "New Very Prive" pump, made with a seductive peep toe and concealed platform, proving he is always one step ahead of his competitors.

BELOW LEFT Black leather "Electropump" shoes with a contoured platform sole and fetish spikes at the centre back of the heel from Christian Louboutin's Autumn/Winter 2015 collection.

BELOW RIGHT "Ulona" multicolour suede platform shoe with padded gold leather straps and striped heel, originally inspired by the Maasai tribe in Kenya, and a favourite with celebrities such as Khloe Kardashian.

WEDGES

No collection is complete without a wedge, but to design an elegant wedge shoe takes artistry. The "Bodrum" wedge sandal, made in handwoven braided cotton with a leather-trimmed upper of criss-cross straps set on a sculpted platform sole, balances elegance with altitude. This is a glamorous shoe with a dramatic, contoured silhouette that elevates the humble espadrille into an exotic yet comfortable ultimate summer sandal. Constructed with a wide strap with a buckle fastening at the ankle, this shoe comes in several heights.

BELOW Low-cut bootie with sculptured wedge heel, made from velvet and decorated with strass crystals on display at The Corner boutique in Berlin, Germany, in 2010.

OVERLEAF A "Pigalle Spike" shoe from the Hawaii Kawaii Spring/Summer 2016 show. It captured the mood of 1950s Hawaii through a bright colour palette and exotic tropical prints sprinkled with coloured spike studs, with a neon-yellow patent "Pigalle" pump in the background, showcased at Christian Louboutin's store on Madison Avenue in New York in 2016.

The Sneaker
Revolution

OLD SCHOOL &
ULTRAMODERN

Renowned for leading trends rather than following them,
Louboutin has been as influential in designing sneakers as
his stiletto heels. He has, in fact, embraced sneakers, one of
the biggest modern trends to emerge that has revolutionized
footwear, whether on the catwalk or the street.

The brand was quick to be one of the first luxury dress-shoe
designers to add the more casual – but no less original and
well-crafted – sneakers to his ranges. Available in a multitude
of colours, fabrics and textures, the shoes exude Louboutin's
sense of fun and *joie de vivre*. They have added a new dimension
to his classic red soles, and most styles appear across both his
men's and women's ranges, creating a non-gendered approach to
his footwear that appeals to a wider, more diverse audience.

His sneakers can be divided into old-school, vintage-inspired
styles or his more ergonomic performance sneakers. Styles like
the "Vieiro", "Pik Boat", "Louis Junior", "Happy Rui" and

OPPOSITE Punk references abound in Louboutin's sneakers. These
gold calf leather, lace-up sneakers from 2016 have an upper covered in
matching gold spike studs and a minimal white rubber sole.

BELOW The "Pik Boat"
slip-on sneaker has
a chunky sole that
references a deck shoe.
This version has an
orange woven upper,
accented with a line
of black spike studs,
elastic side gussets and
a leather lining.

"Louis Orlato" sneakers form part of Louboutin's old-school
low and high-top sneakers. These focus all the attention on
decorative uppers, with a simpler clean silhouette for their
soles inspired by tennis, deck or classic basketball shoes in a
range of different thicknesses. These timeless sneakers are given
a contemporary reimagining through the Louboutin punk
aesthetic, with studded embellishments at the toe and heel, that
transform simple designs into something uncompromising.
The styles support trends in athleisure and easy styles of dress,
working just as well with jeans, sweats or chinos.

In 2019, Louboutin launched the "Run Loubi Run" range in
a bid to take over the performance-sneaker market. He redefined
the concept of luxury sneakers in this range of three styles: the
"Spike Sock", the "123 Run", and the "Red Runner". Each style
encapsulated a high-energy urban lifestyle, blending creativity
with innovation.

Always interested in hybridity, Louboutin has incorporated technology into his next generation of sport-inspired luxury performance sneakers. The "Loubishark", named for its red-ridged sole, is a bold, uncompromising design referencing architecture. It set a new standard for a decorative trainer that incorporates functional elements and sportswear fabrics, like neoprene and mesh, with leather. The Loubishark was originally launched as a limited-edition exclusive of 200 pairs. Each shoe had a concealed serial number, but proved to be so popular that it found a permanent place in his men's and women's ranges and became a gateway design into the world of performance sneakers. The entire Run Loubi Run range featured shock-absorbing and cushioning technology in a six-part sole, which was developed over three years and designed to embody the spirit of movement in a static object through its distinctively

ABOVE These ostentatious sneakers displayed at Galerie Véro-Dodat in Paris, France, show Christian Louboutin's love of colour and texture. The multicoloured calfskin, glitter and studded high-tops have contrasting green laces and show two different toe caps: on the left, a glitter version and on the right, a spike-studded version.

BELOW Styles like the "Spike Sock" have established Christian Louboutin's place in the luxury sneaker market. The "Spike Sock" has an upper made from neoprene and easily slips onto the foot with all-over tonal spike studs.

futuristic silhouette. The sole is outlined in signature Louboutin red and has the brand signature embossed into it. This first collection of running shoes represented a further move towards performance sneakers for the company.

Designed to merge a functional running shoe with the luxury Louboutin is known for, the Spike Sock screams effortless elegance, comfort and flexibility, and it rapidly became one of the brand's most iconic models. The Spike Sock features a sporty neoprene fabric upper adorned with trademark studs. Although drawing influences from sports footwear, it tells a sophisticated, textured story of matte upper fabrics and embellishments in a pared-back sports style.

If the Loubishark was inspired by Louboutin's interest in architecture, the 123 Run references his time designing costumes at the Folies Bergère. It comes in bold colours, exotic leathers

LEFT Actor Robert Downey Jr. poses on the red carpet at the 2013 People's Choice Awards at Nokia Theater in Los Angeles, wearing an understated monochrome version of the "Louis" high-top sneaker.

and satins, featuring embellishments like studs, crystals, ribbons and prints that characterize Louboutin shoes. It shares the same sole as the Spike Sock and comes in styles for both men and women. The success of the 123 Run proved to be the inspiration behind Louboutin's Red Runner sneaker, the final shoe of his design trilogy to find its way out of the gym.

ABOVE On display at Neiman Marcus in New York, this "Red Runner" sneaker shows style features borrowed from performance running shoes. The lacing system makes the shoe fit close to the foot. The upper mixes breathable mesh with glitter materials, a logo tab over the laces, and an iridescent toe cap. It also comes with a signed red rubber sole.

The Red Runner is the star sneaker to be created by Louboutin. Taking inspiration from technology-driven sports shoes, he created a quirky and eccentric sneaker. It optimizes comfort and wearability through an interesting mix of eye-catching materials and bold graphic colours and has Louboutin's signature embossed into its sole. The Red Runner merges contemporary sneaker technology to create a running shoe with all the style and attitude we have come to expect from Louboutin.

The Run Loubi Run range has firmly established Christian Louboutin as the go-to luxury footwear designer for performance sneakers that exude edgy glamour. His old-school low- and high-top sneaker ranges so successfully reimagined the vintage sneakers of the 1970s, 1980s and 1990s that they have made him the master of casual footwear that has wit, charm and style. His sneakers may come with a shock-absorbing price tag, but they are proof positive of a level of detail, original use of materials and embellishments and avant-garde design that makes them well worth the investment for men and women.

The trends for more casual footwear and luxury performance sneakers show no sign of slowing down and it is certain that Louboutin, who has played a central role in transforming sneakers into a truly luxury fashion item, will continue to lead the way.

BELOW Much of Christian Louboutin's work revisits moments in his life that are infused with important memories. This "Vieiro Spike Orlato" sneaker from 2019 has a spike-studded toe cap and printed quarters that show images from the 1980s of the young Louboutin and his muse Farida Khelfa.

Something
for the boys

MEN'S SHOES, BOOTS & LOAFERS

The truth behind Louboutin's decision to branch out into men's shoes may never be known, but as far back as 2009, a few styles for men crept into his collections or were made for private clients and, of course, for himself.

He initially turned his attention to menswear when pop star MIKA asked Louboutin to design all the shoes for his world tour. At first, the designer was bemused – why ask a women's shoe designer to design men's shoes? MIKA claimed his three sisters were so excited by Louboutin shoes that he wanted to capture the same excitement for himself in his tour outfits, and was convinced Louboutin could fulfil this brief. From that point on, Louboutin started to design men's shoes, and full collections followed in 2011. As they had so often in the past, his instincts proved right: the collections flew out of his stores, igniting the same passion for red soles in men as already existed in his female clients.

OPPOSITE Philanthropist, DJ, songwriter and performer will.i.am poses in a pair of gold leather "Dandelion" spike-studded shoes at a photo shoot in Australia in 2013.

BELOW These rich,
burnished dark brown
brogues fasten with
monk straps, gold side
buckles and fringing
over the vamps. Gold
chains decorate seams
at the front and on
the quarters of the
shoes, in place of the
traditional patterned
perforations, and the
shoe rests on a thick
sole and raised heel.
Worn by Louboutin
himself at the Elton
John AIDS Foundation
Academy Awards
Party in 2015.

Like his women's collections, the Louboutin must-have men's shoes include a range of established styles, like Oxfords, Derbys, loafers, monk straps and boots that he regularly remixes in different leathers, colours and details.

Louboutin's best-known men's dress shoes include "Greggo", "Simon", "Hubertus", "Alpha Male" and "Corteo". They come in his usual eclectic range of materials, from the standard patent leather and calfskin of a traditional evening shoe to soft velvets, suedes, neoprene and canvas, plus a range of Louboutin's favourite embellishments, studs, strass and embroidery. His men's shoes have subtle differences that set each style apart and many of his dress shoes come as an Oxford or Derby construction.

The Oxford shoe, named after Oxford University, is usually a formal shoe teamed with a suit, dinner jacket or worn for special occasions. It is made with a "closed lacing" system, which means the sides of a shoe where the holes for the shoelaces are punctured (quarters), are sewn under the front part of the shoe (the vamp). In the hands of Louboutin, we see the classic leather or patent Oxford construction in a range of styles, but we see it as a more daring shoe for the contemporary Louboutin man. The Greggo has an elegant slender toe, and comes in leather or suede with tone-on-tone studs, grosgrain-ribbon edge treatments or an eccentric mix of patent leather, velvet and metallic fabric. These combinations give an urban but sophisticated style to the Oxford, along with an uncharacteristic informality. The

BELOW Classic Oxford-style "Greggo" city shoes made from brown patinated calfskin, with a square toe. The shoes have edges finished with tone-on-tone silk grosgrain bindings and lace across the instep to fit comfortably. Photographed at Men's Fashion Week in London, 2017.

RIGHT Suede and leather Derby-style shoes from the Spring/Summer 2017 collection. They feature a prominent round toe shape and wide vamps with leather leopard-print detailing and a dark purple suede wall across the toes. They lace up with a keyhole design detail across the instep. The collection drew inspiration from bikers, and debuted in Milan, Italy, in a private bikers' club.

same can be said for his Corteo, with its squared toe and stacked sole, which subverts the formal Oxford shoe into a resort style using luxurious suede and strass.

The Derby shoe is an evolution of the Oxford but has a more informal look and can be worn with a suit or with more casual clothes. It is often made in suede as well as leather, giving it a relaxed feel. Unlike an Oxford, the Derby has "open lacing", meaning that quarters are stitched on top of the vamp. Open, looser lacing makes the Derby shoe more comfortable and ideal for walking around town. His iconic Alpha Male reinvents the

casual Derby as a tapered, chic urban shoe in patent calfskin or butter-smooth, sleek black leather. Designed to fit onto a slim last with a wafer-thin elegant red sole, Louboutin's Derby is equally at home at both formal and informal events.

It would be a mistake to think that Louboutin's menswear range could be divided up into a neat set of just dress shoes or sneaker styles, so what else does he have in his footwear armoury? Louboutin's desire to disrupt has been satisfied by his breakthrough technical shoes that bridge the gap between dress shoes and sneakers. Formed on a chunky, square-toed

BELOW Elegant dark
grey patinated calfskin
loafer with an almond
toe and a tongue-in-
cheek handkerchief
tucked into a pocket
placed across the
vamp. The top line of
the shoe is finished in
black grosgrain ribbon.
Taken at the Louboutin
store in Geneva,
Switzerland, in 2020.

last, his technical shoes use sportswear fabrics like neoprene and herringbone canvas to create a futuristic shoe. They often have a thicker lug sole that has deep indentations in a pattern designed to provide grip, usually seen in an outdoor hiking boot. They incorporate subtle details like padded collars around the ankle – commonly found in sneakers – to blend comfort with the refined Louboutin handwriting.

Louboutin's eye for easy elegance is perfectly expressed through his loafers and slipper styles. The loafer dispenses with laces, straps and ties of his dress, technical and monk-strap shoes to create the ultimate slip-on shoe. Louboutin loafers

BELOW Elegant dark grey patinated calfskin loafer with an almond toe and a tongue-in-cheek handkerchief tucked into a pocket placed across the vamp. The top line of the shoe is finished in black grosgrain ribbon. Taken at the Louboutin store in Geneva, Switzerland, in 2020.

ABOVE Inspired by a
traditional Moroccan
slipper, these
"Youssefo" backless
loafers are made from
navy raffia woven in a
herringbone design and
include a tassel detail
on the vamp and a low-
profile leather sole.

fit low around the ankle, and have a short heel and either a slipper-style construction or a bar fastened across the instep like a more traditional loafer. Styles like "Dandelion", "Nit Night", "Dandy" and "Rivalion" have become the luxury loafers of choice and undisputed champions of a laid-back city look.

Louboutin's monk-strap styles and boots complete his menswear collections. His monk-strap styles like "John",

LEFT "Burma
Potpourri Dandy"
slip-on flat loafers
with a slim silhouette
and textured leather
uppers, mixing long
and short triangular
spike studs that
cover the uppers.
Photographed at
New York Fashion
Week in 2011.

RIGHT Black matte calfskin loafers with round toes and contrasted platinum-plated, spike-studded uppers with black leather soles and heels.

OPPOSITE London-based blogger and influencer Chris Burt-Allan attends the opening of the *L'Exhibitioniste* during Paris Fashion Week in 2020 wearing chunky round-toed "Trapman" boots. Made from buffed calfskin, with tonal laces and a padded collar around the top of the boots for extra comfort, they sit on a thick rubber lug sole.

"Mortimer" and "Dear Tok" have a single broad strap that closes across the instep of the foot with a stylish buckle on the outside, but they sometimes come with a double monk strap. His boots range from sleek pull-on elastic-sided Chelsea boots like the "Melon" through to his thick-soled hiking boot styles like "Trapman" and "Citycroc". They feature square, pointed or round toes and are always outlined in his famous red sole in fine leather, or chunky rubber lugs. It is a testament to his original muse, pop star MIKA, that styles in the Louboutin range (such as the "Mika Sky" derby) are still named in honour of him and have become true icons.

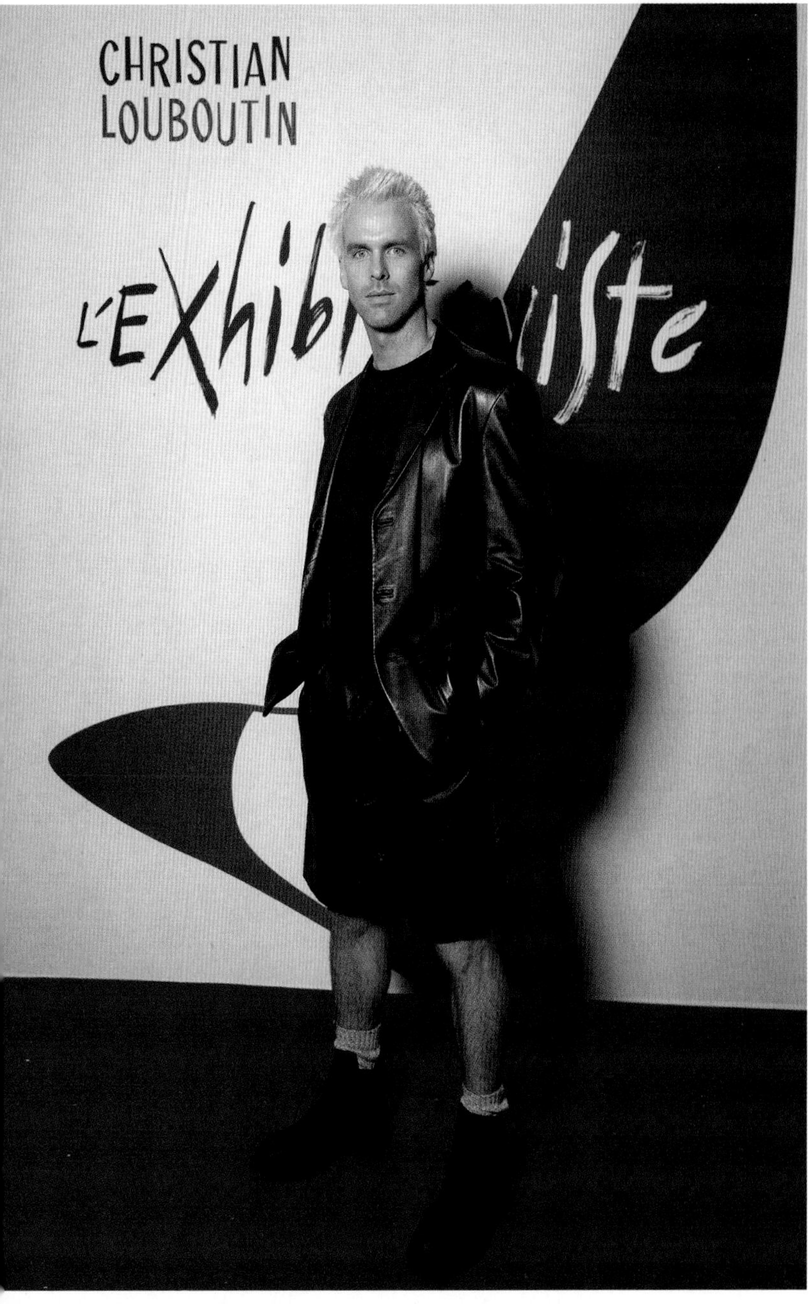
CHRISTIAN
LOUBOUTIN

Collaborations

CREATIVE PARTNERS

Christian Louboutin thrives on collaboration as a means to explore his creative process and celebrate his artists. He has collaborated with numerous fashion houses, including Alexander McQueen, Roland Mouret, Jean Paul Gaultier, Lanvin, LVMH, and Viktor & Rolf. However, some of his most interesting work across the creative spectrum has involved a multidisciplinary approach working with craftsmen, filmmakers, and dancers to maintain his creative momentum.

DAVID LYNCH COLLABORATION, 2007

Louboutin has often remarked that his interest in shoes goes beyond the shoe as a functional object. Sexual undertones have always been prominent in his work and in 2007, working with film director David Lynch, he created an extraordinary collection of images of shoes that reflected his interests in the shoe as a sexual object. The images and shoes formed *Fetish*, an exhibition at Galerie du Passage in Paris, that reflected the fetishism and sexual myths that surround women's footwear and spotlighted Louboutin's interests in shoes as "the ultimate sexual tool".

OPPOSITE Louboutin lays bare his obsession with extremes in footwear by producing a series of "foot-objects", including "Siamoise", a pair of shoes joined at the heel. Displayed at *Fetish*, 2007.

ABOVE Christian
Louboutin and David
Lynch at the opening
of the *Fetish* exhibition
at Galerie du Passage,
Paris, in 2007.

The *Fetish* exhibition cemented the creative partnership of two visionaries from different disciplines, the shoe designer Louboutin, and the filmmaker Lynch. They had both explored desires and extremes of human nature in their work, creating a natural collaborative space for them to fill. Originally, David Lynch had asked Louboutin to design a series of shoes for an exhibition at the Fondation Cartier in Paris. As is his wont, he abandoned notions of practicality or comfort to create shoes that push the extremes of fetish footwear. The collection included 26-centimetre heels and Louboutin's famous "Siamese" heels (two shoes fused at the heel). These bespoke designs were the inspiration for a series of photographs by David Lynch, which developed into the *Fetish* exhibition at La Galerie du Passage Paris

Lynch's surreal television drama *Twin Peaks* inspired Louboutin to started testing the idea of merging shoes together to solve the age-old problem of packing a pair of shoes. He experimented using the "So Kate" last shape which he used to make one of his most popular shoe styles. By placing a pair of lasts on top of each other heel to toe, Louboutin created a container which, after three years of development, became "Shoepeaks", a lightweight aluminum clutch bag. The clutch is finished in either black lacquered metal or gold polished metal enclosed

BELOW A visitor looks at images created by David Lynch and shoes created by Christian Louboutin, which were designed to push the boundaries of footwear, presenting shoes as objects of sexual desire. *Fetish* exhibition in 2007.

between two red soles. The interior of the bag is also reminiscent of a shoe, with a soft lambskin-leather lining and a removable chain so that it can be worn both over the shoulder or across the body.

BOLLYWOOD COLLABORATION WITH SABYASACHI MUKHERJEE, 2017

More light-hearted but no less fruitful was the 2017 Louboutin collaboration with Sabyasachi Mukherjee. Louboutin has always been inspired by travel and the desire to work with the best global craftsmen. He has built a network of artisans around the world who contribute to his collections, so a chance meeting in Mumbai with Indian textile designer Sabyasachi Mukherjee was an opportunity to fuse the artistry of Mukherjee with the

OPPOSITE This heelless fetish pump evolved into the "Conquilla" shoe, designed for Autumn/ Winter 2014.

BELOW American burlesque star Dita Von Teese and Christian Louboutin admire a pair of his fetishistic, sculptural patent-leather ballet shoes with 20-centimetre heels at *Fetish*, 2007.

OPPOSITE Christian Louboutin and Indian jewellery designer and couturier Sabyasachi Mukherjee reveal their limited-edition collection of clothing and footwear at Just One Eye gallery and boutique in Los Angeles in 2017.

Parisian chic of Louboutin. The pair bonded immediately over a shared passion for craft heritage and a love of the glamour and spectacle of Bollywood films. They started to work together on various projects that grew organically into a much bigger collaboration.

Mukherjee is best known for his richly embroidered and embellished bridal dresses and stunning evening gowns. His dedication to exquisite artisanal techniques has elevated Indian craftsmanship onto the global fashion stage. Together, Mukherjee and Louboutin collaborated to create a collection of luxury items. Taking inspiration from Mukherjee's archive of quintessentially Indian materials, which Louboutin later described as "a type of Ali Baba's cave", this profusion of texture and colour led to a tapestry of design ideas and techniques. Fifteen designs for women and four for men were created using exquisite sari fabrics combined with leather, Louboutin's signature studs and hand embroidery. The results were exclusive, original shoes that were predominantly about cultural exchanges and respect for craftsmanship and heritage. The collaboration also gave rise to the "Piloutin" bag, made from sari ribbons to resemble an ornate precious pillow.

"SLEEPING BEAUTY" ROYAL BALLET COLLABORATION, 2019
Louboutin's love of dance led him to his next collaboration, with London's renowned Royal Ballet. Louboutin was inspired by one of the main performances from the company's world-famous production of *The Sleeping Beauty*. "Dance has always been central to my work, I was inspired by the magic of their performances, and *The Sleeping Beauty*," Louboutin said to *Vogue* of the collaboration.

The designer's desire to encapsulate the world of fairy-tale princesses in his shoes first drew inspiration from themes within

LEFT Sabyasachi
Mukherjee's richly
embroidered
collections were
teamed with Christian
Louboutin shoes to
open Amazon Indian
Couture week in New
Delhi in 2015.

the performance, and key scenes like "The Rose Adage", where Princess Aurora dances with four different suitors to decide which one she should marry. The choreography involves her performing the same dance steps with each suitor to see who would be the best partner. This inspired his "Sleeping Rose" shoe, which has a design referencing the most famous element from *The Sleeping Beauty*, the rose. The rose was used as a motif on the shoe, which also had a spiked golden heel inspired by the spindle that poisons the princess and the thorns that grow up around her as she sleeps. Created in delicate blush or in black, with a red decorative rose on the upper and a gold heel, Sleeping Rose captures the romance, tragedy and ultimate triumph of the ballet.

BELOW A shared love of sumptuous fabrics and handcrafted embellishments adds glamour and elegance to Sabyasachi Mukherjee and Christian Louboutin's collaborative menswear and womenswear collections.

RIGHT Louboutin holds a shoe with a cutaway sole that reveals the instep, celebrating the curve of a woman's foot. In the background, an image of a dancer chosen for the unique arch of her feet models the shoe, wearing the seemingly unwearable "foot-objects".

OPPOSITE Satin ballerina pointe shoe embellished with sequins and married with an extreme high heel. *Fetish*, 2007.

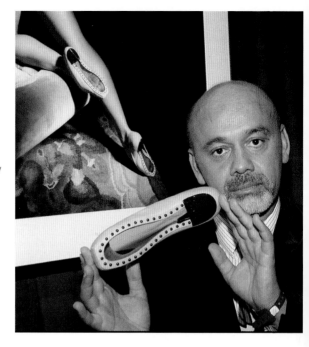

Not content with taking themes from the ballet, Louboutin turned his gaze to the dancers themselves. Their elegant pointe shoes gave the illusion of being an extension of their legs and were an obvious reference point from which to design. The resulting "Miragirl" shoes used clear PVC and leather to create the same illusion, and the chiffon ankle ties mirror the ribbons of the ballerina's shoes. Delicate strass crystals sparkle across the toe, adding a fairy-tale quality in both high heel and elegant flat shoe versions. The Royal Ballet dancers are estimated to use 6,000 pairs of pointe shoes a year, so for every set of Louboutin shoes sold from the collaboration, a pair of pointe shoes was donated to The Royal Ballet.

BELOW *Dolly Forever*
Barbie© Doll was the
second doll created by
Christian Louboutin.
Released in 2010, she
came complete with
a collection of shoes
with red soles, but the
pride of her collection
was her miniature
"Lionne" tasselled
knee-high boots.

THE DESIGNER AND THE DOLL COLLABORATION

"Barbie is an icon; how could I resist
such a collaboration?"
Christian Louboutin, *Vogue*

The most humorous of all Louboutin's collaborations must be
with Barbie, who has long been a muse to famous designers and
artists. Not only does she have a passion for fashion, but also
an obsession with shoes. It seems only natural that Louboutin
would become her footwear designer of choice to create an
enviable collection of shoes. Initially, Louboutin created a
collection of nine pairs of shoes featuring his signature soles,
each pair coming with a matching miniature shoe bag and box.
In 2013, having previously created a pair of classic peep-toe

Louboutin shoes in hot pink for Barbie's 50th birthday (2010), he continued to be inspired by her. Louboutin invited Barbie to spend time at his studio, in his country house and on his boat, captured in a series of photographs. As the collaboration continued, Louboutin designed a series of limited-edition Barbie dolls inspired by Nefertiti and Marilyn Monroe. They have a differently shaped ankle and a more curved foot than conventional Barbie, in order to show off their Louboutins to best advantage. The three dolls came packaged in Louboutin shoe boxes with four pairs of Barbie-size Louboutin shoes. This collection consisted of the Christian Louboutin Barbie Cat Burglar, a safari-themed Barbie, and a Barbie that goes to the Cannes Film Festival. The limited-edition collector's sets were available from internet retail giant NET-A-PORTER.COM, who also offered a Christian Louboutin Barbie shoe collection of 12 pairs.

BELOW All dressed up and somewhere to go! Louboutin's first (and catsuit-wearing) Barbie© and her successors *Anemone* and *Dolly Forever* Barbie© Dolls have specially designed ankles and feet to show off their Louboutin shoes to best effect.

Celebrity
Success

FAMOUS
FANS

Christian Louboutin is famous the world over for
his innovative footwear and red soles. It would be impossible
to extricate celebrity clients from his success; his brand
has become synonymous with A-lister glamour,
popular culture and craft heritage.

He is an unstoppable creative design force within the
fashion industry and rightly holds the crown recognizing
him as the world's most influential footwear designer. His
creations transcend differences to speak to a global audience
through his collections of men's and women's shoes. In
creating exciting brand extensions through accessories,
cosmetics and perfumes, he has collaborated with iconic
artists, brands and craftspeople. In this way, Christian
Louboutin as a brand has entered popular culture through
music, dance and film. So who are the celebrities and
influencers who have supported his success?

OPPOSITE Model and socialite Kendall Jenner proves that lingerie for the
feet exists by wearing a pair of tantalizing "Galativi" mesh and leather
pumps with pointed toes and elevated heels to attend the Met Gala in 2017.

Princess Caroline of Monaco is credited as being Louboutin's first celebrity client back in 1991, when she stumbled across his first store in Paris and was so wowed that she quickly spread the word about this master shoemaker and designer. She has worn his shoes at banquets and state functions in Monaco, and remains a loyal customer and personal friend of Louboutin's.

Madonna is widely reported to have said "It takes a real man to fill my shoes", and as a client of Louboutin for decades she must surely be one of his most iconic muses. She has worn his heels and boots both on and off stage, making numerous red-carpet appearances in them. The Queen of Pop even featured his red-heeled boots in her music video with Maluma for "Medellín". She is kept company by Lady Gaga, who wore Louboutins in her "Million Reasons" video; Miley Cyrus, who wore 14-centimetre peep-toe Louboutin ankle boots performing the launch of her album *Can't Be Tamed*; and Britney Spears, whose Louboutins appear in her "If U Seek Amy" music video.

Jennifer Lopez, singer-songwriter, actor and philanthropist, has also become a loyal customer of Louboutin's shoes and handbags. Her 2009 song "Louboutins" sent a positive message to women who need to leave bad relationships. She famously sang, "I'm throwing on my Louboutins", using the luxury footwear as a metaphor for empowering women. "Louboutins" eventually topped the US Hot Dance Club Songs.

In popular culture, designer items have become the lyrical markers of wealth and sex appeal. Rapper Cardi B's 2017

OPPOSITE Recording artist and fashion entrepreneur Rihanna hosts Cartier's annual Loveday celebration at the Empire State Building in 2008, wearing black calfskin suede spike-heeled ankle boots with a patent-leather buckle fastening.

RIGHT Actress Blake Lively and Christian Louboutin leave the Four Seasons Hotel in New York in 2017. Lively wears silver sandals with a slim heel and minimal asymmetrical straps that buckle at the sides of the feet, while Christian wears his classic "Monana" loafers in black and white leather with a signature red-strap detail across the vamp.

diamond-certified track 'Bodak Yellow' pays homage to Louboutin in her lyrics by referencing his red soles and his shoes also feature in her video for the song, which topped the US Billboard Hot 100 for several weeks.

The company estimates that about 3,000 women have around 500 pairs of Christian Louboutin shoes each. Christina Aguilera owns 300 pairs but his biggest client is American writer (and queen of romance novels) Danielle Steele. Steele reportedly owns over 6,000 pairs. She is known to have purchased up to 80 pairs at a time when shopping at his store, setting an astounding record for red-sole addiction by acquiring dozens of shoes every year. The value of Steele's collection is estimated at close

LEFT Actress Cate Blanchett steps out in a pair of Louboutin "Gwalior" flat pumps featuring a heart-shaped topline and double-tassel details on the vamp.

OPPOSITE Actress Naomie Harris arrives at the 2013 Academy Awards in Hollywood, California, wearing gold-glitter leather "Gwynitta" sandals with high block heels, a single strap across the toes and fine double straps fastening at the heels.

to £2 million. Wwd.com reports Louboutin describing her as "supertop" and says, "She comes to Paris, and she literally buys everything. Then she flies back to New York, says, 'I'm a little disappointed there's nothing in the store,' and walks out with 80 pairs."

At 19 months old, Suri Cruise, the daughter of Tom Cruise and Louboutin fan Katie Holmes, became the youngest ever client of the footwear designer. Cruise had a pair of shoes specially commissioned: moulds of her tiny feet were made and sent to Paris, where a handmade pair of bespoke shoes were created for her.

Talk show host, television producer, actress and author Oprah Winfrey is on the serious wing of Louboutin's celebrity following, not only for her cultural significance and extensive and influential media empire, but for her philanthropy and support for charities that empower and uplift women. In 2015, Winfrey's autographed pair of Louboutin scaled silver stilettos sold for almost £12,000 ($17,000) after a week-long auction for an Australian charity that focuses on women's education in developing countries. Winfrey has since repeated this personal gift and auctioned more autographed Louboutin shoes.

OPPOSITE Media mogul Oprah Winfrey flaunts her red-soled "Bianca" black patent leather platform pumps with dainty peep toes during a press conference in Pasadena, California, in 2011.

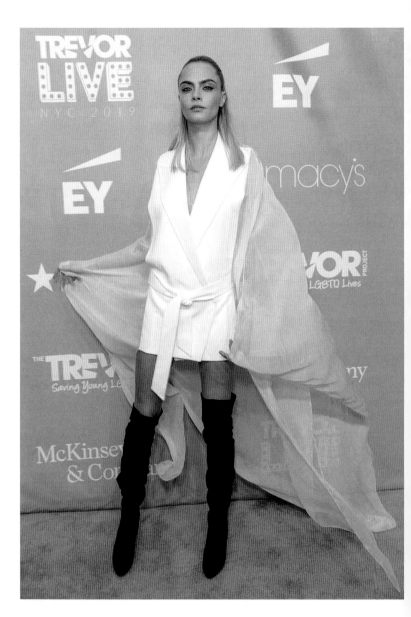

OPPOSITE Model and actress Cara Delevingne strides out in a sumptuous, attention-grabbing pair of over-the-knee "Epic" calfskin suede boots with ice-pick heels to attend the TrevorLIVE New York Gala in 2019.

RIGHT Fashion designer Victoria Beckham leaves a restaurant in New York wearing a pair of statuesque black leather ankle boots with contoured, covered platforms and ultra-high spike heels.

A plethora of celebrities, including Carey Mulligan, Rita Ora, Katy Perry, Gwyneth Paltrow, Rihanna, Angelina Jolie, Cate Blanchett, Cara Delevingne, Nicki Minaj, Dita Von Teese, Victoria Beckham, Billy Porter, Ryan Gosling, Pharrell Williams, and Rami Malek (to name just a few) have regularly worn Louboutin. But one celebrity, Sarah Jessica Parker, has championed Louboutin both on and off screen more than any other. Through her character Carrie Bradshaw in the TV series *Sex and the City*, Parker made cutting-edge fashion choices that are still relevant to this day. Barely an episode was made without a strong footwear theme, and it was Carrie Bradshaw that first brought Louboutin to a wider audience. In one episode in season three, Carrie stepped out of The Standard hotel in Los Angeles in strappy Louboutin sandals that were mismatched, metallic red on her right, and a teal on her left, leaving fans unsure if this was a real fashion faux pas. It took 19 years before the mystery of the mismatched Louboutins was finally solved when Sarah Jessica Parker admitted it was intentional. The actress has had a lifelong love affair with Louboutin thanks to the *Sex and the City* stylist Patricia Field who decided on the wardrobe for each character in the series and introduced her to the footwear brand. Field is the creative brains behind the Netflix hit show *Emily in Paris*. Like Carrie Bradshaw before her, Emily has a shoe fetish and living in Paris she of course wears Louboutin's shoes, specially requested by lead actress Lily Collins.

Louboutin is no stranger to real-life royalty; his shoes have been worn by many princesses from royal houses around the globe. Former actress Meghan Markle became a British princess after her marriage to Prince Harry in 2018. Now known as The Duchess of Sussex, she is no stranger to Louboutin's footwear. She has favoured both the So Kate 12-centimetre black-leather

OPPOSITE Style icon and actress Sarah Jessica Parker, famous for her sartorial inspirations in the hit TV show *Sex and the City*, wears delicate two-tone cream and black leather T-bar strappy sandals with slim high heels for filming on location in New York in 2009.

OPPOSITE Singer Katy Perry performs on stage at Madison Square Garden, New York in 2010, looking every inch a showgirl in a pair of thigh-high cream leather "Supra Domina" boots.

LEFT Rihanna flashes her red soles as she walks the red carpet in an elegant pair of "So Kate" pumps in simmering patent leather at the Metropolitan Museum of Art's Costume Institute Gala, informally known as the Met Gala, in 2012.

heels and the exquisite "Tricolor Suspenodo" ballerina flats in patent leather, for less formal occasions.

Musical royalty – the late, great Queen of Soul, singer Aretha Franklin – was buried in a gold-plated casket after fans were invited to view the legendary singer for one last time before her burial. She was dressed head-to-toe in red, including her nails, lipstick, and of course in her red Louboutin 12-centimetre patent-leather shoes, which were deliberately chosen by her family to make the statement that "The Queen of Soul is a diva to the end."

With so many achievements during his career, it is impossible to predict what Christian Louboutin will do next, but his high-octane creativity burns as brightly as it ever did, and he will continue to create beautiful shoes for many years to come.

LEFT Rapper and singer-songwriter Nicki Minaj wears monochrome-printed snakeskin "Daffodile" Mary Jane shoes with concealed platforms, 16-centimetre heels and thin straps across the instep for the 2013 season premiere of *American Idol*.

OPPOSITE Actor Ashton Kutcher wears an elegant pair of black patent leather "Alpha Male" Oxford dress shoes with silk grosgrain trim and square toes to attend the Screen Actors Guild Awards in 2017.

OVERLEAF Rapper, record producer and entrepreneur Sean Combs attends the 2017 Met Gala in black patent leather "Dandelion" slip-on loafers with the trademark red sole and half-black, half-red heel details.

INDEX

(Page numbers in *italic* refer
to photographs and captions;
bold to main subjects)

Académie d'Art Roederer 22
Aguilera, Christina 33, 141
"Alpha Male" shoe 108, 110–1,
    152
Amazon Indian Couture week
    2015 *128*
Andrieux, Emmanuel 72
Anemone 133
ankle boot 138, *141*, *147*
athleisure 16
"Azimut" booty *89*

B, Cardi 138, 141
Babylon 38, *38*
bags 123, 125
    "It" 10
    "Piloutin" 126
    "Paloma" 36, *36*
    "Shoepeaks" 123
ballet shoes
    flats 65
    "Miragirl" 130
    pointe shoe 130, *130*
Bande de Bandeaux 22, *25*, 26
"Bandy" stiletto 86
Barbie™ **132–3**, *132*, *133*
Barneys department store *50*
Barthes, Roland 26
Batallure Beauty LLC 37
Beckham, Victoria *147*, 148
Belfast Telegraph, 10
Berlin *91*
Beverly Hills *50*
"Bianca"pumps 90, *145*
Bikini Questa Sera 38
black lace knee-length boot *61*

Blanchett, Cate *142*, 148
"Bodrum" sandal 91
"Body Strass" shoe 86
Bollywood 125, 126
boots 89, 113–6
    ankle 138, *141*, *147*
    "Azimut" *89*
    black lace knee-length *61*
    calfskin suede high-cut ankle
        59
    "Citycroc" 116
    "Dear Tok" 116
    "Epic" *147*
    "Fifre Corset" *89*
    flat knee length *65*
    "Guerilla"" *89*
ivory leather mid-calf-length *59*
    "Jennifer" 89, *89*
    "Let Me Tell You" *55*
    "Lionne" *132*
    low-cut *91*, 138
    "Marale" *63*
    "Melon" 116
    "Mortimer" 116
    "Psybootie" *51*
    "Supra Domina" *151*
    "Trapman" 116, *116*
BRIT Awards 2010 *38*
brogues *108*
"Burma Potpourri Dandy"
    loafer *115*
Burt-Allen, Chris *116*

calfskin high-top sneakers *99*
calfskin loafer *112*, *116*
calfskin suede high-cut ankle
    boot *59*
Cambridge, Duchess of 10
canvas "Damier" 68
Caroline of Monaco, Princess

    10, 32, *32*, 138
cashmere 11
Chanel 27
Channel 4 55–6
Cher 22, *22*
"Citycroc" boot 116
Collaborations
    Barbie Doll **132–3**, *132*, *133*
    David Lynch **121–5**, *122*,
        123
    "Loubi World" 17
    Royal Ballet **126–31**, *130*
    Sabyasachi Mukherjee
        125–6, *126*, *128*, *129*
    Yves Saint Laurent 56–7, *57*
collections
    Autumn/Winter 2014 *125*
    Autumn/Winter 2015 *90*
    Loubibaby 38
    Nudes 2013 65, *65*
    "Nudes for All" 2019 65
    Showgirl retrospective, the,
        2012 *57*, *59*, 61, *61*, *63*
    Spring/Summer 2016
        Hawaii Kawaii *91*
    Spring/Summer 2019 16
    Spring/Summer 2020 *31*
    Spring/Summer 2017 *110*
Collins, Joan 33
Collins, Lily 148
colours *16*
Combs, Sean *152*
"Conquilla" shoe *125*
coolhunting.com 12, 16–7
"Copte" flats 85
Corner boutique, The *15*, *91*
"Corteo"shoes 108, 110
Couture Council Award for
    Artistry of Fashion 68, *71*
Crazy Horse 62, *62*

Cruise, Suri 145
cutaway sole shoe *130*
Cyrus, Miley 138

"Daffodile" pump *57, 152*
"Damier" canvas 68
"Dandelion" loafers *107*, 113, *152*
"Dandy" loafer 113
De la Falaise, Loulou 26
"Dear Tok" boot 116
Delevingne, Cara *147*, 148
Deneuve, Catherine 33
Derby shoe 108, 110–1
Design Museum 55, *59*, 61, *61, 63, 65, 75*
designmuseum.org 09
Diana, Princess of Wales 35, *35*
Dior, Christian 27
Doll, The 132–3
Dolly Forever Barbie™ *132, 133*
Downey Jr., Robert *101*
Duff, Hilary *83*
Dusseldorf *85*

Egypt 09, 26
"Electropump" shoe *90*
Elton John AIDS Foundation Academy Awards Party 108
Emaer, Fabrice 26
Emily in Paris 148
"Epic" boots *147*
Evening Standard 14
Exhibitioniste, L' 65, 71, 72, *72, 73*, 116

Face, The 26
Fashion Footwear Association of New York 55
Fetish 121, *121*, 122, *122, 123, 125, 130*
"Feu" (Crazy Horse show) 62, *62*
Field, Patricia 148
"Fifi" pumps 68
"Fifre Corset" ankle boot *89*
FIT (Fashion Institute of

Technology) Museum 56, 57
flat knee-length boots *65*
Flowers 43
Folies Bergère 15–6, 26, *65*, 100
Footwear News 22, 71–2
fragrances 38
France 09
Franklin, Aretha 151
"Freddy" shoes *138*
Frizon, Maud 27

Gaga, Lady 138
"Galavati" pumps *137*
Galerie du Passage 121, 122, *122*
Galerie Véro-Dodat 99
Game, The 44
gardens 31
Gaultier, Jean Paul 26
gold calf leather lace-up sneaker 97
Goop 38
Gosling, Ryan 148
"Greggo" men's shoes 108, *109*
"Guerilla" booty *89*
Guinness pumps *73*
"Gwalior" pumps *142*
"Gwynitta" sandals *142*

handbags
  "Monogram" 68
  "Rougissmie" 36
"Happy Rui" sneaker 97
Harper's Bazaar 22
Harris, Naomie *142*
Heatherwick, Thomas 38
Heels (killer) 86
"Hot Chick" shoe 86
"Hubertus" shoe 108
Hullin, Bruno 62

India 26, 35, 35
"inseparables" pump 35
insole *10*
"It" bags 10

Italy 10
ivory leather mid-calf-length boot *59*

Jagger, Bianca 26
Jagger, Mick 26
Jenner, Kendall *137*
"Jennifer" boot 89, *89*
Jolie, Angelina 68, *68*, 148
Jones, Grace 26
Jourdain, Charles 27
Just One Eye gallery and boutique *126*

Kardashian, Khloe *90*
Kardashian, Kim 33
Kenya *90*
Khelfa, Farida *103*
Kutcher, Ashton *152*

lacquer red 44, 48, 49, 51
Lapp, Alexandra *85*
last *10*, 12, *12, 13*
lasts "So Kate" 123
leather 11
Leather Spa, the 48
Lee, Kiwi *44*
"Let Me Tell You" boot *55*
"Lionne"" boot *132*
lipsticks *38*
lipsticks Rouge Louboutin 38
litigation 50
Lively, Blake *141*
loafers
  "Burma Potpourri Dandy" *115*
  calfskin loafers *112, 116*
  "Dandelion" *107*, 113, *152*
  "Dandy" 113
  "Nit Night" 113
  "Rivalion" 113
  "Youssefo" *113*
London 68, 126
London Fashion Week *89*
Lopez, Jennifer 10, 33, *36, 89*, 138
Los Angeles *126*

"Loubi World" collaboration 17
"Loubishark" sneaker 99, 100
Loubou 138
Louboutin, Christian 9, *9*, 10, *10*, 11, 12, *12*, *13*, 14, *14*,15, *15*, 16, *16*, 17, *17*, 21, *21*, 22, *22*, 25, 26, 27, *27*, 31, *31*, 32, *32*, 33, 35, *35*, 36, *36*, 37, *37*, 38, *38*, 43, *43*, 44, *44*, 48, 49, *49*, 50, 51, 55, 56, *56*, 57, 61, 62, *62*, *63*, 65, 68, 71, *71*, 72, 74, *75*, 81, *81*, 82, 85, 86, 89, 90, *90*, *91*, 97, *97*, 98, *99*, *99*, 100, *100*, 101, 102, *103*, 107, 108, *108*, 111, 112, *112*, 113, 116, 121, *121*, 122, *122*, 123, *123*, 125, *125*, 126, *126*, 128, 129, *129*, 130, *130*, 132, *132*, 133, *133*, 137, 138, *138*, 141, *141*, *142*, 145, 148, 151
  Beauté, 37
  for Yves Saint Laurent Haute Couture, 1962–2002 56–7
  The World's Most Luxurious Shoes 35, 55
"Louboutins" song 138
"Louis Junior" sneaker 97
"Louis Orlato" sneaker 98
"Louis" high-top sneaker *101*
"LOVE" shoes 35
low-cut boots *91*, *138*
Luxury Brand Status Index 55
LVMH 68
Lynch, David **121–5**, *122*, *123*

Madonna 10, 33, 138
Maison du Vitrail, La 72
"Malangeli" shoes 68 *68*
Maleficent 68, *68*
Malek, Rami 148
"*maquereau*" shoe 31–2
"Marale" ankle boot *63*
Marketer of the Year 2015 55

Markle, Meghan 148
Maxima of the Netherlands, Queen 10
"Melon" boot 116
Men's Fashion Week, London 2017 *108*
Men's Fashion Week, New York 2011 *115*
men's shoes 107–117
Met Gala *137*, *151*
Miami 138
MIKA 37, *38*, 107, 116
"Mika Sky" shoe 116
Milan *110*
Minaj, Nicki 33, *145*, *152*, 148
"Miragirl" ballet shoe 130
"Monogram" handbag 68
"Mortimer" boot 116
Mukherjee, Sabyasachi **125–6**, *126*, *128*, *129*
mule-style backless shoe *65*
Mulligan, Carey 148
Musée des Arts Afrts Africans et Océaniens 21–2, 27

Neiman Marcua *102*
NET-A-PORTER.COM 133
New Delhi *128*
New York *83*, *102*
"New Very Prive" pump 90
Newsweek 27
"Nit Night" loafer 113
"No stilettos" 22, *22*
Nudes 68, 72, *72*

"123 Run" sneaker 98, 100, 101
Ora, Rita 148
Oxford shoe 108, 110

Palace, Le *25*, 26
Palais de la Porte Dorée *21*, *22*, 31, 71, 72, *73*, 74
"Paloma"" tote bag 36, *36*
Paltrow, Gwyneth 10, 33, 38, 148
Paris 21, 22, 26, 62, *62*, 65,

71, *72*, *73*, *74*, *83*, *99*, 121, 122, *122*
Paris Fashion Week 2020 *116*
Parker, Sarah Jessica 10, 148, *148*
pensée"" shoe *32*, *44*
Perry, Katy 148, *151*
Picasso, Paloma 26
"Pigalle Follies" pump 82, *82*, 86
"Pigalle Spike" shoe *91*
"Pigalle" pump 81, 82, *83*, 86, *91*
"Pik Boat" sneaker 97, *98*
"Piloutin" bag 126
Pop Art silkscreen flowers *32*
Porter, Billy 148
Portugal 09
"Psybootie" boot *51*
pumps 65
  "Bianca" 90, *145*
  "Daffodile" *57*, *152*
  "Fifi" 68
  "Galavati" *137*
  Guinness *73*
  "Gwalior" *142*
  "inseparables" 35
  "New Very Prive" 90
  "Pigalle Follies" 82, *82*, 86
  "Pigalle" 81, 82, *83*, 86, *91*
  "So Kate" *81*, 82. 85, 86, 148–51, *151*
punk rock 09, 22, *27*

Race d'Ep 22
Rapid Response Collecting gallery 68
red soles 43, *43*, 44, *44*, 48, 49, *49*, 50, *50*, 51
"Red Bottoms" 44, *49*
"Red Runner sneaker 81, 98, 101, 102, *102*
Rihanna 10, *141*, 148, *151*
"Rivalion" loafer 113
"Rose Adage, The" scene 126, 128
"Rose Amelie" shoe 90

Rouge Louboutin lipstick 38
"Rougissimie" handbag 36
Royal Ballet, The 126–31, 130
"Run Loubi Run" sneaker 98, 99, 102

Saint Laurent, Yves 27, 50, 56–7, 56
Saks Fifth Avenue 38
sandals 85
    "Gwynitta" 142
Sex and the City 148, 148
"Shadow Theatre, The" 61
"Shoepeaks" clutch bag 123
Shoes
    shoes "Alpha Male" 108, 110–1, 152
    "Body Strass" 86
shoes
    "Conquilla" 125
    "Corteo" 108, 110
    Derby 108, 110–1
    "Electropump" 90
    "Espelio" 37
    "Freddy" 138
    "Greggo" 108, 109
    "Hot Chick" 86
    "Hubertus" 108
    "LOVE" 35
    "Malangeli" 68 68
    "maquereau" 31–1
    "Mika Sky" 116
    mule-style backless 65
    Oxford 108, 110
    "pensée" 32, 44
    "Pigalle Spike" 91
    "Rose Amelie" 90
    "Siamoise" 121, 122
    "Simon" 108
    "Sleeping Road" 129
    "Ulona" 90
Showgirl, The exhibition 75
"Siamoise" shoe 121, 122
silk grosgrain 11
silver sandals 141
silver stilettos 145
"Simon" men's shoes 108

Sleeping Beauty, The 126, 129
"Sleeping Rose" shoe 129
Sneakers 97–103
    gold calf leather lace-up 97
    "Happy Rui" 97
    "Loubishark" 99, 100
    "Louis Junior" 97
    "Louis Orlato" 98
    "Louis" 101
    "123 Run, 98, 100, 101
    "Pik Boat" 97, 98
    "Red Runner" 81, 98, 101, 102, 102
    "Run Loubi Run" 98, 99, 102
    "Spike Sock" 98, 100, 100, 101
    "Vieira" 97
    "Vieiro Spike Orlato" 103
"So Kate" last 123
"So Kate" pointy pumps 81, 82, 85, 86, 148–51, 151
Sole Desire: The Shoes of Christian Louboutin 57
soles 14
SOS Children's Villages charity 68
Spears, Britney 138
"Spike Sock" sneaker 98, 100, 100, 101
Steele, Danielle 141, 144
Steele, Dr Valerie 56
Stefani, Gwen 36
stilettos 33, 35, 86
    "Bandy" 86
stitching 10–11, 16
stores
    Berlin 15
    Geneva 112
    Greater Manchester 14
    Jakarta 33
    Las Vegas 35
    London 14, 33
    Moscow 14, 33
    New York 14, 33, 91
    Paris 14, 32, 33, 35, 36, 138
    Singapore 35

Tokyo 35
Sunday Times, The 15
"Supra Domina" boots 151

Taj Mahal 35, 35
"Tattoo Parlors" 35
toe shapes 12
Tornade Blonde 38
trademarks 50
transparent mesh upper embellished shoe 71
"Trapman" boot 116, 116
TrevorLIVE New York Gala 147
"Tricolor Suspenodo" 151
Trouble in Heaven 38
Twin Peaks 123

"Ulona" suede platform shoe 90
upper 10, 11, 49

Victoria and Albert Museum 68
"Vieira" sneaker 97
"Vieiro Spike Orlato" sneaker 103
Vivier, Roger 27
Vogue 31, 126
von Furstenberg, Diane 33, 71
Von Teese, Dita 86, 125, 148
Vuitton, Louis 68

Waldman, Michael 55–6
Wall nightclub 138
Warhol, Andy 26, 32, 43
wedges 91
Whitaker Malem 72
will.i.am 107
Williams, Pharrell 138, 148
Winfrey, Oprah 145, 145
wwd.com 145

"Youssefo"" loafer 113

Zepeto 17

CREDITS

The publishers would like to thank the following sources for their kind permission to reproduce the pictures in this book.

Akg-images: VIEW/Ed Reeve 14

Alamy: 51; Abaca Press 72, 145; Grzegorz Czapski 98, 112; dpa picture alliance archive 90 (right), 91; Ros Drinkwater 42; Chris Hellier 20; Brian Jannsen 99; Richard Levine 92-93; Patti McConville 90 (left), 102; Reuters 46-47, 65, 66-67; WENN Rights Ltd 153; Xinhua 37, 73, 74-75

Bridgeman Images: © Julien Faure/Leextra 8, 17; Eric Poupe/ArtComPress 62

Getty Images: AFP/Stringer 71, 123; Imeh Akpanudosen/Stringer 152; Neilson Barnard 50, 114-115; Bryan Bedder 150; Victor Boyko 117; Frederick M. Brown/Stringer 144; Larry Busacca 151; Luc Castel 45; James Devaney 83, 141, 147, 149; Fred Duval 57, 58, 59, 64, 76-77, 131; Philip Farone 127; Isa Foltin 34;

Ben Grabbe 110-111; Sean Gallup 30; Asun Gil/EyeEm 12; Steve Granitz 101; Raymond Hall 142; Frazer Harrison 27; Julien Hekimien 124; Rune Hellestad-Corbis 13, 54, 60, 61, 63, 120; Foc Kan 32-33; 133; Rubina A.Kahn 128, 129; Dimitrios Kambouris 136; Jason Kempin 140; Jeff Kravitz 138; Harry Langdon 23; Lily Lawrence 87; Pascal Le Segretain 10, 22, 56; Mike Marsland 39; Kevin Mazur 154-155; Jason Merritt 143; Bertrand Rindoff Petroff 24-25, 122, 125,130; AV 88; Joel Sagat 44; Florian Seefried/Stringer 15; John Shearer 49; Kirsten Sinclair 89 (bottom), 109, 113; Matthew Sperzel 96, 116; The Sydney Morning Herald 106; Karwai Tang 69, 108; Christian Vierig 36, 80, 84, 85; Angela Weiss 70

Kerry Taylor Auctions: 82, 89 (top)

Shutterstock: Dean Drobot 16 (top); Bebeto Matthews/AP 38; Sonia Moskowitz/Globe Photos via ZUMA Wire 146; Papin Lab 100, 103; Startraks 139; Jovica Varga 11; Catherine Zibo 132; Peter Zijlstra 16 (bottom)